*How Strange
It Seems*

. . .

How Strange It Seems

0 0 0

The Cultural Life of Jews in
Small-Town New England

0 0 0

Michael Hoberman

University of Massachusetts Press
Amherst

Copyright © 2008 by University of Massachusetts Press

Printed in the United States of America

LC 2008003194
ISBN 978-1-55849-646-0 (paper); 645-3 (library cloth ed.)

Designed by Sally Nichols
Set in Monotype Walbaum by dix!
Printed and bound by The Maple-Vail Book Manufacturing Group

Library of Congress Cataloging-in-Publication Data
Hoberman, Michael.
How strange it seems : the cultural life of Jews in small-town
New England / Michael Hoberman.
p.   cm.
Includes bibliographical references and index.
ISBN 978-1-55849-646-0 (pbk. : alk. paper)—
ISBN 978-1-55849-645-3 (library cloth : alk. paper)
1. Jews—New England—Interviews.   2. Jews—New England—Social life and
customs.   3. New England—Ethnic relations.   I. Title.
F15.J5H63   2008
305.892'4074—dc22

British Library Cataloguing in Publication data are available.

To the memory of my father,
Dr. Henry D. Hoberman
(1914–2004)

How strange it seems! These Hebrews in their graves,
Close by the street of this fair seaport town,
Silent beside the never-silent waves,
At rest in all this moving up and down!

The trees are white with dust, that o'er their sleep
Wave their broad curtains in the south-wind's breath,
While underneath these leafy tents they keep
The long, mysterious Exodus of Death.

And these sepulchral stones, so old and brown,
That pave with level flags their burial-place,
Seem like the tablets of the Law, thrown down
And broken by Moses at the mountain's base.

The very names recorded here are strange,
Of foreign accent, and of different climes;
Alvares and Rivera interchange
With Abraham and Jacob of old times.

"Blessed be God! for he created Death!"
The mourners said, "and Death is rest and peace;"
Then added, in the certainty of faith,
"And giveth Life that nevermore shall cease."

Closed are the portals of their Synagogue,
No Psalms of David now the silence break,
No Rabbi reads the ancient Decalogue
In the grand dialect the Prophets spake.

Gone are the living, but the dead remain,
And not neglected; for a hand unseen,
Scattering its bounty, like a summer rain,
Still keeps their graves and their remembrance green.

How came they here? What burst of Christian hate,
What persecution, merciless and blind,
Drove o'er the sea—that desert desolate—
These Ishmaels and Hagars of mankind?

They lived in narrow streets and lanes obscure,
Ghetto and Judenstrass, in mirk and mire;
Taught in the school of patience to endure
The life of anguish and the death of fire.

All their lives long, with the unleavened bread
And bitter herbs of exile and its fears,
The wasting famine of the heart they fed,
And slaked its thirst with marah of their tears.

Anathema maranatha! was the cry
That rang from town to town, from street to street;
At every gate the accursed Mordecai
Was mocked and jeered, and spurned by Christian feet.

Pride and humiliation hand in hand
Walked with them through the world where'er they went;
Trampled and beaten were they as the sand,
And yet unshaken as the continent.

For in the background figures vague and vast
Of patriarchs and of prophets rose sublime,
And all the great traditions of the Past
They saw reflected in the coming time.

And thus forever with reverted look
The mystic volume of the world they read,
Spelling it backward, like a Hebrew book,
Till life became a Legend of the Dead.

But ah! what once has been shall be no more!
The groaning earth in travail and in pain
Brings forth its races, but does not restore,
  And the dead nations never rise again.

—Henry Wadsworth Longfellow,
"The Jewish Cemetery at Newport" (1852)

CONTENTS

CONCLUSION.
The Rewards of Hard Work
*How Small-Town New England Jews Might Be Helping
to Reverse a National Decline*

APPENDIX 1.
A Note on Method

APPENDIX 2.
List of Interviews

NOTES

INDEX

Illustrations follow page 16.

PREFACE

How Strange It Seems tells the story of Jews living in small-town New England from the late nineteenth century to the present. It is a story that hasn't been told, in composite form, at least, and it is worth telling because it offers several enhancements of our overall picture of Jewish life in America. For all of their apparent numeric minority, small-town Jews have important things to say to us, both in their words and in their deeds as described by their words, about what it means to live as a Jew in America and in the modern world. The story is also worth telling because of the insights it allows into the unique cultural perspective of small-town New England, where daily life always seems to have as much to tell us about the present and future as it does about the past. This book makes the case that the convergence of Jewish cultural life and of small-town New England itself has been a singularly fortuitous one. Like the Jews, the people of rural New England have long known how to live in a state of perpetual transition. In their daily lives, they are surrounded by myriad remnants of an age-old tradition. Throughout their history, on the other hand, they have also been supple in the face of the many dramatic economic, social, and cultural shifts enacted by modernity.

Although my own is the centralizing voice in this story, I function in large part and quite intentionally as a mouthpiece for the participants themselves, whose oral histories comprise the foundation of the book. The experiences recorded here all derive from the accounts of those who underwent them. My own interpretive overlay, therefore, while it represents my best effort at synthesizing the diverse accounts I collected, is hardly the responsibility of the several dozen tradition-bearers whom I met as I researched this book. I should like to think that the book's greatest merit is its adherence to the letter and spirit of what I learned from the people I interviewed.

I could not have written this book without the generous contributions of the sixty individuals who kindly allowed me to conduct oral history inter-

views with them. Unquestionably, I owe these tradition-bearers the greatest debt; I hardly exaggerate when I assert that the book is as much theirs
as it is mine. Rather than name each of these people here, however, I direct
readers to Appendix 2, which lists the interviews upon which the book is
based and the names and hometowns of the tradition-bearers with whom
I spoke. I should point out that one of the most important contributions
that these sixty individuals made was their universal willingness to help
me to find other people to interview for the book. Nearly all the people
I interviewed were referred to me by tradition-bearers whose names also
appear on the list in Appendix 2.

To complete my research, I received generous funding from my home
institution, Fitchburg State College. Colleagues and administrators at the
college were supportive throughout the process, and aided me by providing course releases, grant money, and—most important—genuine curiosity
and appreciation for the work I was doing. Many of my students have asked
me about the project as well. I wish as always to thank them for keeping me
on my toes in the classroom and for ensuring that my work retains general
interest.

I also feel privileged to have gained the attention and support of several
Jewish community organizations throughout New England, including the
Conference on Judaism in Rural New England, the Springfield (Massachusetts) Jewish Community Center, Temple Israel in Greenfield, Massachusetts, and the Jewish Genealogical Societies of Western Massachusetts and
of Greater Boston. I was invited as well to speak at the Springfield (Massachusetts) Quadrangle, at The Center for the Study of Community (affiliated with Strawberry Banke Museum in Portsmouth, New Hampshire),
and before the University of Southern Maine's Program in American and
New England Studies. I thank each of these organizations for their interest in my research and for having fostered lively discussions after my talks
that, in several cases, helped me to adjust my premises and approaches to
the writing in useful ways.

Three individuals offered invaluable help to me as I drafted the manuscript, posing just the right sorts of questions and giving me just the right
sort of guidance as I sought both to thicken my analysis and to broaden
the book's possible audience. Clark Dougan, my editor at the University of
Massachusetts Press, has been kind, thorough, and encouraging from start
to finish, and has always been willing to supply me with substantive (and

timely!) responses to any portion of the manuscript I have cared to send his way. Abe Peck of the University of Southern Maine, who attended my University of Southern Maine talk, went far beyond the call of duty in agreeing to read the entire manuscript before I submitted it to the Press. Burt Feintuch of the University of New Hampshire has been a fine colleague and generous supporter of my work as well. His encouraging comments let me know that the job was well worth completing.

Transcribing hours and hours worth of audiotape is no small feat, and I must admit here to having done none of that onerous work. Instead, I hired several people, using funding received from Fitchburg State College. These transcribers were Jossely Castillo, Mike Chrisman, AnneMarie Donahue, Carey-Ann Esposito, Carolyn Halloran, Jess Rigollaud, and Moriah Sterling. Each did a superb job of producing clear and faithful written text representations of the audio interviews.

Although I conducted most of the interviews myself, three individuals provided me with additional oral history audiotapes and transcripts of archived interviews. Carrie and Michael Nobel Kline have always shared their fieldwork with me, and I appreciate their having encouraged me to use two of their interview tapes from Sandisfield, Massachusetts. Joel Halpern, a retired member of the Anthropology Department at the University of Massachusetts, Amherst, was kind enough to share his archive (housed at the Jones Library in Amherst) with me as well.

My final debt of thanks goes to my family. Janice Sorensen, whose artful photographs introduce aesthetic grace to the book and give a face to the many individuals whose story I try to tell here, has been boundless in her support, both as co-creator of the book and as a generous wife and life partner. My children, Della and Lang, have supplied inspiration, warmth, and help in the form of their willingness to execute the sorts of daily tasks that keep us all going in our busy lives. I am grateful as well to my mother, Milka Burstein, for her boundless love and abiding interest in my work, not to mention her kindness in helping me to complete the index.

How Strange
It Seems

. . .

A *Shtetl* on a Hill

o   o   o

Jewish life in the United States began as a distinctly urban phenomenon.
When the first boatload of Sephardic Jewish refugees came to New York
(then New Amsterdam) in 1654, they set a precedent. Successive generations of multiple Jewish backgrounds have followed suit, and only in the
second half of the twentieth century, with the rise of so many Jews into the
middle class and their subsequent move into the suburbs, did urban centers
begin to lose their dominant influence over Jewish life—though even then,
a metropolitan consciousness remained prevalent. A countercurrent, however, has always been detectable within Jewish settlement patterns, from
the Colonial period to the present. As one recent historian has asserted,
given the fact that so many of the nation's Jewish communities have been
"smaller ones in less prominent towns . . . [i]t would be a mistake to think
that the full story of the American Jewish experience can be told without
considering the history of small-town Jewish life."[1] In the largely agrarian
South, Jews were among the earliest settlers in several seaboard communities. Many served the Confederate cause during the Civil War. As some
historians would argue, a distinctly southern—and non-metropolitan—
Jewish culture has evolved over nearly 300 years of continual settlement.
Jews also played a prominent role on the western frontier as traders, early
homesteaders, and elected officials. In various regions throughout the
nation, they settled permanently in smaller communities and have continued to do so well into the present, in apparent defiance not only of Jewish
norms but of American patterns as well; in 2005, according to figures from
the census bureau, we were a nation in which 80 percent of the population

lived within a few miles of a city of 100,000 or more residents. This book documents the Jewish presence in small-town New England, largely through oral history interviews. The title, which I have taken from Henry Wadsworth Longfellow's 1852 poem "The Jewish Cemetery at Newport," is meant as a commentary on the apparent oddity of such a prospect.

Longfellow's poem is a Judeophilic commemoration of an apparently vanished Jewish presence in New England. Referring to "the long, mysterious Exodus of Death" undergone by "these Hebrews in their graves," the poet admires what no longer exists, as far as he is concerned. However small and fleeting the Jewish presence in colonial New England may have been, however, historical records point to a consistent, if dynamic, continuum of Jewish residence throughout the six states of New England, even in the hinterlands. What then, was so "strange," from Longfellow's point of view, about the fact that Jewish people were buried in an old Rhode Island cemetery? Was it their apparently alien religious practice—their davening of the "Psalms of David," "the ancient Decalogue," "the grand dialect the Prophets spoke"? Was it their history of persecution—"the wasting famine of the heart" whose only respite could be found in "the unleavened bread / And bitter herbs of exile"? Whatever the case, in Longfellow's view, Jewish history and Jewish history in New England provided an instructive and chastening lesson in preordained obsolescence. One wonders, however, what made New England seem like such an unlikely place for Jews to have settled. And why, given the region's ecclesiastical history, which has been so notably distinguished for its privileging of the Hebrew bible and the prophets, would Longfellow not have foreseen, if anything, a *revival* of Jewish life on the horizon? This book explores the verbal legacy of a long-standing Jewish presence in what people like Longfellow deemed the unlikeliest of places. That "the dead nations never rise again," as Longfellow puts it, is indisputable. A nation that resists death as the Jews have for millennia, on the other hand, is liable to revive itself just about anywhere.

Although most of American Jewish historiography tells a largely urban and, more recently, suburban story, this book tells the story of a relatively unexamined, specifically rural American Jewish demography—a story that many of us don't expect to hear. The stories told here are stories about Jews defying both other people's and their own expectations and becoming recognizable participants in the cultural life of places where, demographically, they constitute a tiny and barely recognizable minority. The stories told here are not, however, depictions of a vanishing presence. In the more than a hundred years since Jews began to settle permanently in small-town New England, they have worked continually to build, sustain, and renew their identity as Jews, even as they have forged strengthening connections to their new homes. As the accounts in the book show, rural New England Jews have acclimated to the cultural life of their hometowns without fully assimilating or relinquishing their Jewishness. The stories in this book suggest that life in small-town New England has allowed Jews to gain meaningful attachments to place and local communities and, simultaneously, to maintain a separate identity as Jews.

How Strange It Seems is hardly the only book to explore the legacy or cultural life of small-town Jews in America. The field of American Jewish history is a rich one, and several authors, both scholarly and more popular in their orientations, have documented the cultural lives of Jewish residents of the rural South, the Mid Atlantic states, and the Far West, and of small-town Jews in general. In some respects, the themes and patterns that emerge from this book echo much of this earlier research. Regardless of their region, small-town Jews in the United States share certain experiences. Jews who settled in smaller towns throughout America did so in search of the sort of economic independence that, at least by the turn of the twentieth century, was sometimes more easily attainable for them outside the nation's industrial and commercial centers. Along with the obvious relief that small-town life brought from urban overcrowding or, for that matter, from suburban *ennui*, life outside metropolitan areas often allowed Jews of an earlier generation to participate more fully than they might otherwise have in all manner of "mainstream American" civic endeavors and, in the current day, allows for greater access to outdoor pursuits. Small-town Jews, regardless of their region, have also worked effectively to overcome many of the sorts of sectarian differences that have plagued their metropolitan counterparts; because they constituted a tiny, sometimes barely visible minority, they could ill afford to disagree pointedly with one another on the proper way to live Jewishly. In a recent *New York Times* article, Mary Winchester—a Jewish resident of Bentonville, Arkansas—explains the underlying context that fuels Jewish unity in small towns: "You have to try harder to be Jewish down here," she says.[2]

As it is the "small-town" and "regional" focus that sets this book apart from other treatments of Jewish cultural life in the United States, I should like to say a few words about these terms at the outset. To begin, they are hardly interchangeable. Despite any nostalgia-driven popular tendency to assume that small towns are where regional differences are most likely to crop up, historians of regionalism have shown quite effectively that a distinct regional culture is the product of dynamic interaction between urban and rural centers. In New England in particular, the apparent distance between agrarian settlements in the uplands and increasingly industrialized activity of various urban centers, at least by the mid-nineteenth century, masked the reality of interdependence and symbiosis. As Stephen Nissenbaum writes, many small New England villages were given a facelift of sorts in the Civil War period; such towns were "re-made," Nissenbaum says, in a self-consciously "pastoral 'antimodern' image," in order to enforce a quickly vanishing distinction between the patterns of rural and urban life. Thus, "it is more than an irony that the pastoralization of the New England town was fueled by the Industrial Revolution."[3] In the present day, although the most recent census classifies "one tenth of southern New England's population and half of northern New England's population as rural," a mere 2 percent of the region's people live in towns of under 2,500.[4] To the extent that it *is* a distinct cultural region, New England is the product neither of rural agrarianism nor of urban industrialism but, instead, of the centuries-old cross-fertilizations and mutualities which unite its people and connect them to a single landscape. The aspects of New England identity that characterize the people whose stories comprise this book were forged in the country, in the city, and in the imagination. Most important, my own focus on a specifically regional experience is meant to offset a tenacious predilection on the part of Jews and other Americans alike to conflate Jewish history in America with, as Mark Bauman puts it, "New York Jewish history writ large."[5]

Likewise, the book's concentration on small-town (I use the term interchangeably with "rural") life is meant not to guarantee its relevance to a sense of New England regionalism but, rather, as a further enhancement of its subject's distinction from the mainstream, so to speak, of American Jewish life. Whether the identity and experiences of small-town New England Jews distinguish them more firmly from Jews in metropolitan areas or from the general population of Americans in regions other than New England, their small-town provenance marks their lives as recognizably separate.

All the same, the challenge of chronicling small-town life in New

England is compounded by the self-same factors that render the region a complex exception to any rule that might separate rural from metropolitan existence in other sections of the United States. Given the relatively small scale of its geography—only the remotest sections of Maine, New Hampshire, and Vermont are more than a few hours' drive distant from the urban centers of central and southern New England—even the smallest of towns are hardly isolated or entirely cut off from the mainstream. Residents of these towns have long engaged in a lively and frequent commerce with adjacent urban areas. For observant Jews in particular, membership and participation in Jewish life have often necessitated frequent and recurrent travel between small-town homes and synagogues that tend to be located in larger towns and small cities. Even small-town or rural Jews, in other words, are likely to spend considerable time in larger settlements. The population I have undertaken to study here is hardly a hermetic one.

Nonetheless, I have drawn oral histories here from residents of relatively small communities such as Bennington, Vermont (population 16,000); Laconia, New Hampshire (17,000); Northampton, Massachusetts (28,000); and Rockland, Maine (8,000). None of the aforementioned towns qualify as backwoods outposts; each has a long and mixed economic history which took shape as agricultural, industrial, and commercial enterprises converged and overlapped. For what it is worth, however, as busy as such places are and have been over the hundred years since Jewish people first moved to them, they hardly qualify as urban centers in and of themselves, nor do they function as bedroom communities for other urban centers. Jewish residents of these towns and towns like them have quite a bit in common with one another. For most of the preceding one hundred years, the more observant among them constituted single congregations. For the first several decades of their settlement, they drew their economic sustenance from itinerant sales, storefront retailing, cattle brokering, and small farming—small-town enterprises all. Although they may very well have had a good deal in common with their urban coreligionists in such places as Boston, Worcester, Manchester, and Hartford, their Jewish life was considerably more circumscribed by their relative distance from these Jewish centers of population.

While urban New England Jews may not have spoken with a Brooklyn accent, their ease of daily access to myriad Jewish institutions, proximity to entire neighborhoods full of other Jews, and large-scale participation in a multiplicity of avocations distinguished their existence quite sharply from that of small-town Jews. Big-city Jews—even outside New York itself—inhabited what Ewa Morawska refers to as a "a large industrial ethnic enclave." They were more likely, as Morawska shows, to attend college as early as the second generation. They participated in increasing numbers in "the decoupling of previously interfused ethnic and religious components in Jewish group life"[6]—in other words, it was easier for big-city Jews to be Jewish outside of the traditional synagogue setting. Even leaving aside Boston, with its dozens of Jewish religious, civic, and charitable organizations, some of which date back to the nineteenth century, attention to the history of a Jewish presence in Hartford, Connecticut, and Springfield, Massachusetts, for instance, offers further insight into the phenomenon of an urban New England Jewish experience as distinct from that of the smaller towns. In the mid 1800s, when Hartford's first Jewish congregation was formed, a local B'Nai Brith chapter was formed as well; shortly afterwards, Jewish women founded the "Deborah Society."[7] Springfield's Jewish history is similarly distinguished for its various and numerous institutions, its long list of kosher butchers and bakeries, its Jewish day schools, and its range of congregations and Jewish organizations, both religious and secular. Being Jewish in such places, over the last hundred years, has not been equivalent to being Jewish in New York, Miami, or Tel Aviv, but neither has it resembled the truly minority experience of Jewish life in the smaller towns of the region.

While *How Strange It Seems* certainly builds upon the work of other chroniclers of small-town Jewry and while the stories of rural New England Jews in many respects resonate with the stories of rural Jews throughout the nation, a distinct perspective emerges in this book—born, I would argue, of the uniqueness of small-town New England history and culture. As I met subjects, interviewed them, and then reviewed the transcripts of the sessions upon which this book is based, I couldn't help but notice that nearly every account gave voice in some fashion to an intriguing and New England-esque dual allegiance to the legacy of the past and the promise of the future. On the one hand, New England's distinct culture and landscape constitutes, as Bernard De Voto put it, "the first old civilization . . . in America."[8] At the same time, however, small-town New Englanders have always ensured their continued viability in a changing world by thinking progressively and by adapting to rather than shrinking from economic and social change. Each of the men and women with whom I spoke expressed some sort of connection to or admiration for the long-standing traditions and institutions of small-town New England life, not to mention his or her own familial and communal ties to a Jewish past. Where both traditions converge, it is the spirit of progress that unites them. In 2003 and 2004, I attended the Conference on Judaism in Rural New England, which for more than twenty years was held annually on a college campus in northern Vermont. Each of the larger meetings at those weekend gatherings concerned the current state of Jewish affairs, both in rural New England and in the world at large, and each of those meetings was run *on the model of a New England town meeting*. Traditions enacted in the present and in pursuit of an improved future, in other words, represent a common interest for both American Jews and small-town New Englanders. The past is valuable for its immediate applications in the present. In narrating their own history as New Englanders, the men and women I interviewed steer clear of sentimentalizing local heritage. Instead, their accounts draw consistent attention to the spirit of renewal and reinvention that has motivated small-town New Englanders for generations, in no small part because this enterprising spirit was what drew them or their ancestors to the area in the first place. As New Englanders and as Jews, the people upon whose stories this book is based all know what it means to inhabit the modern world without entirely leaving tradition behind.

Rural New England's fascinating history as America's own "Old World" and as the font of some of its newest thinking goes back as far as the age of its own founding as John Winthrop's "City on a Hill." The region's consistent homage to historical precedent, on the one hand, and spirit of innovation, on the other, go a long way toward explaining, among other things, the entire history of Puritanism, the origins of the American Revolution, the Abolitionist movement, the rise of industrialism, and, in more recent days, the area's role as a bastion of political liberalism. In contrast to the South, where traditionalism has been less of an adaptive force than a combative one, the historical mindset in New England has generally been applied in the name of forward movement; the *tradition* of "Yankee ingenuity," for instance, has justified all manner of *newfangled* experiments. As poet laureate Donald Hall notes, the New England experience has always taken shape against the backdrop of a landscape that continually collapses past and future. "New England," Hall writes, "is empty mills, new inventions, wooden scythes, a Mother Hubbard wrapped in paper and stored in a closet, a snow machine, biotechnology and contrails from Logan and Pease Air Force base streaking the blue air above the cellar hole of a farmer who came north after the Revolution to build his land."[9] Among the Jewish residents of small-town New England with whom I spoke, adherence to tradition has meant, aside from retaining one's own Jewish connections, living in proximity to an old landscape and in accordance with preexisting patterns of small-town life. Progressive thinking has meant, among other things, developing and tapping new markets, farming in accordance with new technologies, and adapting religious practice to the conditions imposed by life in an area where Jews must overcome any barriers to cooperation with one another if they are to have any Jewish life at all.

The earliest generation of Jewish small-town New Englanders—men and women who arrived in the area at the turn of the twentieth century— came from worlds in which a connection to the past was an all-powerful, often stifling force. The Eastern European *shtetls* from which so many of them immigrated were richly steeped in religious orthodoxy and in an age-old *Yiddishkeit*, but they were also restrictive landscapes in which Jews were prevented, as Jews, from owning land and, as a tradition-bound people, from attaining a modern education. On the other hand, many latter-day Jewish small-town New Englanders came from places where an opposite effect was at work. In the cities and suburbs of the modern United States, the sorts of communal ties, both within and outside the Jewish community, that are afforded by the face-to-face encounters inherent in small-town life, are distinctly lacking. Thus, rural New England's unique balance of past and future prospects, in which tradition and dynamism act as balancing forces, represents a sort of middle ground, an appropriate destination. Moreover, the region's relative proximity to some of the nation's largest urban centers has long enabled its residents to maintain a rural or semi-rural existence without cutting all ties to the surrounding national Jewish culture. For rural New England Jews, ease of access to urban areas has made all sorts of necessary things available, from kosher foods to college educations.

One noted historian of New England has gone a step further and insinuated that New England's Puritan heritage made it a particularly fitting locale for Jewish life. The region's apparent Arnoldian "Hebraism," as Andrew Delbanco puts it, took shape as a result of its "questing, disputatious quality of mind" and its people's tendency to "seek the future through a dialectical process of debate with themselves." [10] To the extent that such a mindset actually exists, the similarities between it and a distinctly Jewish perspective are unmistakable. The centrality of language, law, and disputation, which grew out of Puritanism's noted preference for the Hebrew bible, lends another occasion for parallelism. "Even though the Puritans' intolerance of heresy, blasphemy and just plain orneriness is what the modern imagination still associates with colonial New England," argues the historian Stephen Whitfield, New England's legalism "did not discomfort the legatees of a people that had lived the Book." [11] By the time that significant numbers of Jews began to settle in the region, Puritanism itself lay in the distant past, but its vestigial remnants—the face-to-face democracy of the town meeting, the emphasis within village life of thrift and hard work—were still plainly in evidence. That one could prosper or even thrive through adherence to such codes of behavior was hardly lost on the immigrant Jews who came to such places. A few of my sources for this study spoke directly to their own ancestors' admiration for and adoption of such characteristically small-town New England attributes. Many others offered indirect commentary on similar themes—words to the effect that they or their parents or grandparents had earned the respect of neighbors, Jewish and non-Jewish alike, through their unostentatious achievement of economic independence and community respect.

Whatever such resonances may be, attention to them begs the question: why should region matter in the first place in the context of the American Jewish experience? In the last ten years, historians have engaged in a lively debate over this question. Scholars have asked whether varying regional affiliations among American Jews are important or incidental aspects of Jewish identity. If they are important, the implication is that Jews, like members of many other ethnic groups in the United States, have achieved (or fallen into) a sort of assimilation. Local style has affected them to such a degree that it has influenced their cultural existence in powerful ways; they have been fully accepted by their non-Jewish neighbors, and they have embraced their neighbors' way of life in turn. If regional affiliations are merely incidentally significant, on the other hand, it is because Jews throughout the United States have much more in common with other Jews than they do with their gentile neighbors wherever they live. Though they may live fairly comfortably in small-town New England, or in the rural

South, or in any number of other cultural regions of the United States, their Jewishness has precluded both their acceptance by others and their own embrace of local culture. The debate has thus far centered on the South, where the *appearance*, at least, of a distinctly regional Jewish culture has been most prevalent as Jews there seem to have acquired southern accents and dietary practices. Mark Bauman and Bobbie Malone refer to this as "'the shalom y'all' factor" and are somewhat dismissive of its relative importance. How, they ask, can serving fried rather than baked chicken on Friday or bagels with grits on the side "define a distinctive Southern Jewish identity"?[12]

Bauman first challenged the prevailing view of a separate and identifiably southern Jewish culture in an intentionally provocative pamphlet published in 1996. Its central assertion—"Where regional contrasts appear, they tend to be superficial"[13]—might seem to fly in the face of a study such as this one, in which the regional focus is a defining element. Indeed, Bauman's central premise is that southern Jews, for all of their historical affiliations with the southern experience and their adoption of even the accoutrements of southern folklife, have throughout their history adhered still more closely to the patterns of Jewish life found throughout the United States and to American trends in general. The overall relevance of folklife and vernacular style, Bauman argues, is not sufficient to counter Jews' simultaneous tendencies, in their social and cultural behavior, to mirror national trends. Their survival and prosperity in the South have been a result of their long-term participation in a delicate balancing act, in which adherence to (or deviance from) regional norms has served a larger motivational purpose. Moreover, as Bauman points out, sub-regional differences, such as whether a given Jewish population lives in metropolitan Atlanta, for instance, or central Charleston, or in the upland South, may very well be of greater significance than whether that population is identifiably "southern."

"If Jews in Boston ate beans and had a Boston accent, or if Jews in the Southwest ate Mexican food, learned Spanish and adapted local clothing styles," Bauman asks, "would the historian offer these factors as evidence of regional distinctiveness?"[14] Presented in such a way, indeed, the traditional folk trappings of regional style do strike us as transparent and superficial. Non-Jews who eat beans or "pahk the cah in Hahvahd Yahd," according to such a formulation, are hardly more regionally distinct than Jews would be. So if regional distinction is important, its outward trappings in and of themselves can hardly be counted as central factors. Moreover, regional affiliation among Jews, superficial or otherwise, has been a minor component of a much more significant tendency on the part of Jews to maintain a necessary equilibrium within the larger context of national life between being Jewish and being American. Eating in accordance with local foodways or pronouncing words in certain ways has had less to do with Jews' desire to express a strictly local or regional solidarity than it has with their eagerness, when necessary, to blend into whatever environment in which they have come to settle.

Ultimately, the question of whether or not regional style has impacted Jews is of less importance than another line of inquiry, which motivates this book: what are the various ways in which Jewish people have been shaped by and, in turn, come themselves to shape, the places where they have lived in America? One has to expect a range of answers to such a question. Adherence to or deviation from a regional "norm" presupposes a unitary or fixed set of cultural behaviors which, given the inherent complexities that govern the cultural existence of a place, is an unlikely prospect. Accordingly, this book does not argue that Jews have either become or been prevented from becoming "real" small-town New Englanders. Nor does it argue that Jews who grew up in or moved to places like New Hampshire or Maine are fundamentally different, on that basis alone, from Jews in similarly sized communities in Minnesota or Alabama. What the book does suggest, on the other hand, is that the particularities of local experience do matter, even if they are merely enhancements of or catalysts for the broader Americanization of Jews, or, for that matter, if their alienness prevents such acts of assimilation. In his response to Bauman's pamphlet on southern Jews, Eric Goldstein observes that although regions, like "historical time periods," are based on "artificial" and, indeed, "porous" boundaries, they can often constitute helpful tools of analysis as we seek deeper insight into the significance of place within the American Jewish experience.[15]

The exigencies of small-town life in New England—closeness of past and future prospects, of tradition and innovation—do "translate" well from a Jewish perspective. Though the existence of such a pattern hardly guarantees the existence of an absolutely singular small-town New England Jewish experience, it has influenced Jews and non-Jews alike in their fashioning of a placed-based mentality. Rural New England's unique geography—its comparatively small scale, its history of mixed agricultural and industrial uses, its proximity to areas of dense settlement—is bound to have instigated a range of results for the various people who have settled there. Regardless of whether small-town Jewish New Englanders are more Yankee or more American, more American or more Jewish, their experiences offer insight into the unique history of what has been, arguably, the nation's most dynamic cultural arena. Likewise, sustained attention to the life of such places reveals the profound ambivalence that underlies Jewish existence in the modern world. If the collective experiences of small-town Jews in New England are unique, it is not because Jews have either acquired one identity or discarded another but because they have undergone a discrete set of exposures to a combination of geographical, economic, and social circumstances in living there, and these exposures have precluded any sort of simple result. In many important respects, Jewish life in rural New England has been similar to Jewish life everywhere else in the United States; in others, it has departed from such norms. Its affinity for or defiance of regional norms, to the extent that such norms can be said to exist at all, should be of equal interest to anyone interested in Jewish life in the United States or in the history of one of its most integral regions.

Though some version of oral history figures as an element in many foregoing studies of small-town Jews, in this book it constitutes the central core. *How Strange It Seems* renders a heretofore untold story in the very words of the people whose story it tells. I have chosen to tell this story through oral history interviews because, though written accounts of small-town Jewish life in New England do exist, they are too fragmentary in nature and constitute too small a sample to represent anything like a composite view. Notwithstanding Bauman's and others' warnings against excessive attention to the "superficialities" of regional accent or foodways, I also adhere to the view, perhaps best expressed by the folklorist Barre Toelken, that concentration on vernacular experience is ideal to the study of a non-metropolitan context in particular. As Toelken writes, the "invisible" products and processes specific to the folk context are of particular value as indices of a rural culture because, unlike the "written and material products of intellectuals," they emerge from frequent and ubiquitous interactions among the quiet, but hardly silent, majority.[16] Small-town life itself, by virtue of all its face-to-face engagements, close-knit institutions, and place-specific traditions, can be most clearly delineated in the forms of "ordinary" talk that can be best elicited in the course of an interview.

How Strange It Seems is an ethnography modeled on the work of folklorists, oral historians, and other documentarians who have sought to depict a group's cultural life on the basis of evidence yielded by a collection of first-hand accounts. I conducted my research for the book first by reading every written source I could find pertaining to the cultural lives of small-town New England Jews. When I had exhausted that rather limited supply of bibliographical sources, I began to seek tradition-bearers for oral history interviews. This I did, initially, by contacting Jewish communities throughout the region (roughly defined, for my purposes, as Maine, New Hampshire, Vermont, and rural portions of Massachusetts and Connecticut) and asking them to announce my study. A handful of immediate responses led to an opening round of interviews in southern Vermont and western Massachusetts. As anyone who has conducted ethnographic research well knows, each interview yields multiple possibilities for additional contacts. After three years of work, I had conducted over 50 separate interviews with 60 individuals. These people were fairly evenly distributed in terms of age, gender, occupation, and New England state of origin or current habitation.

The questions I posed in the interviews were immediate outgrowths of the sorts of questions that motivated the study itself. In the interest of learning how and why my tradition-bearers and their ancestors had come to small-town New England in the first place, I asked people to tell me where they and their families had come from and how they ended up here. As I wanted to know what sort of work small-town New England Jews had engaged in for sustenance, I asked subjects to tell me about their own, their parents', and their grandparents' occupational lives. My interest in Jews' involvement and implication in the civic and cultural life of rural New England led to questions about their participation in town governance and the sorts of customary traditions that continue to inform the communal life of small-town New England. Finally, my interest in tracing out the evolution of Jewish religious observation and folklife within the milieu of small-town New England led to questions about, among other things, synagogue formation, Hebrew education, Sabbath-keeping, dietary practices, and the use of Yiddish in the home.

Once I completed the interviews, each of which I had recorded on audiotape, I sought out professional transcribers to develop written texts.

The transcribers with whom I worked did minimal editing; aside from the excision of the inevitable false starts, multiple word repetitions, and "um's" and "uh's," the transcripts are verbatim replications of the actual audiotapes. Reading the result—a stack of transcribed interviews that comprises approximately 750 single-spaced pages of text—occupied my sustained attention for several months. As best I could, I sought to label portions of interviews in keeping with my discrete interest in small-town New England Jewish settlement history, agricultural activity, economic endeavor, civic involvement, religious expression, and folklife. The patterns and themes that emerged from this large compendium of "raw" data are the sorts of patterns and themes I have spoken of above. Jews came to rural New England because they sought new prospects and livelihoods *and* a stable, historically situated environment in which they might be able to retain the sorts of tight-knit communal structures they had known in the Old Country. Those few among them who lived—or, in the present day, live—agriculturally did so by combining traditional practices and mores with new methods motivated by economic necessity and an interest in sustainability. Tradition-bearers' descriptions of non-agricultural occupations, such as peddling, retailing, and work in the professions occasioned accounts of livelihoods sought and found in which a proper balance between the maintenance of a traditional neighborliness and an innovative mindset could be achieved. So too did my tradition-bearers' descriptions of their religious and cultural lives as Jews speak at once to their dual allegiance to a historical consciousness and to the need for constant adaptation to changing conditions.

For all its focus on oral traditions and personal anecdotes, *How Strange* does address itself to an underlying historical and geographical reality. Jews have been visible participants in the cultural life of small-town New England since the late nineteenth century. Demographic research compiled by the historian Lee Shai Weissbach indicates that, as of 1927, New England itself contained 66 "triple-digit" Jewish communities whose population, in turn, comprised 13 percent of the region's 250,000 Jews.[17] Sizable Jewish communities could be found not only in small towns in the densely populated (and immigrant-heavy) states of Massachusetts, Connecticut, and Rhode Island, but in Maine, New Hampshire, and Vermont. Of the dozen or so communities represented in this book as a current home for Jewish families, each had a significant Jewish population as far back as the early twentieth century. In 1927, towns as small as Bennington, Vermont (total population 7,000), and Rockland, Maine (total population 8,000), hosted populations that were 7 and 8 percent Jewish, respectively, even as the national Jewish population was well under 5 percent.[18]

In the current day as well, small-town New England's Jewish population continues to thrive, even as the national trend among American Jews is toward an overall decline in population. New England itself, as of the 2000 census, is home to nearly 400,000 Jews. Most Jews continue to live in or immediately outside of the region's major cities, but up to 35,000–40,000 live in the upland districts that comprise the geographical focus of this book. Within upland New England, western Massachusetts has the highest concentration of Jewish residents; Jews represent between 1 and 5 percent of the total population in all three rural counties of western Massachusetts, even as the national Jewish population (approximately 6,000,000) has slipped below 3 percent. Parts of northern New England are marked by a similar Jewish demographic. Of Maine's 15 counties, 5 host a Jewish population that ranges from 0.5 to 5 percent. Three of Vermont's 13 counties are home to a 1–5 percent representation of Jews. Three of New Hampshire's 10 counties host between 0.5 and 1 percent, and another 2 counties in that state are home to a 1 to 5 percent Jewish population.[19] In recent years, a significant Jewish population increase has been tracked in both New Hampshire and Vermont, where growth at a rate of 10 percent or higher has been recorded, even within the context of the shrinkage in the national Jewish population and a trend away from the northeastern United States in general.[20] Where the larger demographic trend among Jews seems in the last several decades to have favored the western and southern states, small-town New England persists nonetheless in attracting a Jewish population.

Notwithstanding the demographic patterns that underlie the stories in this book, the emphasis here is on individual and family experiences. I readily acknowledge that interviewing 60 people is hardly equivalent to conducting a comprehensive or scientific survey. Rather, the close concentration on a relatively small sample allows for another sort of achievement—a human-scale, integrally verbal portrait of an otherwise hidden historical and cultural phenomenon. Indeed, the best existing studies of small-town Jews in America thus far have been broadly based social histories, in which the experiences of a large number of people are filtered through a discriminating, but often distant voice of historical objectivity. I have sought in this book to work on a less daunting scale and in the interest of introducing a more humanistic perspective and bringing about a more immediate and palpable effect. Though my voice is consistent throughout, the physical presence of my subjects' own words exercises a powerful balancing influence and is meant to create a textured reading experience. If the result is more impressionistic than exhaustive, it is nonetheless meant, in the historian Gary Okihiro's words "to capture the human spirit of the people" who lived the experiences recounted here.[21]

Stanley "Pal" Borofsky, owner of Sam's Outdoor Outfitters, Brattleboro, Vermont.

Steve, Maxwell, and
Andy Pyenson, Otis,
Massachusetts.

MIDDLE AND RIGHT: Postcards from
Otis Poultry Farm.

TOP: Charlotte and Julius "Zeese" Goos, Augusta, Maine.
BOTTOM: Suzie Laskin with her dog, Sam, Chatham, New Hampshire.

TOP: Rabbi Howard Cohen, formerly of Congregation Beth El, Bennington, Vermont.

BOTTOM: Bob and Amy Jo Montgomery in front of Congregation Beth El.

Work and
prayer at site
of sugarhouse/
shul, Halifax,
Vermont.

Work and
prayer at site
of sugarhouse/
shul.

Noon davening
at sugarhouse/
shul worksite.

Frame raising of
sugarhouse/shul,
February 2006.

Rabbi Shmuel
Simenowitz at
sugarhouse/shul
frame raising.

Sugarhouse/shul
frame raising.

TOP: Rabbi Max Wall, Burlington, Vermont.
BOTTOM: William and Mary Markle,
Randolph, Vermont.

TOP: Natalie Cohen, Augusta, Maine.
BOTTOM: Edwin "Sonny" Chertok, holding
a portrait of his late wife, Pauline, Laconia,
New Hampshire.

TOP: Natalie Cohen lighting the Shabbat candles, Oakland, Maine, 1947 (courtesy of Natalie Cohen).

BOTTOM: Eli and Betty Gordon, Freedom, New Hampshire.

Beala Stark Schiffman, Great Barrington, Massachusetts.

The Gan (Garden), Adamah
organic farming project at
Isabella Freedman Center,
Falls Village, Connecticut.

Steve and Julie Chamay with son Zeke, Pownal, Vermont.

TOP: Sumner Winebaum with the author, under his father's old neon sign, York, Maine.

BOTTOM: Sumner Winebaum with one of his castings.

Milton Adelman and Ray Gribetz in front of Aroostook
Hebrew Community Center, Presque Isle, Maine.

Yoga workshop at the Sweet Harvest Festival, Sukkut 2006, National Yiddish Book Center, Amherst, Massachusetts.

TOP: Timberframe sukkah at the Sweet Harvest Festival.
BOTTOM: Building the timberframe sukkah at the Sweet Harvest Festival.

CHAPTER 1

Settling the Landscape of the Present and Future
Jewish Migration to Small-Town New England, 1900–2000

o   o   o

Rural New England's hills, forests, and villages have been home turf for Jews for more than a century. In many cases, Jewish settlers in the region came from cities and had to acclimate to a new landscape, its occupational patterns, and its folkways. Other Jewish arrivals in rural New England immigrated, directly or indirectly, from agrarian communities in Europe. For these settlers, as well as for the many others who may not have been farmers per se but had subsisted in sparsely populated farming communities, milking cows and bidding on farmland came easily, even as learning a new language and new customs posed challenges. Like all newcomers, the Jews of rural New England have adopted local cultural templates. They have had to learn place names, conform to work patterns, and negotiate local town governance. Permanent settlers do more than merely assimilate to preexisting behaviors, however. For generations, the Jews of small-town New England have inhabited a land whose physical contours and cultural norms have also been made to "fit" their own singular history and traditions. In most respects, then, these Jews have undergone many of the same sorts of transformative and transforming experiences as their non-Jewish neighbors. In a region whose own past has long been marked by cultural dynamism, economic flux, and a tradition of resourceful stick-to-itiveness, Jews have been fitting participants.

Jewish New Englanders of the past century or so trace their roots to various places both in the Old Country of Eastern and Central Europe and, more recently, to the cities and suburbs of the United States. Wherever they came from, however, the present-day Jewish residents of small-town New

England whose stories I collected consider themselves to be *at home* where they are now. Places of origin, in this view, tended to be either unstable (as was the case for the persecuted Jews of tsarist Russia who came here at the turn of the twentieth century) or spiritually unsatisfying (such is the story of the urban and suburban Jews of the latter half of the twentieth century). Tradition-bearers' stories about how they came to their current home communities, on the other hand, tend to emphasize the idea that the rural New England they inhabit represents a sort of provisional destiny. Small-town New England is a resting place and, often enough, a font of economic, cultural, and political wholeness in the face of oppression and, more recently, fragmentation and malaise.

In this regard, perhaps it can be said that Jewish newcomers to rural New England have reversed an existing pattern in which Americans of diverse origins look upon the region as a place of origin rather than as a place of destiny. Rural New England has long served non–New Englanders as a sort of imaginary attic. As the historian Dona Brown puts it in her book *Inventing New England*, American tourists, beginning in the nineteenth century, "sought out the isolated or remote parts of New England looking for an imagined world of pastoral beauty, rural independence, virtuous simplicity and ethnic homogeneity . . . a trip to New England came to mean an escape from the conditions of urban and industrial life."[1] The long-time popularity of *Yankee* magazine throughout the United States, as well as the region's status as a major "heritage vacation" destination, speaks in more contemporary terms to this idea of rural New England as an aspect of the nation's nostalgic yearnings.[2] It is worth noting, however, that the accounts of Jewish newcomers to the region, over the last hundred years at least, tend to highlight their experiences in the present and prospects for the future. Although the Jewish New Englanders with whom I spoke express a nearly universal appreciation for the sorts of small-town, "traditionally" New England values celebrated by the nation at large and its heritage industry, such appreciation is expressed with a certain amount of psychic detachment. Rural New England Jews make no claims on the region as embodying *their* heritage. Rather, they might mention its historical attractions in the same breath as they might refer to its architectural charms, its resources for outdoor recreation, or its highly regarded educational institutions.

Plenty of Jewish New Englanders, especially in the last three decades or so, have similarly gravitated to the region's quieter corners because they sought escape either from the physical confines of urban life or from the psychic confines of a perceived suburban consumerism and cultural uniformity. But even these apparent refugees from the hustle and bustle of life in post-agrarian America have hardly sought escape from modernity itself. Late nineteenth- and early twentieth-century Jewish immigrants to small-town New England came here, in every case, because economic opportunity beckoned, and because a rural location seemed to offer the promise of untapped markets, affordable properties, and an enhanced civic engagement. Like many of their coreligionists who settled in the nearby Catskill mountains of upstate New York, Jews in small-town New England gained "gradual entrance into the cultural lives, businesses and local governments" that shaped rural life.[3] More recent Jewish arrivals in rural New England can only be so retrospective. Even if the Anglo-American mainstream may view New England as "a storied place"[4] which unchangingly awaits the nation's Thanksgiving Day return, Jews—whose "homeplace" will always be a far more distant and storied land of origin—experience places like small-town New England as lands whose meaning can be sought and located only in the present and future. Nostalgia is hardly an integral element in the narrative repertoire of rural New England Jews speaking about their places of origin, and it rarely figures into their generally enthusiastic expressions of allegiance to their current homes either. In this respect, Jewish inhabitants of small-town New England seem to have stood outside the regional mainstream, in which loyalty to the past legitimates actions and identities in the present. Where local heritage could be made useful in the present, on the other hand, and the institutions of small-town life were found to be conducive to continued prosperity and growth in an ever-changing cultural and economic milieu, rural-dwelling Jews embraced it. New England's history may not have been *their* history, but the contemporary legacy of that history inspired continual engagement on their part.

Research on Italian and Irish, as well as other immigrants from Europe in the latter half of the nineteenth century and first two decades of the twentieth, suggests that the promise of a new life in America was quite often darkened by the sadness that resulted from the immigrants' reluctant relinquishing of ancestral homes. Traditional Irish songs and stories that bear the sad tale of banishment from the green fields of Erin constitute a considerable portion of the Irish-American folk repertoire. Such elements

within the Irish oral tradition speak in direct and often very specific terms
to a centuries-old attachment to an actual landscape, as well as to the perceived loss of an entire set of rural folkways that could hardly have been
replicated in the new land. The Jewish newcomers to America, most of
whom journeyed across the same North Atlantic at a later stage of the same
age of massive immigration, did not bear a similar folk heritage. As Philip
Roth writes in his recent novel *The Plot Against America*, "Though Ireland
still mattered to the Irish and Poland to the Poles and Italy to the Italians,
we retained no allegiance, sentimental or otherwise, to those Old World
countries we had never been welcome in and that we had no intention of
ever returning to."[5] Deprived for so many generations not only of their own
fabled homeland but in the ensuing diasporic centuries of the privilege of
landowning *anywhere*, the Jews of Eastern Europe who immigrated to the
United States were not nearly as intent on retaining vivid folk memories
of their lands of origin. Even Jewish immigrants who came to America
from rural areas seem not to have been terribly eager to communicate their
memories of such places to their children or grandchildren.

Folk memory has a way of testifying to the deepest truths regarding a
group's psychic connections to places of origin, as well as its attachments
in the present to the landscape underfoot. As a folklorist trained to seek
out the elements of a living and time-borne oral tradition, I made sure as I
was conducting my field study to ask the sorts of questions that might best
prompt my tradition-bearers to act as the *bearers* of bounded, established
narratives or family legends that would speak to the experiences of parents
and grandparents. Early in any given interview, I asked people to tell me
about any retained memories or images of the Old Country that they had
received while growing up. Not surprisingly, the immediate offspring or
grandchildren of first-generation Jewish immigrants from Eastern Europe
share an almost universal account of Old Country woes or, quite often,
of grandparents who were tight-lipped on matters concerning their Old
Country origins. By contrast, the composite effect of these same people's
accounts of coming to rural New England suggest that Jews whose parents
and grandparents settled in the area at the turn of the twentieth century
view themselves as the fortunate inheritors of and participants in a lively
rural commerce, dynamic cultural life, and, more often than not, vibrant
Jewish milieu whose greatest attributes derive not from a picture-postcard
pedigree but from a sustained engagement with the conditions of the

present. Particularly for the earlier Jewish settlers in the region, life here couldn't help but have been an improvement, economically and socially, over what had preceded it.

Population figures for the two decades between 1907 and 1927, a period during which the German Jewish immigration of the mid-nineteenth century had long since tapered off and been largely replaced by Eastern European immigration, show that New England's total Jewish demography more than tripled, from a regional total of 120,000 to 370,000.[6] The Russian influx was of course primarily an urban phenomenon; even Jews who had come from the comparatively rural *shtetlach* in Eastern Europe usually found their way into urban settings once they arrived in the United States. The migration was a massive one; between 1881, when Tsar Alexander II was assassinated, to the eve of World War I in 1914, 2 million Jews came to the United States from the Pale of Settlement.[7] But the rural impact, while it took place on a much smaller scale, was considerable. The respective 1907 Jewish populations of the northern New England states—5,000 in Maine, 1,000 in New Hampshire and 1,100 in Vermont—had more than doubled by 1927.[8] Census figures for specific rural communities are useful indicators of the change as well. Between 1905 and 1918, for instance, Pittsfield (the central municipality in predominantly rural Berkshire County, Massachusetts) saw its Jewish population multiplied by six, from 250 to 1,500.[9] Between 1878 and 1927, the Jewish population of Rutland, Vermont, saw a proportionally similar increase, from 24 to 160.[10] Indeed, as early as 1927, besides being home to two cities with Jewish populations of over 1,000 (Portland and Bangor), Maine was host to nine additional communities, as Lee Shai Weissbach measures them, numbering in three digits.[11]

Jews in places like these had come for all sorts of reasons, but in the main, their *economic* livelihood was tied to their activities as merchants to the non-Jewish industrial workforce in the respective towns in which they had settled. James Gelin, in his history of the Springfield (Massachusetts) Jews between 1840 and 1905, chronicles the initial influx. Although Gelin describes the early stages of an urban Jewish community, his account mirrors the story of Jews who settled in any number of other small New England towns during the period and the decades following:

Between 1880 and 1885, several Jewish men, most of them peddlers, believed to be of Russian origin, arrived in Springfield. Tanchin

Ivorovitch . . . arrived in Springfield in the late 1870's, settled on Carew Street and continued in his occupation as a "commercial traveler." Leaving the city for several years in 1881, he returned in 1886; throughout the rest of the century, he would find himself peddling ice and eventually running a junk business. He would also dabble in the meat market. The peddler Isodore Cohen arrived in Springfield at the age of thirty two in 1881; he would continue peddling "dry goods" throughout the next decade. Louis Alpert . . . was first peddling his rags in the city in 1884, but later, he decided that tin would be a more profitable item to sell. Alpert was one of the first Jews to live in the North End, and by the start of the twentieth century he would be a successful cattle dealer.[12]

As increasing numbers of itinerants gathered enough capital to establish stationary businesses, Jews across the region began, in the years following 1900, to found congregations and communities.

"That's as Far as the Train Went at That Time":
How the First Generation of Jews Came to the Countryside

Initial arrival in rural New England, whether it was the result of happenstance or of a carefully plotted sequence of events, was, for many small-town Jews in the region, momentous. The descendants of "early" settlers have effectively retained, through family oral traditions, the memories of their predecessors' first arrival. This circumstance seems to result from at least two related factors. First, long-time Jewish residents of rural New England districts are accustomed to being asked how they ended up in those communities in the first place. In anticipation of such inquiries, so it seems, many of the current-day "oldtimers" are well equipped with seemingly ready-made anecdotes which, over the years through telling and retelling, have taken on the status of deliberate, bounded narratives within a larger folk repertoire. Moreover, insofar as the stories tend to have a thematic core or purpose to them, their frequency of retelling also seems to stem from their retention of a sort of object lesson in the challenges and rewards of finding one's and one's family's geographical destiny. The circumstances surrounding the retelling exert a natural effect, of course, on such things. When the descendants of the early settlers describe their parents' and grandparents' initial arrival in rural New England, the land-scape in question still lies before them, a reminder replete with latter-day reference points.

Jews who came to rural New England before and after the turn of the century came there for economic opportunity. In some cases, their choices seem to have followed from a specific desire to try life outside the major cities. Some of the men and women who became rural New England Jews had been, in the Old Country beforehand, residents of rural districts. The relative frequency with which these immigrants became cattle dealers, for instance, seems to have followed from the circumstances of their previ-ous existence in Eastern Europe, where cattle dealing was one sanctioned means by which Jews could earn a living in rural districts. Whether they were sampling rural life for the first time or returning to it after a mediat-ing sojourn in an American city, these early Jewish arrivals became the cen-tral characters in family narratives whose continual telling and retelling into the current age suggests that settlement in small-town New England was a significant identity-forming experience.

In conducting the field interviews, I generally asked tradition-bearers to tell me exactly how their families found themselves settling in the region. Many of the resulting narratives are distinct not only for their framed qual-ity, but few were quite as carefully and lovingly rendered as Milt Adelman's account of how his father, Hiram Adelman, ended up in northern Maine. The elder Adelman, in 1900 or so, had "arrived in New York and spent a year working in a hardware store, but didn't like it because he wasn't used to the city life, and he asked everybody where he could go where it was [a] more similar climate to what he came from." Milt continues, "They told him to go north as far as he could go in Maine. So he took his sav-ings and he got on a train and went to Houlton, Maine. That's as far as the train went at that time." After serving another town-bound apprenticeship working in a store in Houlton, Hiram Adelman went on to become one of Aroostook County's largest potato farmers. He and his family became per-manent settlers, in other words, but the inception of their move to Maine, as Milt Adelman indicates, was an almost entirely arbitrary one. What if the people he had asked had sent him to Minnesota, for instance? In the imagination of his family, in any case, Maine constituted a more sensible home than New York where, by all accounts, as a young man who had been raised in a rural area of Russia, he didn't fit in. According to Hiram's

son-in-law Jack Mazer, "Jobs for unskilled people [in New York] were limited. After painting a building, sewing sleeves in a loft and trying other
dead end jobs, Hiram said, 'This is not for me.' " [13]

A remarkably similar story emerges from the recollections of another
family of agricultural Maine Jews, the Gooses. Zeese, or Julius Goos, grew
up in Bangor, where a considerable Jewish population (of German origin,
primarily) had been in residence, intermittently, since the 1840s. As Zeese
Goos explains, the family's origins in a rural area in Europe had a direct
bearing on their choice to settle in a rural community in New England. His
father, "left Poland and landed in Boston and started to work there by picking rags, sorting out rags. He tried that for a while, and then, the story goes,
while he was working he heard this cow mooing. He had been in the cattle
business in Poland, so he said, 'What am I doing here? This is time for a
change.' So he took off and went to Bangor . . ." Zeese Goos's story—and
he identifies it as a narrative in traditional family circulation—offers a case
in point of the forceful and enterprising individual who knows just what he
wants and needs. The story's celebration of individual will and resourcefulness resonates with all manner of traditional family pioneering narratives
that center around a moment of truth as experienced by one founding pro-
genitor or another.

Zeese Goos's wife Charlotte tells a similar story. Her grandparents
had immigrated as young adults from Russia to Chelsea, Massachusetts.
The grandmother's sister was living in Skowhegan, Maine, and, as Goos
explains, "kept asking her to come because she was not too well and she
thought she would have a better life. She'd have a home there and not be
in a tenement in Boston." Bennet and Razel August, according to their
nephew Bob, "didn't really like being in New York City at all [because] it
wasn't a healthy environment." They moved to Northampton, Massachusetts, on the suggestion of a relative who was already there. Bob August
describes himself as a "product of western Massachusetts in a very literal
sense." On his mother's side of the family, both Kronicks and Kramers had
moved to North Adams and later Greenfield, Massachusetts, for similar
reasons. Steve Steinberg recounts the story of his own pioneering grandfather's settlement atop Kimball Hill outside the tiny village of Whitefield,
New Hampshire. Steinberg's grandfather had left his native Lithuania as a
youngster, moving first to South Africa and then to England. From there, as
a British subject, he was able, according to the story his grandson recalls, to

enter Canada, where he "traded with the Indians and the islanders." Somewhere in the Maritimes, he fell in love with a Canadian girl and arranged
to marry her. He left both the girl and Canada on the eve of his planned
conversion to Catholicism, however, and immigrated this time to Portland,
Maine. From there, he made his way inland through family connections
toward northern New Hampshire. He bought a farm on "one of the higher
spots in Whitefield, which is near Mt. Washington. It was a small, little
town," Steinberg explains, "that had no particular claim to fame. People
were farmers, worked in the woods, had a couple of little factories there.
And he had a little farm. . . ."

In Sandisfield, Massachusetts, Jewish immigrants were motivated to
settle on parcels of farmland owing to a large-scale Jewish Agricultural
Agency sponsorship. Jack Pevzner, though he was born in New Jersey, was
raised in Sandisfield. His mother's father had come there early on, "from
Ellis Island[, where] a land agent sold him a whole farm for $800." Another
Sandisfield settler, Abraham Moskowitz, came to Sandisfield from New
York where, as his daughter-in-law Irene Moskowitz tells it, he "would get
bottles of beer and climb up on a building and sell them to the [construc-
tion] workers." Jack Sandler, the late husband of Sandisfield tradition-
bearer Lena Sandler, made his original purchase of farmland while still
living in New York City. His, as Mrs. Sandler recalls, was the typical immigrant's dream. Jack Sandler, "used to be in New York City and worked all
his life. . . . And then [he thought] he would come [make money in the
country], and he thought he would be a big man in Europe. . . . He was
working like ten horses here to accumulate his money. . . . So he bought
this piece of farm, through a neighbor right next door. . . ." It took Sandler
some time to accustom himself to farm ownership; his wife recounts that
before finally settling on the land, he first sold it back to the neighbor from
whom he had bought it. For all of its promise of removal from urban squa-
lor, rural life, especially when one faced the prospect of tilling the thin soil
of the Berkshires, was hardly paradisiacal.

Ruben Tablitz, who eventually became a business associate of Sandler's,
supplies a broad retrospective view of Sandisfield's original settlement by
Jews. The people who came there from New York had been "very, very
poor. Very, very poor. Finally, the [First World] War broke out," Tablitz
explains. "A lot of Jewish people . . . were operating in clothing and this
and that, you know, in New York. And of course, everybody gets tired of

what he is doing. They come . . . to Sandisfield. This one had a father, this one had a mother. And they bought a farm." A noteworthy pattern in Tablitz's account, which happens to echo both Milt Adelman's and Zeese Goos's, is its suggestion that a rural geography was a welcome and sustaining antidote to the urban existence that most Jews, for better or worse, had found upon immigrating to the United States. The same was true for the Pyenson family, which settled also through assistance from the Jewish Agricultural Society, in Otis, Massachusetts (adjoining Sandisfield). Maxwell Pyenson, who was born on the family's farm in 1916, tells the story of how the family came there:

> My folks came here in 1904 or '05. My mother came [to America] first and worked in the garment district in New York and saved up enough money to send for my father. . . . He came [to America] the following year and they stayed for a while in Brooklyn and were associated in a candy store . . . and that didn't work out and they somehow got the word that people next door to where we live now had a large farm and used to keep boarders and they needed a farmer and my father was trained in Russia . . . in agriculture. So somehow they got acquainted and hooked up that he should come here as a farmer and my mother came along as a domestic and they stayed there for possibly a year or two at the most. And they were sort of discouraged with the situation there and . . . found out that the place next door, which is the present farm, was for sale and they bought it for $800.

Many of the Jews who moved to rural New England districts, Charlotte Goos explains, "came from farm countries, so they didn't want to go to New York City. They weren't accustomed to city living; they were more rural people." The Goos, Sandler, Tablitz, and Pyenson accounts also remind us that Jewish newcomers to rural areas were often moving into already existing, if fledgling, communities.

In other words, for every immigrant who, by force of individual will and spurred on by a nostalgic or whimsical or practical moment of truth, left the urban frontier for a rural place, several other immigrants can be counted upon to have chosen a rural resting place because it was already home to some other family member or members. So Evelyn Slome, whose grandparents settled in the Lewiston/Auburn area of Maine, surmises: "They married where there were Jews and they also went to where there were

Jews . . . where there was someone from their village or somebody they knew." The August and Michelman families of Northampton, Massachusetts, settled in that town because, as Jack August describes it, one branch of the family would settle and then tell the other branches, "Sure, come to us." "They had knowledge of a family member in Northampton," Jack's nephew Bob points out, "and said, 'That's where we're going, honey.' " The eventual consequence of this gradual settlement, Bob August indicates, was that the family "reproduc[ed] a *shtetl* right here in Northampton, similar to what they had left." Lillian Glickman's parents Samuel Shapiro and Annie Kronick came to North Adams, in the northern Berkshires of Massachusetts, first immigrated to Boston and New York, respectively. "My mother's family had relatives here," Glickman explains, "My mother had older brothers who settled here and came here. My father . . . had a brother here too, before he came. . . ." According to the oral tradition, the entire Jewish community of North Adams, which by 1937 had grown to include 750 individuals,[14] had its origins in the decision of one man, a tailor, to settle in the town after hearing upon his earlier arrival in the nearby Hudson Valley of New York that rapidly industrializing North Adams was in need of a tailor. The origins of North Adams's Jewish community lay primarily in various economic enterprises that arose directly from the town's role as an industrial center and, by the 1870s, the western portal of the Hoosac Tunnel, whose completion created a dependable rail link between Boston and Albany. The town was also immediately adjacent to farmland. Samuel Shapiro, like his counterparts in Maine, dealt in cattle and horses.

On the other side of the Berkshires from North Adams, Phyllis Nahman grew up in similar circumstances; her American-born grandfather had been drawn westward from Worcester, where the family had originally settled upon immigrating: "My dad's father had to come to the country because of his health," she explains—"for fresh air. So he came to Turners Falls because he had a sister there. And my dad and his parents settled up near what is now the airport, which was pretty much wilderness when they came." Prospects for improved health were also a primary factor in the Richelson family's move from the Lower East Side of Manhattan to central New Hampshire. Selma Mehrman's younger brother, Irving, "was sort of sickly," and his parents had been advised by their doctor to "take him to New Hampshire." Some of their relatives were already settled in Laconia. Before long, the family moved to Ashland, 30 miles away. The enticements of the countryside, along with the area's promise as a place to go into business, constituted a considerable draw. "They looked around," Mehrman says, "and they took a ride up into what was Ashland, and that's where they decided to settle, because my uncle was already in business."

Jewish newcomers to rural New England in the turn-of-the-century period arrived for the most part one family at a time, and tended to pursue the more "traditionally" Jewish occupation of retailing. As Sonny Chertok explains his family's having settled in Laconia, New Hampshire, his father's establishment as a retailer stands as the point of departure for both the family's history and its connection to Laconia. The elder Chertok had come first to Worcester, where he met his wife. "They married on Thanksgiving Day in 1914," Chertok relates, "and that year he had purchased an old secondhand store in Laconia, New Hampshire and brought my mother there as a bride." In many cases, Jews began their forays into the area as traveling peddlers. In *Small-Town Jews*, Howard Epstein's recent collection of first-person accounts, Gertrude Crockett Shapiro, a resident of Stonington, Maine, tells the story of her father, who, like Hiram Adelman and Sam Goos, chose Maine: "Somewhere between the ages of 9 and 12, my father borrowed 90 cents and started peddling along the coast of Maine. At that time, it was even more sparsely populated. He went on foot from house to house until he made enough money to buy a horse and buggy." [15] Pal Borofsky's grandfather had moved from New York to Bridgeport, Connecticut; his son reversed the move but, upon entering the produce business in New York, decided to begin a career in peddling and took to itinerant sales. The history of the Borofsky family not only mirrors the history of any number of other small-town New England Jewish families, but also sheds light on the history of an entire business—that of Army/Navy surplus. "Ultimately," Pal Borofsky explains, "one of my father's brothers came to New England and they started a store in Keene, New Hampshire, and he bought a store in Brattleboro, Vermont, and he coaxed my father into coming up here to run the store, and my father came up here and he ultimately bought the store from my uncle and then they were in business together and they opened other stores. . . . They were basically work stores; they were called Army and Navy stores, and they served . . . the immigrants." The history of Jewish retailers in rural New England is replete with accounts like Pal Borofsky's. Unlike the traveling peddlers of the nineteenth century, how-

ever, the Jews who came to small New England towns immediately before
and after World War I often stayed. They never expected to be warmly
embraced, but the driven among them learned to manage a comfortable
living and succeeded, after a period of time, in insinuating themselves into
the community.

As Judith Goldstein describes it, Jewish peddlers could not have helped
becoming closely acquainted with the rural New England landscape by the
mere practice of their routine. "Five days a week," Goldstein writes, "and
every week of the year, except for Jewish holidays, the peddlers went out
from Bangor in Maine's harsh winter days and the warmer months of late
spring, summer and early fall. They walked on the dirt roads, trekking up
and down long hills, looking for farmhouses placed on tidy strips of cleared
land. Often screened sedately behind a straight line of maples or oaks, the
small white houses stood in peaceful and lovely landscape." [16] By the early
1900s, whole Jewish communities were taking shape in the wake of peddler
activity throughout the region. Such was certainly the case for the Plotkins
of Orange, Massachusetts. When Louis Plotkin's family first came to Massachusetts, they spent time living in two different towns. Plotkin's father
"heard that in Gardner there was a place . . . where he could find a job,
with a junk dealer, a Jewish junk dealer. He came there and he got some
work, but it wasn't very satisfactory. So he put a pack on his back like many
of them did in those days and peddled for rags, and rubbers, and iron, and
metals and eventually landed . . . in Athol[, Massachusetts]." Obviously,
ease of mobility was a key factor in a given peddler's decision to "settle" in
any particular area. In his 1976 interview, Maurice Carlson explains that
the first Eastern European Jews to live in Northampton, Massachusetts,
actually lived in outlying areas in the interest of being able to have equal
access to the goods they supplied and the scattered markets they served.
"The original Jewish people . . . other than the three or four German Jews
[who had long since become downtown merchants since their arrival in
the 1860s and 1870s] . . . didn't come to Northampton [proper] right away.
They were living in Haydenville and Leeds," Carlson says. "They were
all peddlers, and they could go from [those outlying villages] and spring
out . . . into the country—the hills—with their horse and wagon and
peddle." Eventually, as these peddlers became merchants, actual Jewish
communities began to take shape.

Rabbi Max Wall, who came to Burlington, Vermont, after serving as a chaplain in the American military during World War II, presided over a congregation whose roots, as far as he was able to tell, lay in the peddling profession. "Like most other [Jewish] communities in the country," Wall says, "Burlington's story started off perhaps with a peddler."

> Peddlers are a very important element in American history. They bound the communities together in many ways. And when those peddlers starting coming, most of them came directly from Europe. Most of them came from Eastern Europe and most of Eastern Europe was still basically a very observant community. So kosher and Shabbat meant a great deal to these people. And they go out into the wilderness, and what are they going to eat for kosher? Well, the farmers gradually learned about it, so they would give them eggs, give them milk. They managed, they had to make a living. And pretty soon, they were much more comfortable, so they'd stay for the whole week, or they'd rent a room somewhere, and before long a bunch of them found themselves in a town like Burlington, and they said, "Why don't we make a minyan? We've got eight people here already; we need two more families." And that's how it got started in Burlington.

Sonny Chertok offers an account that both corroborates Rabbi Wall's Burlington narrative and creates a larger context for it. Speaking of another burgeoning industrial center, his hometown of Laconia, New Hampshire, Chertok explains that Jewish retailers came to the area because of the multiple opportunities that beckoned. Laconia itself was a centralizing node that, like other New Hampshire manufacturing towns large and small, had a geography that drew people in:

> Laconia grew and the mills grew along the river, not only in Laconia, but in Franklin. The growth has always been along lines of transportation and water power—you take the Connecticut River. And Haverhill, New Hampshire, was famous for its growth, one of the first settlements up here, near Dartmouth College. That whole area was very flat fields, flooded fields, and the agriculture was good. The Merrimac River, of course, with the tremendous mills, and mills in Manchester, down through Lowell, that whole area.

Peddlers who came there were capitalizing on such towns' growing base of immigrant labor. Their early presence might pave the way for others who would follow in their wake but choose different lines of work:

> I think our Jewish community probably was typical of most of them. Why were people here? An opportunity to work. Why did people come to Laconia? Because the textile mills all of a sudden got busy, the lumber mills were busy, there were job opportunities. And where there's job opportunities, there's always a chance for people to sell them goods and services. Our downtown had many Jewish retailers. Some didn't make it; others did. Some of the older people came. They were actually in agriculture. There were some farmers over there in Gilmanton. One of the big families was the Kaman family, and yet the old man, Kaman, had a house on Hoyt Street, had his cows in back and all of that.

The pattern was replicated in any number of places, as Jewish immigrants sought to create permanent communities wherever they could. "This is Laconia," Chertok is eager to point out. "You could say the same for Franklin [New Hampshire] or Portland, Maine or Rumford[, Maine]. This is the history of the Jewish people."

In Natalie Cohen's story of how the two halves of her family came together, we hear not only another version of how a peddler came to stay, but about the quirky vicissitudes of rural life in the farthest reaches of Maine and New Brunswick, Canada. That a New England Jewish family owes its very existence to the agrarian regulations that evidently apply in the story may be a testament to just how firmly entrenched such apparent "newcomers" came to be in their rural surroundings. "My father came over from Russia to New York," Natalie Cohen says,

> and a cousin of his who lived in Woodstock, New Brunswick, needed somebody to help him peddle. So my father went to Woodstock and he peddled in Plaster Rock and all around, but his home base was Woodstock. Now my mother was born in Fort Fairfield, Maine, and this story has to be true because two of my aunts have told me the same story. Fort Fairfield is very close to the border, and at one time, all the farmers were allowed to graze their animals on either side but at sunset, the animals had to be returned. Well, one night my grand-

father didn't get his animals returned, so he had to end up moving to New Brunswick, so he moved to Woodstock.

In its telling, Natalie Cohen's account reveals itself as a traditional family narrative; it is a true story, as she is sure to explain, because its has been told and retold, and for good reason. The story of how her people came to settle in rural New England (or, as the case may be, rural New Brunswick) is of great importance to her family's sense of identity both as farm people and as Jews living far from any centers of Jewish population.

Occasionally, a Jewish family arrived ahead of any others and single-handedly established a presence that could serve to make the next family feel a little less isolated. At the earliest stages, however, this would not necessarily have been the case. As May Schell describes her family's coming to a small western Massachusetts town at the turn of the century, she suggests that the town's other Jewish family played a limited role in making her own feel more at home or enhancing any broader sense of a Jewish community or religious life. The mutual support network *had been* important, however, *before* May Schell's family, the Magriels, settled in Easthampton: "I guess the thing was that families who immigrated were helpful to one another," says May Schell. "My mother's family helped find a position for [my father]. And as he had no profession, they found a job in a . . . shoe store in Easthampton . . . where there was only one other Jewish family and a family that were older and larger, of course, than we were." Easthampton, in fact, was well on its way in the early days of the twentieth century to becoming a major manufacturing center. Although it did not, at the turn-of-the-century period, develop a large Jewish community, it was relatively close to several towns and cities where Jews had been long established.

May Schell remembers her hometown quite affectionately, and recalls her father's evolution there from employee to employer, as well as her own developing sense of place as a child. Easthampton was

> a small manufacturing town—very small. It manufactured small materials like elastic ribbons. There were several factories which got their energy from the Nashawannuck River. My father, in a few short years . . . started a shoe store of his own and it backed onto the Nashawannuck River. So we children became familiar with it because we would walk over there . . . when I was born, my parents and their children lived in an apartment in the very center of East-

hampton, but they soon moved out to a small house. . . . We lived in
this house for a few years; then we moved to a large two-family house
in a very different and very nice area where our neighbors were certainly higher on the economic scale and it was at the foot of Mt. Tom,
which is a small mountain.

Although her family left Easthampton for Springfield immediately after
World War I, May Schell is able, on the basis of specific place memories
such as these, to recall the aspects of small-town life that made it an appeal-
ing, if unusual, backdrop for a Jewish upbringing.

Notwithstanding the attractive idea that the Puritans and their descendants had some sort of Judeophilic tendency, the central underlying factor
behind Jewish settlement in the era beginning a century ago was a simple
one—economic opportunity. Nonetheless, Jewish immigrants to small-town
New England in the early 1900s found themselves on familiar ground. The
area's culture of resourcefulness and thrift was evidently a fortuitous counterpart to the *shtetl*'s tradition of communal survival on limited means. By
dint of countless acts of economic innovation and adaptation, the earliest
generation of Jewish immigrants succeeded in transforming what may
they first have experienced as alien territory into home. In the case of some
families, the gradual settlement of Jews within the region led to the development of ever-expanding kinship ties from one community to the next.
Bob August describes his family's divergent strands that—in composite
form—suggest a broad Jewish presence throughout western Massachusetts. "The August family is an enormous family," he says, speaking of his
paternal relatives in Northampton. On his maternal side, another strand,
the Kronicks, were dominant in North Adams and yet another, the Kramers, settled in Greenfield. Over time, other Jewish families would develop
similar kinship networks throughout small-town New England, rendering
the entire region all the more familiar.

*Back to the Land: Renewing Jewish Cultural Life in
Post-1960s Rural New England*

Jews who have settled in rural New England in the years since the 1960s
fall into two fairly well defined categories. The first group, which began
arriving in the wake of the social and political ferment of the 1960s, but

which—to a somewhat lesser extent—continues to trickle in, —has con-
sisted in large part of idealistic, generally younger "refugees" from urban
and suburban America who, in various ways, have sought to simplify their
lives. Some of these men and women have cultivated a closer connection to
the land itself, seeking the benefits of life lived on the smaller, healthier
scale made possible by small-town New England life. Writing in 1986, R. D.
Eno, a co-founder of the Conference on Judaism in Rural New England
and a Vermont resident, marked the apparent trend, noting the connection
between the "new" Jews of upland New England and the post-1960s counterculture. "Schooled in the expressive, often ecstatic, spirituality endemic
to the radical political scene," Eno wrote, "a nostalgia for a Yiddishkeit
to which they were heirs began to supplant the adopted nostalgia for the
Yankeekeit of a tribe in which they could never be fully enfranchised." [17]
The constituents of this back-to-the-land trend have, in intriguing ways,
reversed the preceding generation's attempt to improve its economic
existence; rural life in the late twentieth and early twenty-first centuries
quite simply offers fewer opportunities for financial gain than a metropolitan existence does. The second group, which might best be understood to
comprise an older subset of the first group, consists of recent retirees from
urban and suburban areas—men and women who have chosen, like the
back-to-the-landers of the 1960s and 1970s generation, to take advantage
of their post-retirement mobility by settling into the peaceful existence of
rural districts. Small-town New England often attracts this group, as well
as the larger contingent of ex-urban and suburbanites, because of its rich
cultural, educational, and medical care resources, as well as its easy proximity to many larger cities both within and on the outskirts of the region.
The essential difference between the two groups stems directly from the
difference in age. Back-to-the-landers, whose settlement in rural New
England coincided with their youth and prime, were reasonably assured of
the opportunity not only to reinvent their own lives but to raise a generation of rural children.

Interestingly, both groups have been active collaborators in the revival of
existing Jewish communities in the area and in the establishment of new
ones. Where long-established synagogues had, by the 1970s, had their ranks
depleted by the gradual winnowing of early Jewish communities and the
dispersal of younger rural-born Jews to colleges and cities far from home,
the influx of back-to-the-land Jews, as well as the more recent phenom-

enon of Jewish retirees moving to the area, reinvigorated those same synagogues and helped to create new ones. As far back as the late 1980s, active
congregations could be found in dozens of towns throughout rural sections
of northern and western New England, including Northampton, Amherst,
Greenfield, Pittsfield, North Adams, and Great Barrington in western Massachusetts; Bennington, Brattleboro, Montpelier, and Manchester, Vermont;
Bethlehem, Keene, and Laconia, New Hampshire; and Augusta, Bangor,
and Rockland, Maine. Jewish newcomers rarely found themselves having
to create Jewish institutions from the ground up, but over time their ranks
have filled not only emptying pews but—importantly—desks in Hebrew
schools. Jews who have come to rural New England communities since the
1960s did not, for the most part, come with the express intention of foment-
ing a Jewish revival in the area. In many cases, however, their arrival and
involvement have done just that. Having moved to the country for all manner of reasons, this "second wave" of rural Jews has almost inadvertently
helped to shape the area's viability as a vibrant host for Jewish culture.
R. D. Eno draws a comparison between the Jews of this second wave and
a long-standing but once "foreign" icon of the upland landscape. "The
renewal of Jewish life in the hills of New England," he suggests, "is certain
to make Judaism an important social and ethnic presence in a region where
it was as alien and exotic as the apple tree." [18]

Much in the same way that their predecessors have preserved the
memory of exactly how Jewish families came to settle in rural parts, latter-
day rural New England Jews often have clearly bounded narratives to supply when they are asked how and why they chose to live in the area. The
stories contrast significantly with their accounts of where they or their parents were brought up. For the most part, the decision to settle in the region
had little if any overt connection to an individual's or family's Judaism.
Quite often, however, the renewed connection to land, sometimes coupled
with the raising of families, converges in these narratives and makes them
directly relevant to the idea of a rural Jewish revival.

Bob Rottenberg's account suggests that he came to several realizations
at once. Moving back to the land, for him, ended up being a very Jewish
thing to do:

Early in the summer of 1974 I found myself at a yoga retreat in
Newport, Rhode Island, with the swami Sachem Nanda—ten days of

silence and meditation and chanting and discourse and so on. And at the end of that retreat I had the summer free, and I was planning on spending the summer just traveling around, visiting people . . . and the first friends I wanted to visit were in Bennington, Vermont. And I got a ride, after that retreat, with three people who lived in Colrain[, Massachusetts]. It was after ten days of having absolutely no . . . real conversation—and we had a long ride from there to here, and we were just talk, talk, talk at that point, you know. "This is a really beautiful area around here; there's a lot of neat things going on; you should hang around . . ." That was 1974—June of 1974—and here it is, February of 2003, and I'm still here. So basically, I never left. And that summer I discovered I found everything I'd ever been looking for was here. So why leave? . . . These three people, who were all Jewish, were living in a house with other Jews . . . and that first Friday I was there I said, "Hey, it's Friday; we've got *shabbos* coming; I'll make a *challah*; let's do a *shabbos* thing."

Rottenberg's Judaism, which in 1974 had been a sublimated aspect of his larger spiritual quest, was a factor in his decisions both to visit and to stay in western Massachusetts. As he explains it, the spiritual quest and the desire to settle close to the land were one. Rottenberg gives voice to a sentiment that I find to be latent in the accounts of many other latter-day rural New England Jews. "What I started," he says, in reference to the Colrain Shabbat gatherings and the larger Jewish revival that happened around them, "it started becoming clearer and clearer as I was here and I was living in a very rural setting, that Judaism started coming alive."

Helene Meyerowitz's movement into rural Judaism was even less deliberate. Nonetheless, like Rottenberg, she *found herself*, and her Jewish connection as well, in the course of *leaving* the geographically concentrated urban Judaism that she had grown up with in New York City. She began the process by marrying a man who, though his biological mother had been Jewish, had been raised by his Irish Catholic father and grandmother.

My parents, of course, wanted to see their daughter marry a Jewish lawyer or a Jewish doctor, whatever. I broke the mold; I was the black sheep for a while. We proceeded to get married and we had a son, David, and I was married in 1964 soon after graduating from Hunter College. In the summertime of '72, we moved ourselves to Presque

Isle, Maine, [a] very rural part of the country—12–13 hour drive
up an interstate that had one lane north and one lane south going
through potato country, and we settled in . . . Presque Isle. Talk about
minority: there was . . . a building that they considered a Jewish center. It was not opened all year long. There were not enough Jews to
warrant that happening, but there were a few of us, and came the
High Holy Days in September, they flew a rabbi up to Presque Isle,
so we did have services.

Where Bob Rottenberg succeeded in very short order in helping to build
a *havurah*, or Jewish friendship circle, and even branching out and teaching Hebrew aleph-bet to unaffiliated Jewish children in "the hills," Helene
Meyerowitz's journey into her Judaism has occurred over a much longer
term. Nonetheless, it was the movement into rural exile, so to speak, that
began the process for her. Maine's apparent tolerance has helped her along
in the process. "I like the friendliness," she remarks. "After many years of
being in Maine," she says, she "realized, 'Hey, I like it here . . . ' I'm unique,
but it's the uniqueness that people come to want to know more about."

The land itself, or a specific piece of it, seems in most cases to have been
somewhat less important than the *idea* of land. Those latter-day rural New
England Jews who have chosen to live agriculturally clearly have a more
important stake than the majority who appreciate an immediate proximity to the outdoors and a daily connection to the cycle of nature. For Joe
Kurland, also of Colrain, Massachusetts:

In having grown up in New York City but having spent some time as
a kid going camping and being out in the woods and having a summer home in, I wouldn't call it a very rural community, but in a rural
area, I just came to really appreciate being away from the noise and
bustle of the city and also the outdoors, and just being on the land is
a very spiritual thing. I think I also felt something about the history
of the Jews in Europe not being allowed to own land for many years
and feeling that this is a thing that needs to be done—to have a piece
of land to take care of as best I can.

Reversing the centuries-old prohibition on Jewish land-owning, as well as
the accompanying acculturating tendencies that have added to the general
assumption that Jewish life in the United States is a strictly metropolitan

phenomenon, would seem to underlie all manner of small-town New England Jewish psyches.

Rabbi Shmuel Simenowitz has always had an awareness of how un-Jewish rural life *seems*. Indeed, he jokingly refers to himself as the "President of the Jewish Chainsaw Owners' Club." To illustrate, he recounts the following anecdote:

> I remember my brother came in from Israel once and he saw a plastic case in my garage. He said, "What's that?" I said, "my chainsaw." And he said, "Jews don't have chainsaws." And that was actually one of the titles I was thinking for a book I was going to write. Another incident was very similar. I had a position as an adjunct rabbi in Rosedale, Queens for many years. And I bought a horse property out in Suffolk County. And the rabbi says, "Why are you living out there?" I said, "We have horses." And he replied, "You know, Jews don't have horses."

Simenowitz is happy to acknowledge the apparent anomaly and even empathize with the dismissive or at least quizzical views he occasionally encounters. "The Jew in an urban setting has more trouble visualizing," he remarks, how easily—and appropriately—rural-dwelling Jews like himself can be both at home in the country and, at the same time, strongly Jewish in their religious and cultural identities.

Gen Uris, who grew up in Waitsfield, Vermont, was raised "in a small old converted farmhouse that [her] family had renovated. We had about 6 acres," she explains, "and probably about 20 protected acres less than a mile from Sugarbush [ski area]." Uris's father, an attorney, moved to Vermont as a "lifestyle choice" that appears to have had little to do with his having been raised Jewish in Queens. As she describes, "It was probably '69 or '70 that he moved up and wanted to get out of the city, making choices of where he'd rather be, what he'd rather be doing—Vermont, skiing, golfing . . . And I guess he was caught up in, as he said, the 'tuning in and dropping out,' so he moved up here." As connected or unconnected as he may have been to a sense of himself as a New York–raised Jew, Gen Uris's father had a special appreciation for the opportunity to become a landowner. "Your dad used to come home from work," Gen's friend Trudy Wolf interjects, "throw his jacket or whatever over his shoulder and say, 'This is my land.'"

The connection to the land, and the underlying connection to one's Judaism in that context, is a significant factor, not only in first-hand accounts by latter-day rural New England Jews, but in the familial narratives that are carried forward by the children of those back-to-the-landers. In this respect, a rural Jewish sensibility attains to a sort of inherited, or at least provisionally traditional status. Elizabeth Lerner, of White River Junction, Vermont, explains that, after earning his degree in library science at Columbia, her father, who had grown up in suburban New York, made a deliberate choice. "I don't quite know why he liked Vermont," she says, "but he really did." Perhaps owing to his having spent some time living in upstate New York, he had "fallen in love with the area." Cale Weissman, whose parents had also grown up in the suburbs, marks what he sees as his own—perhaps unwitting—participation in a larger movement. Having spent his entire life in Colrain, Massachusetts, he envisions leaving rural New England upon going to college. "I believe it's a cycle," he says, "living here. My dad grew up in the suburbs, on Long Island, and he got so tired of it that he decided to live in the country, and the same with my mom." David Arfa and Kim Erslev chose the western Massachusetts village of Shelburne Falls for a range of "lifestyle" reasons, not the least of which was the area's apparently rich Jewish life. As Arfa puts it,

> I discovered this region and this whole beautiful place here. It's gorgeous here . . . this whole region of small towns with universities and progressive values all combined together, and Jewish life, for that matter. Not big city Jewish life but Jewish life of having synagogues and offerings and scholars coming in for a little bit. And those were all perks. That wasn't the deciding factor, but that was definitely part of it. I mean if we were in rural, beautiful rural America that had no Jewish life or was the heart of fundamentalist belief, it certainly wouldn't feel the same, and I doubt we would've stayed.

With the possible exception of a few of the turn-of-the-century agriculturalists, the rural New England Jewish settlers of the earlier generation had not made the "choice" to come to the region for anything resembling a spiritual or ideological reason. Their marginal economic and social existence, as first- or perhaps second-generation immigrants, precluded any such luxuries. Latter-day rural Jewish newcomers, on the other hand, emerging from relatively comfortable circumstances, could do just that.

What is remarkable about their having done so is that so many of them, acting simultaneously and for divergent reasons, arrived so fortuitously at the same conclusion at once: that rural life could at once afford them a provisional escape from urban and suburban malaise and, at the same time, offer them an ideal context in which to revive and reinvent their latent Judaism.

Rabbi Howard Cohen of Bennington, Vermont, offers the broad perspective of someone who comes into frequent contact with a large cross-section of the rural Jewish population. Though the synagogue in Bennington has been in existence since the 1920s, very few of its current-day members trace their origins to southern Vermont's early influx of Jews. "I'm dealing overwhelmingly with people who have moved to New England," Cohen observes; "some as recently as a couple of years ago, and some 20 years ago." Rabbi Cohen acknowledges the apparent oddity of any self-consciously Jewish person deciding to live away from a Jewish population center, but he embraces the challenge of serving that exact constituency. The geographical choice that they have made is one aspect that distinguishes the members of his southern Vermont congregation. They are, as Cohen puts it, "highly self-actualized people. They're doing what they want to be doing with their life. They're living where they want to be living."

Jews who have come to rural New England have, as a rule, done so as a result of the exact sorts of personal choices that are in keeping with a post-1960s mentality. Suzie Laskin moved to the White Mountain region of New Hampshire in the 1990s, in the midst of what she calls her "midlife crisis":

All through the '80s, I was single in downtown Philly and doing all of the typical single things, and then . . . I had gotten involved in kayaking and started going away camping every weekend. . . . When I turned 40, I said, I just got to get the hell out of this city, I just can't stand the city any more. All of a sudden, it was just like this overwhelming urge to get out of the city. It just overtook me, and I came up here on a vacation and just fell in love with the mountains up here and fell in love with this area, and I just said, "I've got to move up there; that's where I want to be. It just feels right. It feels like home. It feels good to me."

The personal or self-actualizing choices of the back-to-the-land generation of rural New England Jews, like the more family-oriented choices of their turn-of-the-century predecessors, were only inadvertently Jewish choices. Only out-and-out utopians, in other words, would have been likely to think that country life would reawaken their Judaism.

Retirees, too, have stumbled into the same circumstances, and moved to remote sections of New England only to discover afterwards that there was a Jewish life to be had. The self-actualizing tendency that Howard Cohen describes would appear, in this respect, to preclude a communal mentality. "Self-actualized people," Cohen says, "tend not to have as much need for what religion has to offer." Naturally, retirees who have the luxury of organizing their lives around all manner of individual pursuits might make the most self-actualizing of geographical choices. "As Jews," Betty Gordon suggests, "our whole mentality is based on being ostracized, on being the minority. . . . If you're up here, and you like the country, and you want to ski, and you want to be out in nature, you can't expect to be among your own ilk."

Bill and Mary Markle came to Randolph, Vermont, in 1979 because they had a daughter living in a neighboring town. Both daughter and parents acted on personal whims that seem to have borne no direct connection to their Jewish allegiances. "She had worked with me out in the Midwest," Bill says of his daughter, "and decided she wanted to live in Vermont. . . . She was working making wood burning stoves up here in this town for a company called Vermont Castings and she had an executive job with them."

Though their adult daughter had moved to Vermont, Bill and Mary Markle saw no immediate reason to do so in her footsteps. Their eventual move had an almost arbitrary feel to it. Bill Markle provides the unlikely account of how he and his wife did, before long, decided to give up on suburbia and renew their existence in Vermont. He had been visiting his daughter, who had decided to take an hour-long break in her workday to do some laundry in town.

I said, "Okay, I'll go with you. Where are you going?" She said, "I'm going to Randolph . . . which is the next town over." So we got to Randolph and she said, "I'm going to be doing my laundry for an hour. What are young going to do?" I said, "I don't know. I'll walk around some to keep me busy." So I said, "I'll see you back in an hour." And I looked around and had an hour to kill and I saw a sign, "Realtor." So I felt it was a good way to kill an hour. So I started this conversation with this very suspicious salesman who thought I was really bs'ing him and asking about real estate, and he was pretty sure I was wasting his time. I finally got him to put me in his car and start showing me some properties. . . . And so I saw this house and I really liked it and I called Mary up in Chicago and she said, "Where are you?" I said, "I'm visiting Penelope up in Vermont." I said, "I saw a house up here and what would you think if I bought it?" She said, "Where's this house?" And I told her. "Oh," she says, "I know exactly where you are. . . ." Anyway, so we went back to this guy's office and I said, "Okay, here's my offer," . . . and I went. I said, "Oh, I got to get back to meet my daughter."

Having chosen Vermont as a home, the Markles shortly afterwards began to make inquiries in the interest of creating a Jewish life for themselves. Partly as a result of activity already underway, and partly as a result of their own activism in this direction, they soon found that life in rural Vermont could, in fact, be lived in a richly Jewish way.

Whether they were helping to establish the first Jewish presence in the hills of New England or unwittingly touching off a latter-day Jewish revival, the Jews who came to such places have been a forward-looking group. Their traditional ties both to Judaism and to the patterns of regional life were a springboard to a dynamic existence in which they might bring about a betterment of their lives, economically, culturally, or spiritually. No matter their origin or their destiny, for that matter, arrival in rural New England implicated them in adjusting to life in a new *place* surrounded by a promising, if long-inhabited, landscape. The conditions of life as they found them had been shaped, in large part, by the evolving particularities of that landscape. Those who took up the work of peddling found it to be an at least temporarily sustainable pursuit because rural settlements were sufficiently remote and decentralized as to call for traveling sales but also easily accessible to the cities where one bought one's stock. Immigrants who graduated from peddling to retailing took advantage of the area's many small industrial centers, each of which was located on some sort of waterway and supplied a diverse population of immigrant factory workers who required dry goods and staples at affordable prices. Current-day Jewish arrivals in small-town New England have been no less influenced by local geography. In the face of an urban and suburban expansion that has been underway for over a hundred years, recently arrived Jews have chosen to make their homes in rural New England *because of* the relative remoteness of locale and the ready access to the outdoors it has also afforded its residents. A rural existence has necessitated and occasioned both acts of conformity and acts of invention in accordance with the patterns of New England history. None have been so aware of this as those who have lived closest to the land itself—the farmers whose story we turn to next.

CHAPTER 2

"I Remember Being in the Barn"

The Story of Jewish Agriculture in New England

o   o   o

Jewish participation in New England agriculture, which spans approximately a hundred years, takes its place within a continuum of non-Anglo ethnic farming. Beginning around the middle of the nineteenth century, and accelerating in the aftermath of the Civil War, members of such immigrant groups as the Irish, French Canadians, Poles, and Italians began to buy up increasingly available, untended farmland throughout the region. The Yankees' movement away from the land occurred at an ever-increasing pace. The historian Lisa Krissoff Boehm points out, for instance, that in the 1850s alone, Hampshire County, in western Massachusetts, was drained of a third of its residents, even as the state itself continued to grow in population.[1] A similar trend could be seen in the northern Vermont community of Chelsea. In 1860, according to the historian Hal Barron, there were resident in that town 153 boys between the ages of 5 and 14.[2] A mere twenty years later, only 36 of the same individuals remained in Chelsea, so many of them having been drawn off by the enticements of the cities and of the West. Large numbers of the original Yankee farmers, with so few sons left to inherit their holdings, sold off their farms; eager immigrants could often be found to take their places. Over time, as immigrant farmers both acclimated to the conditions of farming in New England and helped to extend its long-term viability into the twentieth century through new methods, technologies, and business savvy, they stopped being newcomers. Jewish families, though their numbers were relatively small, were participants in this succession.

A significant number of Jewish farmers, beginning in the turn-of-the-twentieth-century period, became quite successful. They managed to surmount the difficult task of remaining connected to a single place and generating a competitive income from it. During the period immediately before and after World War II, a second generation succeeded to the proprietorship of these farms and added onto the first generation's achievements. Economic success can cut two ways, however, and by the 1960s and 1970s, what few original Jewish farm families were still in existence began to leave the land for many of the same enticements that had drawn previous generations of rural New Englanders away from the countryside.

Jewish agriculture would have passed into nonexistence at this juncture except for the arrival, beginning in the late 1960s, of a new influx of largely countercultural, urban- and suburban-reared Jews. While most of the participants in this movement did not go to the country in order to take up full-time farming, a few have, and the result is that Jewish people, once again, are recognizable, if not large-scale, participants in the region's farm economy. If a common thread unites today's Jewish farmers with those of previous generations, it is that their farming is influenced not only by preexisting local methods and tendencies, but by a grounding both in science and in community economics. Many of the "new" Jewish agriculturalists farm organically, and are part of a movement that, in a broad sense, is attempting to revive bygone small farming practices in the service of an environmentally and community-spirited global awareness. Notwithstanding their idealism, these farmers are also just as pragmatic as their predecessors were. In this respect, the history of Jewish agriculture in New England forms a continuum and also conforms to a pattern found throughout the region among all farmers—success is predicated on a combination of traditional values and progressive practices. New England farmers have long distinguished themselves as mavericks and as individualists. Innovation is intrinsic to their endeavor. In the words of Mark Lapping, "They farm the sides of hills, take gambles on weather and markets like a pack of riverboat cardsharps and . . . consistently fly in the face of a conventional wisdom which says that there is no New England agriculture." [3]

Coming to rural New England was, for most turn-of-the-century Jews, a fortuitous endeavor. Jews found their way into rural districts and small towns, but very few of them were or thought of themselves as part of a deliberate movement or even an informal settlement pattern. An exception would be found, however, in the history of those few rural New England

Jews who were "brought" to the region by the Rothschild-funded Jewish Agricultural Agency, which sponsored Jewish farming initiatives in central and eastern Connecticut, as well as southwestern Massachusetts. These efforts were often underwritten by the Bavarian-born philanthropist, Baron Maurice de Hirsch (1831–1896). Baron de Hirsch devoted his initial attention to Jewish farming prospects in Russia, where—according to a Jewish Agriculture Society pamphlet of 1954—"he went so far as to offer the Russian government 50 million francs . . . to establish an educational system for Jews which would include agricultural schools."[4] The tsars, of course, were more interested in ridding themselves of Russian Jews than they were in aiding them, so eventually de Hirsch chose to direct his attention toward establishing a more general fund for worldwide Jewish agriculture.

Many American Jewish farming utopias, as well as the more successful, long-term Jewish rural settlements in sections of rural New England, the Catskills, and central New Jersey were financed in part by Baron de Hirsch's fund. Inspired by the Am Olam ("Eternal People") movement (its counterpart, the Bilu, developed as a movement within Zionism) and fueled by the increasing social and political ferment among Russian Jews in the period preceding the Revolution, the baron and his associates actually steered a significant number of recent Jewish immigrants to the United States into agriculture. Some of these were first-time farming families, but others were people who had known rural life and agriculture first-hand in the Old Country and wished to continue on in that vein. Sponsored or unsponsored, many of the Jews who went into farming beginning at the turn of the century—or at least those who were able to sustain their efforts through two or three generations—were more businesslike than they were utopian. Jewish farmers learned the long-standing lesson of New England agriculture—that viability increases with adaptability to changing times and needs. Jewish farmers, moreover, were able to set useful precedents in their methods and business models. Some of them, by the second generation, were sending youngsters off to college to be trained in agricultural science and business.

The first decade of the twentieth century saw Jews forming less than one percent "of the nearly 1,400,000 agriculturists who immigrated to the United States."[5] The trend among Jews—as it was for many of the other immigrant groups of the period—was to settle in urban areas. Despite the fact that a significant percentage of Jewish immigrants were coming from

the comparatively rural settings of the *shtetlach*, hardly any of those immigrants came close to replicating the outward cultural geography of that
experience. Nonetheless, as Uri Herscher puts it, a small, yet hardly inconsequential group of Jews "was determined to look up to the bright side of
free America not a from a crowded, malodorous urban pavement but from
the land itself, the fields and forests that lay waiting beyond the borders of
the city."[6] Life in rural precincts of the United States would necessarily be
quite different from rural life in the Pale of Settlement, but in its comparatively small scale, at least, it would reward immigrant Jews who found the
experience of life in the urban centers to be alienating.

The Jewish farmers who came to settle in rural New England were
drawn by disparate forces. Many early Jewish farmers chose agriculture
because they already knew how to farm in Europe. As the historian Morton
Gordon points out, despite long-standing attempts by European authorities
"to deny the Jew the right to farm, according to the 1897 [Russian] census,
2.9 percent of the Jewish population in the Pale of Settlement engaged in
agriculture, fishing and forestry."[7] Moreover, even those Jews from the
shtetlach who didn't own farms were quite used to the patterns of rural life,
including the small-scale husbandry of cows, horses, and chickens and the
cultivation of vegetable gardens. As a result, as early as 1900 there were
some 1,000 Jewish farm families in the United States as a whole. That
number had increased to 5,000 a mere ten years later, and by 1930 to
16,000. Jewish agriculture in the United States reached its high point in
the immediate aftermath of World War II, when the influx of Holocaust
survivors, officially known as DPs, or Displaced Persons, increased the
national number to 20,000.[8] Although the largest numbers and concentrations of American Jewish farmers were to be found in upstate New York
and central New Jersey, several New England communities too were settled
by Jews. The relatively large-scale Jewish agricultural experience in Connecticut has been well documented. In my own fieldwork, I was told about
or met directly early Jewish farm families from Maine, western Massachusetts, and New Hampshire. In every case, the accounts I collected indicated
that versatility, specialization, and technical know-how were key components to a given family's success in agriculture, as well as the cultivation of
neighborly or at least businesslike relations with non-Jews within the community. Jews who began farming in the first half of the twentieth century
in New England appreciated the value of becoming active participants in

the local regional economy and culture. And they knew as well that doing so implicated them in becoming innovators who were willing and able to keep up with and even set local trends. Their farms having lasted for two, three, and even more generations bears testimony, in the words of two mid-twentieth-century historians, "for the belief that there is something in the New England spirit especially responsive and hospitable to Jews."[9]

Perhaps as in no other region in the nation, New England's agricultural history has been marked by an integral dynamism, both in terms of methods and in the ethnic composition of its farm families. Colonial-era farmers took what advantage they could of the region's resource base, but famously disappointing soil conditions essentially precluded large-scale single-cropping, and so the tendency among the earliest generations of New England farmers was to farm on a mixed, subsistence level. By the period of the Revolution and early Republic, however, enterprising farmers in the region went on to adapt to a growing market economy and to specialize as they might. Vast portions of the region's interior and coastline, in the mid-nineteenth century, were given over to large-scale sheep farming. Certain areas specialized in particular products: stall-fed beef cattle were raised in the Connecticut Valley during the early decades of the nineteenth century; palm leaf hat-making was common in many upland communities in the middle part of that century. Over time, the farm economy became still more tenuous, and only those farmers who could refine and diversify their operations remained viable. The famous connected farm buildings of the region, as the architectural historian Thomas Hubka demonstrates so convincingly in his 1983 book *Big House, Little House, Back House, Barn*, give material testimony to the enterprising and resourceful agricultural mindset of the latter half of the nineteenth century. As market conditions worsened but technological advances increased, New England farmers created all manner of back houses, woodsheds, barns, and assorted other contiguous outbuildings in the interest of maximizing efficiency. A back kitchen could accommodate craft production or large-scale food preservation operations. A carriage house and adjacent farmyard could accommodate various wagons, pieces of machinery, and the tools and space necessary to repair them.[10]

The formula brought some success, or at least an extended sustainability, to an increasingly shrinking farm population of Old Yankees. But rising industrialization within New England itself and a westward-moving economy put most New England farmers on the defensive as they never had been before. In the face of such trends, and owing to the enormous demographic changes that were bringing growing ranks of immigrants to the region on a yearly basis, the practice of agriculture continued to shift, especially in the opening decades of the twentieth century. As the agricultural historian Howard Russell writes about the immigrant influx, he enumerates ethnic groups, subregions, and areas of crop specialization. Finns, he points out, came to Worcester County, Massachusetts, and adjacent southern New Hampshire, and raised both "berries and poultry." Norwegians and Swedes farmed in and around Concord, Massachusetts. "Italian workers," Russell writes, "were making their way in suburban market gardens and florists' greenhouses in Rhode Island, Connecticut and Massachusetts. Portuguese had long been taking up dairy and vegetable farms in eastern Rhode Island and southeastern Massachusetts." [11] Although the preponderance of French Canadians were drawn to New England because of its enormous factories and mill towns, some few—nostalgic, perhaps, for the agrarian existence they had known in Quebec—went into farming, especially in the northernmost sections of New England. In southern New England, and particularly in the Connecticut Valley area, Poles and other Eastern Europeans bought all-but-abandoned Yankee farms by the hundreds. It was into this context that the area's small but significant number of Jewish farmers made their way. At the turn of the century, most of the farmers in New England, with the prominent exception of those few who had access to prime floodplain soils in the lowlands, were dairymen. By 1900, a small number of restless urban immigrant Jews might have heard, as the *American Jewish Yearbook* reported, that the old Anglo farmers of New England were all but going out of business. "The farms' abandonment," the *Yearbook* reported, "is due to the death or old age of their owners, whose children, attracted to the cities and to professional occupations, are willing to sell their ancestral homesteads at a great sacrifice." [12]

Whether Jewish farmers followed a programmatic course, as was the case at least at the outset for the de Hirsch-funded agriculturalists, or got their start owing entirely to their own initiative, they could be found in noticeable numbers in many sections of the region, and contributed to the local economy as a result of their sustained interaction with long-standing rural residents. Jewish farmers were sufficiently visible to attract the negative judgment of one noteworthy critic—Wallace Nutting. Nutting, whose claim to fame was a series of antiquarian books published in the 1920s, devotes an entire chapter of *Massachusetts Beautiful* to the topic of immigrant farmers. The skepticism he harbored toward the presence of Italian farmers in rural New England was dwarfed by the apparent resentment he had for Jews, primarily on "aesthetic" grounds: "We remember," wrote Nutting, "instances where farms in the central and western part of the state have been purchased by the Hebrews and become centers around which gather innumerable decrepit automobiles or carts or rubbish until we conclude that a cyclone must have swept through. The Hebrew begins by cultivating the soil ostensibly, but he invariably ends by being a cattle trader or a trader in something, and it is very seldom that one sees him striking his hoe into the soil."[13] Nutting's resentment of "the Hebrew" resonates, of course, with the anti-Semitic views that—during the 1920s in particular—plagued Jews throughout the United States. What is striking, however, about his assessment is the broader realization that it yields him. Like Henry James and Henry Adams, among others, Nutting was discomfited by the apparent chaos wrought by unassimilated newcomers and their perceived assault on American standards of civility and cleanliness. But fear of the Other was equivalent, essentially, to fear of modernity itself. In the paragraph that follows 'his indictment of Jewish farmers, Nutting acknowledges the inevitability of change and of New England's particular susceptibility to modernization. For one thing, he had already witnessed the gradual abandonment of rural districts by successive generations of Yankee farmers: "Perhaps we ought to be glad that anybody wants our country acres," he wrote. "We are in a state of flux at present and the future of farms fifty years hence will be very different. The specialization process will have proceeded farther and there will be more attention to neatness and, indeed, to beauty on the part of those who are now just getting their start."[14]

Leaving aside views like Nutting's, which may or may not have been shared by other "native" New Englanders, Jewish farms could hardly have been dismissed as inconsequential. Notwithstanding the handful of Jewish farming utopias, which came and went, the Jewish farming presence in the region was sufficiently long-term as to have an impact both on New England culture and within the larger Jewish community itself.

The departed utopias serve as fascinating touchstones to the imagination. The rural communities in which Jews have lived for several generations, on the other hand, as equal and fully implicated participants in their towns' cultural and civic life, tend to escape notice. Leaving aside the current day's relatively wide dispersal of Jewish families *throughout* rural New England, we might still note several examples of communities in which Jews have existed in significant numbers for successive generations. Though the degree of documentation has been relatively minimal, we find nonetheless that certain corners of the region have been home, or were, for significant periods of time, to Jewish rural-dwellers. Among these, several sections of eastern and central Connecticut were home to Jews going back to the late nineteenth and early twentieth centuries. An article by Mark Raider published in the *American Jewish Archives* describes the farming community near Rockville, Connecticut, which—at its height, just before the First World War—was home to several enterprising tobacco- and potato-growing Jewish families.[15] In Colchester, Connecticut, also in the eastern part of the state, Jews once accounted for a full 40 percent of all the town's farmers.[16] According to Alexander and Lillian Feinsilver, who wrote an article in *Commentary* magazine about Colchester's "Yankee Jews" in the 1950s, Jews in that town were "closer culturally to the Old Yankee stock than the more recently settled Slavic elements, who constitute 45 per cent of Colchester's population."[17] Central and eastern Connecticut had dozens of Jewish egg farmers as well. A newer community of Jewish farmers was located in the area around Danielson, Connecticut, where there were "more than 100 Jewish farm families," many of whom had arrived in the United States as DPs in the aftermath of the Second World War.[18] As well as Jewish farm families who gained local prominence for their relatively large-scale operations, a certain number of Jews in the region were engaged in farming on a small, homesteading scale or, for a short space of time on an overall continuum of mixed economic endeavors. Phyllis Nahman's father, Meyer Rubin, who worked in the area around Turners Falls, Massachusetts, at various times as a junk dealer and later as proprietor of a bustling scrap-metal business, tried his hand at family farming as well.

My dad was always very ambitious. He wanted to do all kinds of things. . . . He wanted to try everything. And he wanted to become a farmer; when I was a little girl, we had cattle, and we had a big, big garden. What I remember is the tail end of this venture, because my dad, who quit school in the 8th grade, actually went to UMASS, which was Mass Aggie at the time, and took a couple of courses in cattle-something—probably to do with milk—and we drank the milk from these cows, and I think he probably sold some of it. . . . I remember being in the barn and making the rounds with him and learning to stay out of the way of the cows, and I remember the last calf that was born in our barn, which was going to be my calf, but then we sold him, because the cattle was taking too much time, and my dad had to support our family, and the junk business was growing, when I was a little kid during the [Second World] War.

So eventually we got rid of the cattle. But I know that other neighbors got milk from him; whether he gave it away or sold it, I don't know. I remember [that] the pediatrician for all four of us, and for my children . . . was a very good friend of my dad's and we used to go sit in the barn with him. . . . And my dad was very proud of the fact that Dr. Low said his milk was such good, clean, healthy milk for children, and recommended it. . . .

I remember my dad did keep some fields of strawberries and rhubarb, and my mom used to can fruits and vegetables; I mean, we ate that stuff, that was very important in our lives. . . . When we were kids we all got as a job to help take care of the strawberry field, which was pretty extensive, and pick them, and we had a little table that my dad would set up near the roadside to sell some. First, he made sure that we knew how to do arithmetic, and then we all got a turn sitting out there selling things. My brothers got to drive the tractor, and the girls got to be down on the ground weeding and picking and that sort of stuff. At the time, I remember that I didn't enjoy it all that much, but in retrospect it was kind of fun.

It is worth noting that Meyer Rubin was hardly any different from any number of his non-Jewish neighbors in having temporarily experimented with farming. In the marginal economy of turn-of-the-century western Massachusetts, one had to try one's hand at various occupations in order to remain economically viable. Moreover, his practice of setting his boys out to drive the tractor and restricting the girls to the manual work of weeding and picking was absolutely in keeping with the local norm as well. Many Yankee farm families tried to keep girls and women out of the fields altogether. Polish farm families, however, who were rapidly attaining majority status in western Massachusetts by World War II, broke the Yankee taboo on assigning farm labor to females, so Rubin may have been following their example as well.

Not far from the Rubins' home, in North Adams, Massachusetts, Lillian Glickman's father Samuel Shapiro, perhaps in his capacity as a horse and cattle dealer, "had a barn and owned land." Glickman also remembers her brother haying the father's fields. Irene Moskowitz, of Great Barrington, Massachusetts, speaks of her and her husband's having bought a considerable-sized dairy farm in the 1930s from her in-laws, who had themselves been Jewish farmers in the area going back to the turn of the century, when they had participated in the Sandisfield colony. Like many other residents of small towns, May Schell, of Easthampton, Massachusetts, remembers having chickens around the house; she and her siblings were also, as she puts it, brought up to know "the very freshest of gardening food." Growing up in Skowhegan and later Augusta, Maine, Charlotte Goos recalls her mother not only keeping "a beautiful garden" and having a "a green touch," but producing most of her kitchen goods from food that the family raised itself; the chicken soup that the family ate all week was always made from chickens that the family had raised.

Isolated Jewish farms could be found as well elsewhere in the region. Eva August, who came to the United States when she was a young girl in 1915, settled in the industrial town of Holyoke, Massachusetts. But her mother "felt choked up" by the urban atmosphere, so the family "bought a farm in [adjacent] South Hadley." On the farm, August says, "she had her cows, she had her horses, she had her chickens." In Whitefield, New Hampshire—a small village located in a remote corner of the White Mountain region—Steve Steinberg's grandparents Louis and Rachel Blumenthall operated a small farm called Kimball Hill, which eventually went on as well to host vacationing Jewish families from urban areas. In the New England spirit, the Blumenthalls insinuated themselves into the local economy and cultural life by developing several endeavors simultaneously. "He had cows and various crops," recalls Steve Steinberg. "He sold milk, to Hood milk. He brought it down in a horse and wagon every day to the railroad station in Whitefield, and the milk train would pick it up. To supplement that income he had a junkyard of sorts. He would go out and get junk and rags and so forth from various farmers, and he also had a garage in the village, which at one time or another became a gas station." Steve

Steinberg is quick to point out that his grandparents were the only Jewish farmers for miles around; they could hardly be said to have been part of any large-scale Jewish agricultural presence in the White Mountains or in rural New England for that matter. But their presence rendered problematic any notion of early or mid-twentieth-century rural New England as a kind of pristine Yankee holdover. As their grandson describes them, the Blumenthalls were "strange Jewish people with Yiddish accents living in mountains long peopled by French Canadians and the descendants of Yankee colonials." They could hardly live invisibly. "Aside from his religion," as Steinberg describes it, Louis Blumenthall "was fitting pretty good there." Steinberg associates his grandfather's rough physique and boisterous manner with his apparent ability, notwithstanding his status as a flagrant non-native, to acclimate. "He was a very handsome guy," Steinberg points out. "[He] had red hair, blue eyes, [was] a very tough, primitive character. [He had a] bad temper. He didn't take shit from anybody." Three generations later, though the family has long since quitted farming in Whitefield, their original connection to that place has hardly been severed. And for all of the evident isolation that they endured, they maintained their Jewish identity.

A reference to another long-lost Jewish farm also surfaces within the oral tradition in Sumner Winebaum's account of how Jews just arriving in Portsmouth, New Hampshire, at the turn-of-the-century period were acclimated to American life. "In Portsmouth," Winebaum recalled having heard, "there was a man named . . . G-O-U-S-E. And [he] had a farm outside of Portsmouth, just outside. This farm by and large for most Jewish immigrants was a way station. It was the place where they worked for a certain number of weeks, months, for board, and it was the place where they were taught the ropes." Edwin "Sonny" Chertok recalls a Jewish farm family, the Feuersteins, who lived near his home in Laconia, New Hampshire. "I had recollections," he says "as a very little child of being bundled up and being taken in my father's Ford truck with high bordered sides, and we went down to Gilmont, which is about 12 miles on country roads, where Abe . . . and his father had the farm there in Gilmont." Chertok also recalls a Kropp family farm, in Tilton, New Hampshire. He went to a party once at their place, "and Kropp had a barrel of cider. There was a hose and everybody was suctioning the cider out of the barrel," he recalls. "[He was] a real farmer, made a lot of money. Guys that minded their P's and Q's and whatever," Chertok explains, could make a living. Indeed, in the eyes of their non-Jewish neighbors, if people were able to make money honestly, their participation in the local culture was essentially unassailable. Poultry farmer Maxwell Pyenson sums up the terms to which his family was held in their hometown of Otis, Massachusetts:

> I think they found out we were relatively honest people and good neighbors. My mother used to get acquainted with all the farm-women around here and I think we finally got accepted that way. I mean, we didn't interfere with their markets. They had all the markets in Lee and so forth in the small towns around here where they would take the horse and buggy and maybe the automobile later on and go in to peddle it there. Few dozen eggs and whatever else they had. And they were worried that my father with his 3000 or 4000 birds would interfere with their market. And he never did. He had his own market. He went into Springfield and they figured on that score that he wasn't trying to interfere with their business and that probably he was a right guy.

Jewish farmers may not have been warmly embraced by their non-Jewish neighbors. They were, after all, newcomers and automatically suspect, like the many other immigrants who found their way into rural districts. If they might eventually achieve acceptance, provisional or otherwise, it would have to come after a probationary period.

"A Very Fluid Kind of Business": Jewish Cattle and Horse Merchants

Perhaps the foremost means by which New England Jews bridged the gap between their affiliations with agriculture in the Old Country and the conditions of rural life in New England was by working as cattle and horse dealers. "Apparently, that was an easy profession for them to take up," says Julius Goos. "A lot of them had come from farming areas in Europe and so it was sort of natural." Bob August describes his European forbears as "basically very small town peasant people," many of whom, he suspects, "were involved in butchering, cattle-dealing and ritual slaughter[ing]" in their home *shtetl* of Gadisha, in Lithuania. Indeed, the cattle business bridged two other worlds as well—that of the small- and medium-sized farmer and that of the businessman. Jewish cattle dealers, who were thick throughout the region from the late nineteenth century well into the twentieth, traveled far and wide within the six-state region, and they also had to and did establish firm rural roots in the process. New England was not the only region of the United States where Jews attained prominence as cattle dealers. In Appleton, Wisconsin, and Modesto, California—both towns in which the pre–World War II Jewish population exceeded 300—cattle dealing was the primary vocation listed among Jewish heads of household.[19] Cattle dealing, perhaps more than any other agrarian pastime, made strong relationships with local farmers—some of whom had roots going back several generations in the region—a necessary part of one's profession. It was also a means by which Jews with an agricultural bent could participate broadly in the rural economy and culture and build their overall business profiles while simultaneously enhancing their rural pedigree.

Bob August, whose father and uncles were long-time cattle merchants in western Massachusetts going back to their arrival in Northampton in the 1890s, explains what he refers to as the "fluidity" of the cattle business, at least as his father practiced it. Cattle merchants applied a combination of agricultural, veterinary, financial, and interpersonal skills to the work that they did. Their facility with such a diversity of abilities derived in part from their experiences in the Old World, but they were also quite clearly adept at adjusting to and capitalizing on the shifting, modernizing conditions they encountered in small-town New England communities. Their work seems to have epitomized the overall transformation of New England to which all the residents of the early twentieth century were witness. The August brothers

maintained a stock of animals and they either had them in their own barns or their own pasturage facilities, locations, or they were in a farmer's pasture, a farmer's barn. It was a very fluid kind of business. [Some] of the Northampton cousins, D. and I. August—Dave and Izzy—had a barn. They had a fairly substantial milking operation and a dairy. They did some processing in addition to their cattle dealing. . . . They had a stock of animals that they traded in and out of, were constantly replenishing and moving out. My father's, my uncles', grandfather's for that matter, operation was a little more fluid. They had animals and they had animals all over the place. . . .

[At] the end of my father's involvement with cattle, his health was failing and it was getting to the point where there was some risk in terms of his own survival. So Dad had all this cattle all over the place, no one knew where they were. He knew where they were. He ran his business out of his shirt pocket and his pants pocket, literally. He had a very agile mind, and we finally got dad to sit down one day and we said, "Look, let's just put a little ledger together. You tell us where the cattle are, at least we'll know. If you go tomorrow, we're not going to know where they are." . . . Looked at from today's business perspective . . . [it was] an ancient craft. Those cattle dealers were not only knowledgeable about the animals they were working with and had an ability to barter, to trade, and all that went into judging value and what things were worth and all that business which is a real art; but they were also bankers. They financed the purchase of animals. They signed loans, signed notes at the bank for farmers to secure their ability to borrow the money to buy the animals. They loaned their animals out. [In] my dad's case, if he had a cow that was coming due or was going to be producing milk, he didn't want the cow in the pasture. If it was going to do some good to the farmer to have the cow, get some milk, fine—you take the animal, you feed the animal, you take care of the animal, you get the milk, I get the cow back when you're finished with it. It was a very, very fluid kind of economic system, which incorporated all kinds of crafts and skills, and it was very interesting to watch.

The August family's cattle business in western Massachusetts was one of dozens of Jewish-run operations throughout rural sections of New England. In the space of a single generation, Jewish cattle dealers—many of whom had been born and raised overseas—had become intricately involved in the agricultural and economic lives of small-town New Englanders.

Jewish cattle dealers worked throughout Maine, New Hampshire, and Vermont, where, as Rabbi Max Wall recalls hearing when he first came to that state, they lived not only in his hometown of Burlington but in Montpelier, St. Johnsbury, and Newport as well. Lisbon, New Hampshire, according to one White Mountain region tradition-bearer, was home to a Jewish cattle dealer named Fineman. As Julius Goos puts it, throughout rural New England, "there were several Jewish cattle dealers." He continues: "Actually, in proportion, there were probably more cattle dealers for the amount of Jews that were there." In the area around Great Barrington,

Massachusetts, in the southern Berkshires, the late Harry Moskowitz ran a cattle business based at his family's dairy farm. His wife recalls his having brought most of his cattle from Wisconsin and Canada, as well as ponies from Scotland. The same was true, Irene Moskowitz says, for an associate of his, Leon Kaplan. Cattle dealers in the area also included a Morris Goldberg and the Pevzner brothers of Sheffield, Jake and Sam. As Jake explains, referring to the 1930s, "In those days, there was no such thing as supermarkets or big markets. Only the cattle dealers and real estate people . . . had any contact with the farmers themselves, and they would buy anything, whether it was chickens or horses or cows, and bring them to market."

Over time, as the work of cattle dealers was phased out owing to market changes, few remained in that business, Jew or Gentile. A notable exception, as Irene Moskowitz points out, is her son, who still operates a small cattle business in Sheffield. "He has just a few customers left," she explains, "because they've all pretty much left the farming business because the taxes have become too much . . . and the price of milk has been so little."

The late Jack August told his 1976 interviewer about his family's cattle-dealing history; as for many other immigrants, cattle trading was one aspect of a larger and ever-adapting economic enterprise. According to his son, Nyman August "was a cattle dealer and a butcher. He used to go out and buy livestock, and course with it, he bought other little things that came along, that he felt he could turn a dollar on." For August, as for other Jews, cattle dealing did not have to be learned; "he was," as Jack points out, "the third or fourth generation of butchers and cattle dealers and horse traders." When the Augusts first came to Northampton, they took to dry goods peddling. "The cattle thing came on very quickly," however, remarks Jack's nephew Bob August; "that's what he did in the Old Country." Natalie Cohen's father, a resident of a section of New Brunswick that bordered on Maine's Aroostook County, had also carried his profession of cattle dealing forward from earlier days in Russia. "This is what they did in the Old Country," his daughter says, "and that's what they continued to do." Indeed, in her particular area, as she recalls, cattle dealing was a profession shared by most of the Jewish families. Her mother's father, who had grown up mostly in Aroostook County, was in the same business. Sam Goos, who had moved to Bangor because a cow he had heard mooing while he was working in Boston had inspired him to seek a rural home, was a long-time cattle dealer as well. His barn, as his son Zeese explains, "was right smack in the city," and he had space there for "about 12 head of cattle." The business kept his father on the road quite frequently, but it also compelled him to sink roots and purchase land. "He would go around to the different farms," Zeese Goos says, and "pick up and buy cattle; of course you had to have a place to put them. If they were milking cattle, you had to have a barn or something to put them into especially during the cold weather. But he bought a pasture in the Bangor area, and that's where he used to keep a lot of his cattle. Then he had another pasture outside of Bangor where he would keep a lot of his younger cattle." The combination of travel throughout the region and connections to specific places contributed, it seems, to his having good relations with his overwhelmingly non-Jewish neighbors.

The elder Goos's work as a cattle dealer apparently earned him a solid reputation among the small farmers with whom he dealt. For all of his immigrant ways—he was fresh off the boat from the *shtetl*, after all—he gained a good deal of respect and a sure footing in the rural economy, where a personal reputation really mattered. Part of his success was based, apparently, on his own spirit of good faith. "He had a horse and wagon," recalls Zeese. "Of course, he couldn't write, but he learned to write his name. He used to go out and deal with farmers. And he would sign the checks, and the farmer that he bought the cow from would fill in the rest. Thank goodness, the farmers were very honest, [in] the majority." Based, apparently, on his early dealings, Goos gained a reputation for being extremely honest. As a matter of fact, Zeese continues, "he would call the other dealers up and sell cattle over the phone, and they would say to him, 'Sam, is it worth what you're asking?' If my father said, 'Yes,' they said, 'Ship it.'"

Perhaps the positive reputation which these Jewish cattle dealers developed among their neighbors derived from their having been perceived as working in the farmers' interest. Cattle dealers, as Bob August points out, mediated several worlds and, it might be argued, eased their neighbors' passage into a new realm of economic consolidation. They fulfilled a role that has always been somewhat familiar to Jews in many lands and eras—that of the go-between. Indeed, based on the explanation that August gives, the experience of Jewish cattle dealers emerges as a fitting metaphor for the entire Jewish experience in small-town New England. Clearly, the cattle dealers' adjustment to rural New England could have nothing to do with their having lived in the area for a long time; their success, on the contrary, was a direct function of their ease and fluidity within both the Old World and the New, between an agrarian existence and an industrializing economy. "It was a fraternity of people providing a very . . . valuable service to a large community of farm families," says Bob August.

> In order to understand the cattle business, you have to also have a picture of what that rural and what that agricultural world was like back then. There were lots of very small farms, small dairies, just all-purpose farms. A lot of families just had a few animals just for their use. There were a lot of animals out there in that world and there was not a lot of mobility among a lot of those families, so these cattlemen brought something to those small economic family groups that they [the farmers] weren't going to be able to easily achieve for themselves. And they didn't have the ability to sell the cow unless the neighbor wanted to buy it. They had even less ability to replenish the herd stock if they needed it. So that cattle dealer was providing lots of very tangible services to those families in those small farms in addition to providing things that they were going to have a great difficulty achieving on their own, and that's capital access, either in the form of the animal, or in the form of the cash to get the animal. Again, I come back to thinking, there's a very fluid, very responsive kind of system that was represented by that sort of not very meaningful term livestock dealer, or cattle dealer. It really represented a whole lot more that was going on in that economic framework, the social framework of a farm.

August points out that Jews were not the only cattle dealers in the area. "There were some Yankee cattle dealers," he says; "there were some Polish cattle dealers; there were some Italian cattle dealers." Given their miniscule place within the region's overall demography, however, the Jews' role in the business was significant. It brought visibility, and—eventually—that initial visibility was a step in the direction of permanent establishment throughout the region. Geographic mobility was a key element here. As August describes it, his father covered a broad geographic area. "He did a lot in the hilltowns, western Hampshire County—Middlefield, Cummington, Worthington, Goshen, Williamsburg." August's uncle—also operating out of Northampton—operated further south—"into Westfield, Easthampton [and] Southampton."

In Maine as well, Jewish cattle dealers comprised a sort of business fraternity, and they carved up the state among themselves. Even in the remotest places, where Jews would hardly, if ever, be seen at all, Sam Goos worked his cattle business. His particular territory, as it turned out, was primarily the Bangor area, but he frequently ranged as far as Mount Desert Island, where, in addition to buying and selling cattle from and to small farms, he also "haul[ed] baled hay because there wasn't much land on the island there where they could have fields to get the hay." Milt Adelman recalls as well that the Escovitz-Rapport families, who also farmed potatoes "in all these places up around the Canadian border," sold cattle throughout northern Maine and then, like several other cattle dealers, switched to automobiles. In North Adams, Massachusetts, Sam Shapiro eventually made the same move from cattle and horses to cars. His auto dealership went on to become one of the largest in northern Berkshire County. Indeed, as the region made the transition from horses to cars, Shapiro moved back and forth between both realms. "By the time he was selling cars," his daughter Lillian Glickman explains, "a farmer would need a truck and he didn't have the money for the truck but he could give my father cows, and my father would buy the cows and then he would go to a farm and he'd sell the cows."

"In the early days," as Glickman recalls, Shapiro didn't hesitate to apply a business practice drawn from the folkways of Eastern European Jews right in the middle of the Berkshires. Shapiro's brother-in-law had sold him some horses which had to be transported from Sioux City, Iowa. The brother-in-law sent his nephew on the train to accompany the horses and fetch the payment from Sam in North Adams. "My father didn't have too much money to pay him," Lillian Glickman says, "so he [Sam] said, 'I'll pay you a different way.' And he got him a date. And he [the nephew] married her. He stayed here. That's how the story goes, anyway." Perhaps to a greater degree than any other rural Jews of the period, the cattle and horse dealers plied their business with their feet still in both worlds. This circumstance may, at least in one town's case, have been cause for a certain amount of in-group tension. As Max Wall recalls from his early days as the rabbi of a congregation in Burlington, Vermont, shortly after World War II, five local Jewish families were in the cattle business, "but they didn't talk to each other." Bob August, on the other hand, recalls some rivalry among cattle dealers but a generalizing spirit of cooperation among them. "As a kid," he says, "I used to watch some of the dynamics there, you know, and sometimes there was a little of 'Well, that was my customer and this was my customer.' The Jewish cattle dealers tended to stay out of one another's hair." This result, August explains, was achieved through either "territorial segregation" or by "the type of livestock they dealt with."

Perhaps because so many of them had made their living as dealers in cattle in the Old Country and found themselves living and trading each day among New England dairymen, many Jews found the transition to actual dairy farming to be a natural progression. Louis Blumenthall owned and milked a small herd in Whitefield, New Hampshire, and the milk went for more than family use. As his grandson Steve Steinberg explains, "It was not a large operation, you know. A dozen cows. That area is not good for farming. . . . [But] dairy farming was okay." Not surprisingly, Blumenthall supplemented his income as a dairyman by cultivating a potato crop and running a junk business. He was hardly the only Jew or New England farmer, for that matter, to have learned that dairying alone was an unreliable source of income.

In the southern Berkshires, the Pyenson family of Otis, Massachusetts, eventually came to similar conclusions and shortly after World War II began its still functioning, exclusively poultry-raising business. The family had not been alone in its raising of cows. "Within walking distance" of the Pyenson farm, recalls Maxwell, were a few Jewish butchers. Another Jewish family, the Rods, "ran a dairy farm for many, many years" and sold its milk to the Springfield market. As for the Pyensons, it took years before the elder Pyenson gave up his small herd of dairy cows. As Maxwell talks of the sort of farm work he had to do as a boy, he describes the atmosphere of mixed production. "We had three, four or five cows," he explains. "Where the cows went, more shoveling manure and milking. Of course I learned how to milk, not to the greatest extent, but I learned how to milk. Then of course there was cutting hay. We had 35 acres around here but only about 15 or 20 of it was hayfields and you had to cut the hay and cure it and bring it into the barn for the cows, which was a big chore." Later, after Maxwell returned from his World War II military service, he worked on convincing his father to give up the cows.

I says, "You can buy milk." And I says, "You hate to milk; you hate to milk the cow anyway." I says, "Let's get rid of the cow," and I says, "There's milkmen around here that deliver milk. You can buy milk."

And of course my mother says, "Well, they don't make the cheese like I do." And this and that and everything else. I says, "Well, you'll get used to it, you know." So you started buying butter from the milk-man, you started buying your cheese and the milk and everything else and you got away from the diversification and you went into spe-cialization. This is it. You're in the egg business and this what you're going to specialize in. This is where you're going to put your energy.

Elsewhere in New England, Jews remained in the dairy business for a longer period of time. As late as 1966, when Herman Levine's *The Ameri-can Jewish Farmer in Changing Times* was published, there were "about 30 Jewish dairymen in Connecticut, with herds ranging in size from 50 to 300 milkers." [20] In the neighboring Catskills in upper New York State, Jews continued on as dairy farmers for still longer, and in higher concentration. Viability in dairying was a function of one's willingness to move toward an industrial model, and in this regard, Jews could succeed as well as any-one else. As Morton Gordon puts it, in reference to the Jewish dairymen of Connecticut, "Mechanized barns, manure spreaders, electric milking machines and bulk milk tanks took much of the hard work out of being a dairy farmer. On the whole, the Jewish dairy farmer who enlarged his herd of cows and modernized his equipment did well financially." [21] Doing well financially, in turn, could lead to an easier social adjustment.

Immigrant Jews Transplanted to the American Farm: The Jewish Agricultural Colony in Sandisfield, Massachusetts

Outside of Jewish concentrations in eastern and central Connecticut, one of the areas within New England in which Jewish farmers settled in larger numbers was the Berkshire region of Massachusetts and Connecticut, beginning in the first decade of the twentieth century, in the wake of the pogroms that followed the 1904 Russo-Japanese War. Tiny Otis, Massa-chusetts, was home to the Rod family, who farmed steadily into the early 1970s. [22] The Pyenson family farmed in Otis as well, raising both chickens and cows in the aftermath of World War I. Indeed, that family's poultry business, now in its third generation of continual operation, continues to thrive, and the family recently marked its hundredth year of continual operation. Jews also farmed in and around Great Barrington during this period, though on a small scale. A more ambitious Berkshire agricultural endeavor was the colony begun shortly after World War I in Sandisfield, Massachusetts. Like the Catskill Jewish farmers, the Sandisfield Jews undertook to gain more than a subsistence livelihood. They opened their farms, which had been largely devoted to poultry raising, to summer guests—Jewish New Yorkers, primarily, who wanted to escape the hot and crowded city. The participants in the Sandisfield colony comprised one of the longer-lived Jewish agricultural communities of the early twentieth century. "By 1921," as the authors of *Jews in Berkshire County* recount, "the Sandisfield colony became congregation B'Nai Abraham"; one of its members purchased a Baptist church, where services were held for the ensuing thirty years.[23] "With the sons and daughters moving off," however, the colony had dissolved by the mid-twentieth century. Interestingly, as Horwitt and Skole write in their account of the Jewish Berkshires, "a resurgence of interest in 1971" made it possible, after successive years of abandonment, for the synagogue to be repaired and used for High Holy Day services.[24] Today, the old synagogue serves the larger community as an arts center, but the legacy of the Sandisfield colony is hardly forgotten, and several of the Jewish families who settled the area in the early part of the twentieth century remain.

The Jewish farmers who participated in the Sandisfield colony experienced a difficult adjustment period. Indeed, when the project first got underway, under its official Jewish Agricultural Agency auspices, some of the farmers themselves appear to have had considerable doubts. As might be expected, the pioneering spirit that went along with such ventures, at least in an American context, where urbanized Jews just recently removed from the East European *shtetlach* were to be isolated and cut off from the larger Jewish community, was accompanied by at least a measure of wistfulness and skepticism on the part of the pioneers and their descendants. The relief that rural life brought from the overcrowded conditions of life, say, on the Lower East Side of New York City, might very well have been countered by a sense of loss. How could Jews—clearly a foreign presence in places like the Berkshires at the turn of the century—hope to become rural-dwelling Americans *and* retain their Jewish identity? The words of a 1935 Jewish Agricultural Agency study articulate the difficult odds facing the immigrant Jewish farmers of the period and also resonate with the view, expressed by Mark Bauman in connection with the southern Jewish

experience, that Jewish life and a vernacular regional affiliation are, at least
in part, incommensurate. "Manifestly," the pamphlet asserts, "the American Jewish farmer is not indigenous to the soil, but simply the immigrant
Jew transplanted from American city to American farm." [25]

In an interview I conducted with three long-time residents of southwestern Berkshire County, Massachusetts, the conversation about that area's
Jewish farming venture of the early twentieth century touched on several
of these aspects. I had asked Irene Moskowitz about her family's origins in
the area around her hometown of Great Barrington. While Mrs. Moskowitz
offered a relatively factual account of the farming colony located in nearby
Sandisfield, her friend Beala Stark Schiffman, who moved permanently
to the Berkshires from Cedarhurst, Long Island, in 1960, contributed a
more pointed version of the same story. The interchange between the two
tradition-bearers gives voice to a profound ambivalence that results, it
seems, from the divergent pressures of Jewish and rural American identity.
To have been an independent Jewish farmer in a world in which pogroms
raged and Jews were still routinely discriminated against and stereotyped as
weak could clearly have been a point of pride. Nevertheless, embarking on a
venture like the Sandisfield experiment was fraught with at least some psychic peril, not to mention a measure of potential folly. The Jewish farmers
of turn-of-the-century Sandisfield were quintessential interlopers—mostly
foreign- and urban-born. To the degree to which they might succeed in
insinuating themselves into the cultural fabric of rural New England, they
would risk being seen by their fellow Jews as outsiders.

IM: My father-in-law's sister . . . had come here years before and
they lived in Sandisfield . . . they were brought. A lot of Jews were
brought here—

BSS: In 1902—

IM: Yeah, by the Rothschilds. Baron Rothschild, who decided that
Jews should learn to be agriculturalists . . . he funded these people.
[Baron de Hirsch, a Rothschild relation, was chief financial instiga-
tor of such Jewish agricultural missions.] A lot of them went into the
chicken business. . . .

BSS: One of the women told me . . . she was the only one [of the
original Sandisfield farmers] living here when we came up in 1960.

And the rabbi in Cedarhurst said to us, "You live in Sandisfield?" I said, "We have a summer home in Sandisfield."

"Oh," he said, "It's in the history books. They brought all the Jews up there to farm and live there."

So I went to her house, and I said to her, "How was it? Was he such a wonderful man?"

"A bastard. He tricked us. He said the farming was good. It was not good for farming in Sandisfield. . . ."

I know of a girl, Anne Hopman, who was Anne Pinsky . . . and when they came up she hated it. And soon as she was able to walk, she went to New York and went to the Village. That's where I met her. But we used from New York to hitchhike to Lenox, to Tanglewood. And she wanted to go with us, and on the way she said, "We can stay at my mother and father's house." So we all looked and we said, "What?" We thought that Jews only lived in New York!

Even Irene Moskowitz's essentially factual account introduces a certain amount of in-group tension. There appears, for instance, in her suggestion that the wealthy financier "decided that Jews should become agriculturalists" to be a significant element of class awareness. Moreover, as Moskowitz uses the verb " 'decided" in association with the philanthropist, she seems to be intimating that the baron had made his pronouncement from on high, from a position of profound aristocratic detachment. Clearly, such wealthy barons were no agriculturalists themselves. The Jews who came to Sandisfield were "brought" there by a guiding force more powerful and less willing to get their hands dirty than themselves.

The rabbi in Cedarhurst, in Beala Stark Schiffman's account, introduces another element of Jewish detachment from the exacting drudgery of rural life. Here, once again, is an example of a non-agriculturalist—in this case, the leader of a comfortable suburban congregation—with a grand, though in this case, retrospective ("it's in the history books") view of Jewish redemption. What little he knows of farming and of rural life is revealed in Schiffman's conversation with the woman she met in Sandisfield in 1960. Several decades after the experiment's inception, a surviving farmer's pronouncement removes all traces of admirable grandiosity from the baron's legacy. He becomes "the bastard" who "tricked us."

I find it interesting, however, that this anecdote's element of Jewish humor introduces as well a significant note of triumphalism. For all their having been "tricked" or even just carelessly misled into the *goyische* wilderness of the Berkshires, the Sandisfield Jews *survived*, and survived *as farmers*, no less. If the rocky mountain soil was hardly conducive to lucrative single-crop farming, as any New England native would have known, the Jews made the best of their situation and undertook to raise poultry. If the neighbors were skeptical or unwelcoming toward the prospect of a Jewish farming colony in their midst (and the accounts of the Great Barrington tradition-bearers suggests that this was the case), the farmers were determined to transcend that condition as well; though admittedly few in numbers, more than a hundred years after the experiment began, it is still possible to find descendants of the original farmers in several southwestern Berkshire County communities. Some of these descendants—including two of the three Great Barrington tradition-bearers—continued to farm well into their adult lives. Indeed, at the end of the excerpted section, when Beala Stark Schiffman tells her story about hitchhiking to Tanglewood with her friend Anne Pinsky, her pride in the very existence of the Sandisfield farmers—again, decades after 1902—is evident. "How strange it seems," she and her fellow Greenwich Village-ites were saying—strange but worth celebrating, that Jews like Anne Pinsky could be *going home*, and bringing their friends with them, to the Berkshire Hills.

Despite the factors that held them as outsiders, the Jewish farmers of Sandisfield and its immediate environs, at least those who remained and outlasted the initial experiment's failure to take hold in the 1920's, cannot be said to have failed entirely to become participants in the rural culture of southwestern Berkshire County. Lena Sandler, who went on to become a permanent settler, began visiting Sandisfield as a child growing up in New York City. As a certifiably Jewish locale in the Berkshires, the area had begun, by the 1920s, to play host to summering urban Jews, as farms opened their houses up to paying guests on the Catskill *kochalein* model. After marrying one of the original settlers, Lena Sandler began to absorb the colony's history. In her recollection, the de Hirsch Fund had not stipulated anything about farming per se. The offer of land "was made on the condition that they [the city Jews] come here, but I don't think there was anything said specifically as to what they should do. . . ." On the contrary, she says, "I did hear people came this way because it was a good idea. From the Old Country, they were used to rural living, and it wasn't as expensive as it is today."

Within a decade or so of the area's original settlement by Jews, several families had taken up occupancy. Lena Sandler enumerates them, mentioning in the process what has become of them. She names several families—the Pinskys, Jenskys, Pollacks, Hamiltons, Springs, Herskovitches, Glassbergs, and Weinsteins. Most of these, she explains, "moved on . . . to New York City" but a few stayed. Families who remained in the area managed to do so by leaving off their previous attempts to farm in accordance with a mixed production model. Instead, many of the Sandisfield farmers, participating in the local trend toward some sort of specialization in agriculture, chose either of two paths—poultry farming or cattle dealing. A significant number, including Jack Sandler, went to poultry farming exclusively after first having pursued mixed production and, at an early stage, owning dairy cows. Economic viability, however, could hardly be sustained by such a course of action, as so many preceding generations of New England farmers, especially in the hills, had already found out. Throughout New England, the Jewish farmers who stayed farmers tended, by the middle of the twentieth century, toward some sort of agribusiness model. As Morton Gordon points out, though, in reference not to Sandisfield but to the Jewish farmers of Connecticut, three goals had been articulated by the Agricultural Agency—"success at farming," "maintaining and intensifying Jewish identity," and "acceptance by the non-Jewish community."[26] It would seem that the second and third goals would have been dependent on the first. And, indeed, wherever Jewish farmers were successful, which is to say wherever they managed to generate actual income and to enjoy a broad, if tentative, neighborly acceptance from their surrounding communities, sound business and innovation were key.

Accounts of Jewish agriculturalists who set the pace for farming in their locales abound. Morton Gordon tells the story of one Connecticut farmer, Jacob Biber, who set records for dairy production. The farmer, Gordon writes, "purchased an old dairy farm from a Yankee farmer who could produce only three cans of milk a day from his twenty-five cows. In less than a year, Mr. Biber had rehabilitated the farm and was producing from seven to eight cans of milk a day from the same cows."[27] Gordon cites dozens of other examples of Jewish advancement in agriculture, from Arthur Cohen, who won the "Chicken of Tomorrow" contest to the "Jewish poultry farmers of Connecticut" who, as he explains it, led the trend throughout the region toward large-scale poultry production.[28] Whether such innovations actually endeared these farmers to their non-Jewish neighbors or, for that matter, contributed to their alienation, is hard to say, but perhaps it isn't relevant either. That the farmers were successful in mastering an efficient model of production that enabled them, if they chose, to *remain* farmers, was key. Participants in the culture of a rural area don't have to be members of a mutual admiration society to be integral to it.

Ruben Tablitz, whose home was in Winsted, Connecticut—just across the state line from Sandisfield—participated in the transportation and marketing aspects of the poultry business. In his 1992 interview with folklorists Michael and Carrie Kline, he tells the story of how that operation got started. A typical farmer would first "build a chicken coop," and then, Tablitz says, "start to raise chickens." For his own part, Tablitz collaborated with Sandler; upon his finding a receiver in New York City, well outside of the Berkshires' usual market, their poultry operation took off. Tablitz and Sandler went to New York "once or twice a week" in a truck that fit two hundred crates or two thousand chickens altogether. Lena Sandler recalls how widespread chicken farming was at one time in Sandisfield and describes the challenges it presented as a way to make a living.

> At one time, there were a lot of people that were in the chicken business. There was Morris Levine; he built his whole chicken coop, and he took the whole thing down. Would you believe that? He was really something, that man. He took the entire building down himself. He put it up, and he took it down. And then I think Pinsky had chickens. I really don't remember. I know Margules had chickens up on the hill, and we bought his farm because at that time we were raising a lot of chickens, and we really needed the space. You really needed a lot of chickens or you really couldn't make a living. And we built the chicken coop here. So we got into the business after that gentleman, our neighbor said it was a good business, so we got into it. But it was a tough business. It was seven days a week, and there was no time for resting. You just had to get out there and clean the eggs and do the eggs and grade the eggs. And my kids had to work.

Eventually, as some of the chicken suppliers had difficulty in raising the necessary feed, men like Jack Sandler and Ruben Tablitz found themselves supplying them with free grain. The innovation had brought extended viability to some, but not all.

Where the Sandisfield colony failed, or so it seems, was in its self-conscious attempt to insinuate, on a large scale, a more or less instant community of urban Jews into a rural district. Anti-Semitism, although of what Irene Moskowitz refers to as a "covert" variety, played a role, to be sure. Even after the original Sandisfield farmers had either gone back to the city or dispersed to various other points in the Berkshires, Jewish residents of the area, as Moskowitz says, "knew that they were not welcome"; real estate agents played a particularly injurious role in this sort of exclusion. An equally debilitating result followed from the infighting that, by several accounts, dominated many of the interactions among the Sandisfield farmers. "They were individuals," Moskowitz explains. "You've often heard . . . that if you need a minyan you need eleven other cars because nobody talks to anybody. . . . In many cases they were in opposition to one another because one wanted a better price, one wanted to sell their goods in a different place, and so on." If, as Jack Pevzner suggests, they could avoid competing with one another by, for instance, selling their milk to New York City's wide-open market, they could bring a positive result.

Outlasting adversity through innovative practice was essential. The farmers who settled in Sandisfield on the terms set by the initial experiment and then failed to specialize in its aftermath had little choice but to give up. When they first came, according to Jack Pevzner, "There was no electricity . . . the kids . . . didn't have enough to eat, so they flew the coop." In his family's case, the tragic death of his two-year-old brother precipitated a move to nearby Sheffield; his parents couldn't cope with staying on the same piece of land where their child had perished. Another family, the Pyensons of Otis, survived and prospered by remaining at an arms-length distance from the Jewish colony at Sandisfield, even though their initial arrival had occurred in the context of the same Jewish Agricultural Society initiative that had brought Jews to Sandisfield. The Pyensons met with success because they saw the danger of clustering. Indeed, a noteworthy pattern among all of the descendants of farmers who had been assisted by the Jewish Agricultural Agency was that those farmers who remained viable were the ones who left Sandisfield for farms in adjacent towns or, like the Pyensons, never settled there in the first place.

Cultivating the Chicken of Tomorrow:
The Legacy of Jewish Poultry Farming

Having just celebrated its one hundredth year of continual operation, the Otis Poultry Farm can make a legitimate claim as one of the oldest Jewish family farms in New England. It was founded, like the small farms of Sandisfield, under the auspices of the Jewish Agricultural Society, which sponsored dozens of Jewish farming enterprises during the first half of the twentieth century. The founding of the Pyenson family farm occurred within the larger context of Jewish agricultural ventures throughout the northeastern United States. Perhaps as an indirect result of the family's Old Country agricultural background, David Pyenson was not the only member of his family to have been encouraged in that direction. As Steve, his grandson, explains it, the other family members were settled in rural areas as well: "[The] Jewish Agricultural Society relocated probably thousands of workers or agricultural background people from Minsk, Russia," Pyenson explains. "A lot of them settled in Sandisfield [and], I believe, Monticello, New York. [My grandfather's] other brother settled in Toms River, New Jersey and was actually president of the New Jersey Poultry Association for 30 or 40 years, and his side of the family stayed in that area around Toms River. . . . Of course . . . poultry was big down there too." Once settled in Otis, the Pyensons began farming dairy, produce, and poultry. They switched to an all-poultry operation after World War II. That decision had come on the heels of difficult economic times. Indeed, like the Blumenthalls of Whitefield, New Hampshire, and many of the Jewish farmers of the Catskills and those in nearby Sandisfield, the Pyensons had already begun to supplement their meager farming income by welcoming summer guests. When Maxwell Pyenson's father came back from his military service in Baltimore, according to his son, he "said that if he couldn't make a living out of this farm, why it was no use holding it."

> So he decided he was going to start in the poultry business raising chickens. . . . Raising young ones for eggs. I know there was a time when he raised them in the house when they were baby chicks so they would stay warm and so forth. I remember we were tearing the house apart and remodeling it and we still saw signs of litter between the floors. He gradually used the milk and so forth and butter and

cheese that my mother made to sell to the summer people. Of course they sold them the eggs from the farm too so there was a little extra source of income there.

But there came a time when he expanded a little bit heavier so that he had to find routes around here where to sell his eggs and through the years he got acquainted with many friends that used to come up here from Springfield and stay at the at the house as room-ers. A lot of them owned grocery stores. . . . So he used to sell eggs all year round to their grocery stores. And of course through one he came acquainted with several others. They were all Jewish grocery keepers and [he] did business with them for many, many years in Springfield, selling his surplus eggs. We used to go there once a week and also bring in some butter and cheese and things like that that my mother made. So this is how they made a living in the early years. They had grown from 300, 400, 500 chickens. I think the most they ever had in early '30s or the middle '30s [was] probably around 3,500, 4,000 chickens, at the most.

Chicken farming was a dependable source of long-term income, as Pyenson describes it, because it served a ready market of egg-buyers in distant cities. The area's non-Jewish farmers, for the most part, sold their produce in local markets. Not until the 1960s and 1970s, when the Pyensons began to set up their own retail store, did they sell large quantities of eggs locally.

The Pyenson poultry business, as we might expect from a business which has lasted so long, has evolved through several different stages over the years. From mixed production to mass production of one product and from the targeted marketing of an urban clientele to the operation of an on-site retail store, the history of the Pyenson farm serves as an illustra-tion not only of Jewish agricultural practice in New England but of New England farming trends as well. In its middle stages, the farm produced an enormous number of eggs. Steve Pyenson, who currently runs the farm, explains the evolution of the place. Interestingly, the farm in terms of acre-age has hardly changed at all but has remained constant at approximately 35 acres. What has shifted over time has been the focus of the family's mar-keting efforts. From the farm's founding, the family has been consistently devoted to making sure that its agricultural practice has been economically viable and business-minded. The Pyenson farm, in other words, was never a utopian scheme, despite its founder's original ties to the Jewish Agricultural Society. Before the family took up retailing, it subsisted by producing not only eggs but hatchlings. Later, they built an extra barn and went into production of both table eggs and up to 25,000 hens a year. Within the always mercurial context of New England agriculture, the Pyensons managed not by maintaining a low profile but by cultivating the largest market possible and by nurturing its ambitions for continued growth and opportunity.

When Maxwell Pyenson took the business over from his father in the 1950s, he set about refurbishing it and building its production capacity. "We had a bunch of old buildings here," Maxwell says, that "were built back in the '30s and were not suitably acclimated to this kind of weather." In 1960, Pyenson "borrowed money from the Farmers Home Administration and . . . tore down the old farm and started rebuilding and . . . put up one big house for 10,000, 11,000 birds." Making the farm work meant increasing not only the scope of production but the farm's efficiency. Having been trained in agricultural science at the University of Massachusetts, Maxwell put his knowledge to work. At the same time, he made the most of his familiarity with local marketing needs and with other individuals in the business. He also knew, as he tells it, when to get *out* of the business. "I developed a pretty good strain of what they call a six link cross," he explains.

> I got acquainted with a hatching egg broker down in Connecticut who wanted all the eggs I could produce for hatching and I became number one on his sales list to purchase hatching eggs. I was selling hatching eggs, or he was selling them for me all over the east coast and towards the end, back in the early '70s I guess, late '60s, the hatching egg business was sort of petering out. They weren't giving me enough money for it. They would give me 30 cents off the wholesale quotation, which didn't amount to much because it costs a lot more to produce a hatching egg. You had to buy. I bought special males that I raised . . . so that I could constantly improve my stock. . . . If the market was good I might get 80. But everybody else was getting at least 90 cents for a dozen for the hatching eggs and I says, "You can't pay me that, I'm getting out of the business."

As Maxwell's son Steve describes it, the business continues to thrive because it has consistently stayed within its means while at the same time following a rigorous regimen of eliminating deadweight and severing all unreliable clients. Severe reductions in the number of chickens they raise come whenever needed.

All of these sound farming and business practices have arisen from the family's adherence to and embrace of a local standard. First-generation immigrant that he was, the elder Pyenson determined early in his farming career that the only valid reason for remaining in the business would be his and his family's ability to achieve economic self-sufficiency from it. As with the surrounding community of Yankee farmers, their tie to the land could hardly have been merely sentimental. Rather, loyalty to place could only follow from that place's ability to yield economic sustainability. The Pyensons did, however, act in accordance with one trend that was more in keeping with American Jewish practice than it may have been with New England farming. The elder Pyenson made sure that each of his sons would leave the farm and attend college. The father himself had evidently benefited from his own agricultural education. Maxwell knows little about his father's life in Russia, but in telling the story of the family's farm in the Berkshires, he doesn't neglect to mention that the elder Pyenson's decision to farm did not occur in a vacuum. "He went to agricultural school there [in Russia]," Maxwell explains. "I have a picture here of his class. . . . What he learned there, I don't know, but it was the rudiments of agriculture that they taught there in Russia. . . . Whether it helped him or not, of course, it couldn't have hindered him." Whatever its applications might have been, the education that the father received may well have influenced both father and mother to encourage their sons in a similar direction. All three Pyenson boys went to college, and all three pursued advanced education in agriculture upon completing their undergraduate educations.

"My mother insisted . . . that we go away and get an education," Maxwell recalls. Indeed, to the extent that rural-born Jews differed in their upbringing from their non-Jewish neighbors, the oral tradition tells us that their tendency to leave home for (and sometimes not return from) college was a primary means by which they held themselves apart. The story proves more complex, however, than we might expect. Although several tradition-bearers speak to the numbers of second- and third-generation rural Jews who left for college and never returned to the countryside, some families sent children off to school and saw those same youngsters return to apply their new technical skills on the farm or in business. Sending young people off to school seems in fact to have served at least a few families as a purposeful means of maintaining agricultural viability. Often enough, the key to viability was in a given operation's movement toward "integration," or the joint coordination by one family or business entity of the entire production process. Abraham Lavender and Clarence Steinberg, authors of *Jewish Farmers of the Catskills*, recount the experience of one upstate New York farmer, Morton Shimm, who articulated the case for integration. Beginning in the 1960s, larger farmers—in the Catskills, these larger farmers were often Jewish—"survived because they were part of an integrated plan where a hatchery and a feed mill would farm out chicks to farmers who couldn't make it by themselves." [29]

Maxwell was the one Pyenson son who returned from college to spend almost his entire career helping to manage the farm, but his two brothers remained engaged in agriculture, and his own son Steve, who now manages the farm, followed a similar course. "I was trained in agriculture in college, UMass, Amherst," Maxwell says.

> I was trained in poultry and animal husbandry and education within the animal industry. So I had that background and one of my brothers was trained as an entomologist and he had his Ph.D., and he taught at the Long Island Agricultural Technical School. And another brother had his Ph.D. from University of Massachusetts. They did graduate [work], one of them at Cornell and the other one at Penn State and the second one got his Ph.D. at Penn State and was in the dairy industry. And he [was] associated for many years with the University of Pennsylvania and the University of Wisconsin at Fond du Lac. And then he got a job at Redi Whip. [He was] the director of research at Redi Whip.

Indeed, the brother who worked at Redi Whip was the inventor of the Redi Whip aerosol can. For his own part, although he was the one who returned to the farm, Maxwell still managed to earn a master's degree in poultry and animal husbandry. In fact, before he came back to the farm after World War II, Maxwell Pyenson worked as an agricultural extension agent with the Jewish Agricultural Society. A generation later, the Pyensons still carried on the tradition of sending children off to school, at least in part in order to better serve their poultry business. Steve attended the Stockbridge Agricultural School at the University of Massachusetts, Amherst, and then transferred to the university proper. After serving a term in the military, he returned to the farm, which he now manages.

This pursuit of higher education in the service of greater agricultural efficiency, as well as the overall goal it served of building sound business plans for their farms, may have distinguished New England Jewish poultry farmers like the Pyensons—as well as the Lipmans of Maine. The same families followed the local practice of putting youngsters to work as soon as they were physically able to handle the tasks and machinery in question. I asked both Maxwell and Steve Pyenson about their earliest introduction to farm work. "Well, we all had to work, naturally," says Maxwell. "I mean, you have a farm everybody has to pitch in and work and we all learned how to pick up eggs, naturally. We all learned how to shovel manure, we all learned how to . . . disinfect poultry houses. And of course the greatest chore . . . was, you know, shoveling manure." For his part, Steve grew up performing his share of farm chores as well and, as he puts it, learning "the whole realm of everything in rural life." He learned to drive a tractor at age 7. On a farm, he says, you "learned to fix almost anything by yourself, whether it was carpentry work, fixing a roof, maybe tinker[ing] and fixing a lawnmower. I never ever liked to work on cars or motors, but we did learn some plumbing and electrical work. We learned how to use a saw, a skillsaw, a power saw. Cut a tree down. You know, shoot a gun, mend a fence." When Maxwell returned to the farm after his own time away in school and in World War II, he knew exactly what he was getting into. Perhaps his time away from the farm had educated him to seek for or expect greater efficiency. One of his first acts upon coming home was to try to convince his father to give up the family's horse in favor of a tractor. Like any farmer, he had been brought up to expect hard work, but that did not mean that he wasn't interested in shifting the farm's focus or accelerating the pace of its production. Before long, the elder Pyenson let go of the horse in favor of a tractor. "The time it takes you to take care of a horse," Maxwell told his father, "is kind of wasted, as far as I'm concerned. . . . You [should] spend more time with what's productive." In the days following World War II, machinery was scarce, as Maxwell explains it. "Me being a veteran," he explains, "they put me on a list and gave me some early indication that I could get a tractor. So with the tractor we got a snowplow. And then eventually we went with the tractor snowplow and mowing machine on the tractor to mow the land. And this is how we went into what you call

mechanization, which was a lot easier than taking care of the animals."
The result, which continues to evolve more than a hundred years after its
founding, is a poultry farm which has long adhered to local standards of
business and production and managed all the same to maintain its familial
and communal ties to Judaism and Jewish culture.

For all their distinguished history as a long-standing Jewish poultry
farming family, the Pyensons were hardly the only representatives of the
phenomenon in the region. As we have seen, poultry raising was widespread among Jews in central and eastern Connecticut from the turn of
the century well into the postwar period. Charlotte Goos's family, the Lipmans of Skowhegan, Maine, also made a go of it in poultry raising, beginning in the 1930s. Like Lena Sandler and Ruben Tablitz, as well as the
Pyenson family, the Lipmans "went into hauling poultry to the market."
As Charlotte Goos explains, "what happened was one of the Lipman boys,
in order to make a living, trucked poultry to Boston [from Maine]. He'd go
and buy it on the farm, and he'd truck it to Boston." From such humble
beginnings, the family expanded its scale of operations. "They used to go
to the farms and buy poultry and through this started expanding the poultry industry," Goos continues. "They were what they call the 'Kings of the
Poultry Industry' in the state of Maine, and they used to raise poultry on
farms and take the live product to Boston or to other markets, ship it. They
decided that they would build a processing plant where they would process
and have the product ready to sell to the wholesaler that sold to the stores."
In her account of the family's poultry business, Charlotte Goos describes
the full extent of the enterprise. Becoming poultry kings meant that the
family had to manage an "integrated product."

Having begun humbly by raising their own birds, they now owned
the entire process and were known by farmers throughout Maine and
beyond; they set a national precedent, as Goos explains. The Lipmans did
"everything from having a rendering plant for the offal from the chicken.
And Purdue, in fact, came to Maine to find out how Lipman was going
through their various phases of processing chicken and feeding chicken.
They had a grain mill; they had a hatchery." The Lipmans were busily
applying in Maine just the sort of agribusiness model that had begun to
take hold farther west. In order to survive and compete in the increasingly
industrializing economy, mid-twentieth-century farmers, in New England
as everywhere else, had to become industrialists themselves. The Lipmans

worked as "contract farmers." As Goos explains, "the farmers would buy all of the feed, the fuel, [and] Lipman would buy this, and then they would pay them." This they did in addition, she says, to running "farms of their own [where] they raised the products." Branching out in this way ensured more than long-term economic viability. It helped as well to establish the Lipmans throughout the Maine backcountry. Like the Pyensons, they also utilized resources in higher education toward such an end. Charlotte Goos, who as a young woman had been controller of the Lipman Poultry Company, had been sent to business college in order to fulfill that role.

"He Just Got Farming":
Jewish Potato-Growers in Aroostook County, Maine

Outside of poultry raising and cattle dealing, agricultural Jews in New England distinguished themselves in the area of large-scale potato cultivation. In Maine's Aroostook County, Jewish families comprised some of the most enterprising potato growers and brokers; one agricultural historian labeled them the area's "largest potato growers and merchants."[30] As Milt Adelman of Mars Hill recounts, "Fort Kent had the Etscovitz family. The Marks family in Limestone was big. . . . There was a Marks and Fish who farmed very big [near the University of Maine campus at Presque Isle], and their land was partly donated to the college and where the university sits. South of us, there's one Jewish farmer left, barely. He was Jake Shur, and his son Arthur came home, and he's still farming some. . . . Those people drifted in for the potato business, buyers or brokers, strictly farming." Potato farming, like poultry raising, was at once big business and agriculture. Jewish families who participated in that endeavor were active participants in the modernization of rural New England. If their existence was precariously balanced on the verge of two worlds, this was so only because the region itself had long before undergone an overall shift away from anything like simple subsistence farming. Large-scale potato growing, on the other hand, which was relatively new to Maine, managed nonetheless to extend the long-term viability of this most rural section of New England.

The Adelmans followed a pattern similar to the Lipmans'. From his humble beginnings "along the First World War" when Hiram Adelman began growing potatoes, to the mid-1980s, by which time all of the Adelman grandchildren had moved to other parts of the country, the family had dynamically reinvented potato cultivation and brokering and had helped to revive and sustain the local economy. Hiram had gotten underway in earnest during the Depression. After a lengthy stint first as a peddler and then as a store owner, according to Milt,

> He just got farming, with another fellow probably. He had a guy named Groop. The two of them starting farming together and buying and selling potatoes. It wasn't just farming. . . . It's all a lateral type of operation, going with farming. We bought farm fields and sold them; we had our own pack and ship. Sold spray material to farmers, fertilizer. And then later . . . in the mid-'50s, my brother and I bought the first mechanical potato harvester in the area, and we became the dealer for that, which led to us getting into a mercenary business.

Hiram Adelman's only prior knowledge of farming, when he got started with potatoes was, as one of his sons recalls, "memories from his childhood in Europe and the scenes of teenagers sowing seeds and singing as they moved across the field." [31] Nonetheless, Hiram, like his sons after him, learned by watching others. As Milt puts it, "You never stop watching what the other guy was doing. If one guy started doing it, everybody was going to do it. Nothing was original. Someone saw someone else doing." It would not be long before the Adelmans were doing perhaps less of the watching and more of the being watched.

For all of their eventual branching out and agribusiness savvy, however, the Adelmans couldn't have been accused of having inherited their bounty without having worked hard for it. To begin with, before the 1950s and the advent of the mechanical harvesters, all of the Adelmans knew the backbreaking labor involved in hand-digging potatoes and extracting stones out of the thin soil of northernmost Maine. "They'd go back one row at a time, go through with horses and lay them [the stones] out for people to pick up," as Milt describes it. Adelman and his children all speak to the apparent laboriousness of the work under such conditions. "Of course it was pretty crude," he says, "because we have a lot of rocks up there." Even with machinery in place to do the harvesting, rocks had to be carefully worked around. "[If] you use something mechanical, how do you separate the rocks [from the potatoes]?"

Many of the offspring of New England farms recall just such a chore as having been their first, and singularly unromantic, specimen of farm labor.

Like the Pyensons, Milt Adelman from an early age was used to having all manner of other difficult tasks assigned him as well.

> [The farm] would keep me busy in the summertime—hand hoeing. We didn't have herbicides to spray to kill weeds, so the only way you could get the mustard—which is a yellow plant that would grow in the potatoes—out of them was to go down and pull the mustard, or you'd take a hand hoe and dig it out. I remember as a kid going out with the crew. One of our farms I remember distinctly had a lake at the end of it. We went in the field, and on a hot day you'd get to the end of the field, you'd go jump in the lake and come back and hand hoe back.

Family members were the most readily available laborers on a potato farm. Small children "picked potatoes, put them in barrel, and the barrel weighed about 180 pounds." Adelman explains how the system worked: "If you were [a child] picking potatoes, you couldn't pick that barrel up, could you? No. So you had to have some adult in there, and you might be getting 6 or 8 cents a barrel, but you might have to pay him a penny or two pennies to load your barrel on the truck." Milt's son Todd grew up putting in a hard day's work as well. "At an early age, younger than [my father], I was working on the farm," he remarks. His first paying job, as he recalls, involved riding the family's "Cub Cadet lawn tractor behind the mechanical harvester picking up the potatoes that fell through the machine." The Adelman children were so much a part of the potato harvest—a period during which the public schools in Aroostook County would always be closed—that they found themselves greatly appreciating time spent at the synagogue for the High Holy Days in a way that their urban and suburban counterparts could not have grasped. As Cathy Adelman puts it, "I think we were probably the only kids who didn't mind spending all day in temple on Rosh Hashanah and Yom Kippur because it was a day off from working in the fields. . . . The holidays always came during harvest, and it was like a vacation day. You didn't have to get up at 5 and be there [in the fields] at 6."

Crude labor as it was, large-scale potato cultivation called for more than a workforce of farm owners and their children. In the heyday of the Adelman farm and of the other Jewish potato growers, according to Adelman, a typical potato farm would range somewhere between 200 and 500 acres.

The enormous and tedious tasks of seeding, weeding, and harvesting potatoes could be accomplished only with large numbers of hired helpers. As if to further underscore the cultural diversity represented by the Jewish-owned potato farms in the midst of the remotest New England countryside, big crews of Quebecois workers would be bused to Aroostook County to assist with the work. Indians were contracted as well; Todd Adelman recalls having worked alongside Passamaquoddys, Micmacs, and Maliseets in his father's fields. Whatever the depth or degree of actual interaction that occurred among such disparate people, the cultural reality of life in the potato fields might go a long way toward establishing just how polyglot the region had become by the middle of the twentieth century.

Potato farming by Jewish families remained viable well into the 1970s and 1980s. Indeed, at their height of production, Milton and his brother Yale "were shipping 200 to 300 trailer loads of potatoes to the Publix supermarkets in Florida."[32] These operations were phased out, as was so often the case for rural New England Jews in general, only because the families themselves, owing to the value they had placed on higher education, became "too successful" to keep the venture going. "The second generation evolved," Irene Moskowitz observes, "and did well and went in to college, and this is a whole different thing." Milt Adelman half jokingly refers to the phenomenon when he says, "I farmed until I was 70 . . . and I enjoyed a good life, bringing up six children in a rural area, but the trouble is, I gave them all too much education, and I couldn't keep them down on the farm." A generation earlier, his own parents had set the precedent, but in their case, as with the Pyensons of Berkshire County, the educational enterprises in question served the farm by supplying it with more expertise. Milt himself "got out of high school in '42, went to college for a year, enlisted in the Navy, [and] got out in 1946, with an engineering degree," which he later adapted to agricultural engineering. His brother Yale left home to play baseball on the team at the University of Alabama. In the next generation, Cathy Adelman left home to attend Simmons College, while her brother Todd attended the University of Maine and Northeastern University. Todd returned from school to give potato growing a try in partnership with his brother, but decided instead to pursue a business career outside agriculture. Reflecting on the history of another Jewish farm family in central New Hampshire, the Kamans, Sonny Chertok tells a similar story. "The . . . children were all brilliant. They went to school. His sons were very successful. . . . the daughters were outstanding teachers, and they married doctors." By the mid to late twentieth century, the first go at Jewish family farming had run its course. "I went into semi-depression when these boys decided to go," says Milt Adelman, "because I realized I was stuck with the farm, and I didn't want to keep on." Jewish farming in New England, in effect, would have to skip a generation, and with Old Country trauma lying so far in the past, its practitioners would have to be refugees from another sort of world.

"Working to Make This a Better Place to Live":
The Organic Revival of Jewish Agriculture in New England

In much in the same way that the ranks of small-town Jewish congregations came to be first emptied by the pattern of young people leaving the area, and then refilled with the coming of the post-1960s back-to-the-landers, the ranks of Jewish agriculturalists in New England, to the extent that they have in fact been replenished, have expanded as a result of back-to-the-land sorts of schemes. Another generation of Jewish farmers now tills the soil of New England, motivated, as their predecessors were, occasionally by ideological but more often by practical interests. Unlike the earlier generation, however, some of these farmers deliberately incorporate their Judaism into their farming practices, while others simply happen to be farmers who happen to be Jewish.

Much of the energy that infuses contemporary Jewish agricultural enterprises in rural New England emerges from the farmers' large-scale participation in the organic farming movement. Beginning in the 1970s, small farmers who were going "back to the land" consciously chose to grow their crops in accordance with older practices, avoiding any temptations to chemical enhancement through either fertilizer or pesticide use. With the growth of the environmental movement and the banning of DDT and other toxic and cancer-causing substances, young farmers in particular began to explore alternative methods of cultivation that would remove the necessity for artificial enhancements. The aftermath of World War II had drastically shifted many farms toward an industrial model, in which technological and chemical innovation were key components in achieving a large-scale and more lucrative specialization. The young people who were leaving the cities and suburbs for rural preserves in the New England hills were in flight from such things, and they quite purposefully sought to farm more often than not in accordance with the older methods, using untreated manure and composts for fertilizer and finding nonchemical means of controlling pests. Where their predecessors might have chosen to specialize in one sort of farm product and to make liberal use both of technological and chemical methods, the organic farmers would choose other means of achieving versatility, including hydroponics, specialty herb crops, and—at least in one case—the raising of kosher produce. Having abandoned the industrial scale of their predecessors and relinquished the desire to replicate actual self-sufficiency, current-day Jewish farmers inhabit a different milieu. As Milt Adelman referred to a friend of his who continues to grow potatoes in northern Maine as "the only active Jewish farmer left," I mentioned my recent fieldwork among the "new" organic farmers of western New England. "Organic, yeah, yeah," Milt said; "another generation." Adelman's skepticism is tempered by what sounds like a measure of respect, at least coming from a native New Englander: "Well," he says, "they're getting their price."

At least one farmer of the "new era" can be said to have gotten his start in the older milieu. Bob August, who grew up assisting his father in his cattle dealing and dairy farming, adhered to the small-town Jewish pattern of going off to college and attended the University of Maine in Orono in the 1960s. The cattle business, as August explains it, "wasn't something that he [the elder August] was going to see his son pursue or have anything to do with his son pursuing." August explains his course of study and where it led him. He ended up gaining not only practical skills but a scientifically informed and environmental sensibility that the previous generation would most likely not have shared. "My major was forestry," he says, "but one of the academic options that I seriously considered before making the decision to be a forester was animal science. So I was still hanging onto that animal thing. That didn't come to pass and I ended up going to school, studying forestry, never to become a field forester, but got involved in natural resources planning and administration and sort of, what I came to describe as the politics of conservation, public policy and things of that nature." After devoting several years to environmental research and advocacy, August came back to western Massachusetts. Looking for a model of sustainable agricultural activity, he and his wife resolved, in the 1980s, to adapt his father's acreage in Whately, which had long supported cows, to a new use. "I applied my special interest in the land and what could be done with it to the pasture," he says. "It's just a rough pasture, basically, and we established a Christmas tree plantation." For what it is worth, August readily acknowledges that there are probably "not too many Jewish Christmas tree growers in the universe"; tree farming made sense to him because it allowed him to put what he had learned about forestry and resource conservation into practice. Indeed, in the years since he and his wife have stopped growing and selling Christmas trees, they have sold their farm to the New England Wildflower Society for use as a nursery.

Leaving aside people like Bob August, among the larger contingent of back-to-the-land rural Jews, present-day New England Jewish farmers tend to be of an urban or suburban background. An agricultural tendency came to them after they had left home, once they were studying in college. Farming was not something that had been passed down to them within the family. Michael Docter, who manages the Food Bank Farm in Hadley, Massachusetts, attended Oberlin College after growing up in suburban Maryland. After working for various nonprofit agencies dedicated to creating opportunities for low-income housing in the inner city, he decided to try something new. Ideologically, he was committed to making a political difference, but living in an urban area tried him. "That was my background," he says, "and I pretty much hated it. I hated being in the city and sitting at a desk." Shortly after moving to western Massachusetts in 1987, he heard from a friend of his about an endeavor at the local food bank called the Chili Project:

Somebody had this idea they were going to grow the ingredients to make a vegetarian chili—the beans, the tomatoes, peppers and everything. So I got involved in it, and eventually with an older farmer woman who had grown up across the street here, we sort of took that project over from the Hampshire College professors who we thought were going to screw it up pretty good. We were definitely not off base on that. And I eventually got hired by the Food Bank, went from being a volunteer coordinator very quickly to being a part-time employee of the Food Bank to turn this Chili Project. We were growing all the ingredients to make a vegetarian chili, freezing it and then distributing it through the Food Bank on Hampshire College grounds. We did that for three years. And I liked what I was doing. I liked growing food; I liked giving it away.

If an ideology was at play here, its relationship to Docter's Jewish background was indirect. Docter does draw an association between a mostly bygone work ethic and his Jewish cultural identity, however.

Like the Zionists of the early twentieth century, he rejects the notion that Jewish success should somehow be measured by the degree to which Jews have managed to avoid physical labor. His family, as he sees it, and thanks in large part to his potato-picking grandmother's example, inherited a different ethic from that of the majority of assimilated, "successful" American Jews.

> Everybody else sort of bought into what is sort of a predominant Jewish norm, which is that work's for other people, and we have to figure out how to raise ourselves, kids, whatever, so that they become doctors and lawyers and they don't actually have to work for a living or do hard labor because there's definitely something wrong with you if you do that. You weren't able to figure your way out of the immigrant stature or whatever, if you still are working or went back to working. And to a certain extent, that's reflective, obviously, in our larger culture in the sense that work is definitely not looked on favorably in our culture, especially [by] Jewish people. [But] that's what we do here: We work and we get dirty and we work really hard, and we do what my grandmother did, which is work for three or four people, especially on this farm because we give away half of what we grow. And we do that without any grant money or subsidies or any other sources of income. We give away half of what we grow basically by being very productive. We still support our family and pay our crew favorably.

If getting dirty and making a living by getting dirty have an ideological origin, that origin would seem to have more in common with Marx and other nineteenth- and twentieth-century prophets of the working class than it would with the prophets of the Hebrew bible. Moreover, as Docter refers to the lack of grants and subsidies, he may unconsciously be invoking the vaunted rural New England tradition of self-sufficiency. "I operate a private company that manages the farm and we pay the Food Bank," he explains.

> Forty to fifty percent of what we grow goes to the Food Bank. That's part of our lease, and then all the operating costs. We pay off their mortgage and insurance and all the other direct costs which comes to about $20,000 a year that we pay to them in cash. Then after that, the business is essentially ours. If we can make a buck at it, it's ours. I deliberately set the farm up and had them spin us off in that way because the farm, if it was going to be successful, had to be run like a business, and it was being run like a business, only it had this non-profit ownership structure that I didn't think over the long term was going to be conducive to its survival.

Jacob Fine's initial experiences in farming also came about through his participation in self-sustaining Community Supported Agriculture (CSA) projects. His first exposure to farming occurred at the Hampshire College CSA in South Amherst, Massachusetts. He went on to find work in a number of similar endeavors afterward including the Delta organic farm in Hadley, Massachusetts, and a farm in nearby Gill, where the main crop was echinacea. These experiences led him, before long, to "using gardening and farming as an educational tool . . . specifically within a Jewish context." Thousands of post-1960s agricultural experiments, Jewish and non-Jewish, have taken shape throughout rural America since the first countercultural exoduses began taking place, many of which were inspired by just such a vision of social justice combined with a sort of newfangled Yankee ingenuity.

Farming by Jews in rural New England is not an entirely secular pastime, as Jacob Fine's account suggests. Lurking behind Michael Docter's very practical sense of commitment to community-supported agriculture is an ethic that even he, a vocal nonbelieving Jew, acknowledges as being rooted at least in part in his valued Jewish heritage. "I'm a Jew," he says, "and I come from this group of people that have been through a fair amount of oppression and to deny that in any way would be really wrong for me."

A significantly more deliberate Jewish farming endeavor can be seen in the work of Rabbi Shmuel Simenowitz, a Hasidic homesteader who currently divides his time between a small farm in Readsboro, Vermont, and a

small enclave of arable land he recently purchased in the midst of suburban East Longmeadow, Massachusetts. I first heard of Simenowitz through
a feature article in the *New York Times* about an attempt by several Hasids
based in Amherst, Massachusetts, to begin operations on Eretz Ha'Chaim
(the Living Land), which was to have been one of the nation's only communally operated, kosher, organic farms. Eretz Ha'Chaim was abandoned in
the face of an insufficient number of families to undertake its purchase and
cultivation, but Simenowitz, who was already operating what he referred to
in a separate news story as "the area's only *shomer shabbos* organic horse-
powered farm"[33] has continued on with his mission of producing kosher
food on his New England acreage.

Simenowitz grew up on Long Island and spent several years leading a
very prosperous life in the New York area—he as a music industry attorney,
his wife as a corporate executive. The family's move to the Vermont countryside did not occur out of the blue, however. Simenowitz had grown up
visiting his uncle Milty's farm in northeastern Connecticut, and remembers
watching the cows get milked. Even as a youth in New York, Simenowitz
developed an affinity for horses. "Even when I went to Yeshiva High School
up in Washington Heights," Simenowitz recalls, "my dad would meet me
Sundays [and] we would go up to Van Cortlandt Park. . . . We were fairly
proficient in horses." For her own part, Mrs. Simenowitz had been raised in
a family that had a summer home in South Windham, Vermont. Among
other agricultural endeavors, the Simenowitzes have raised Scotch Highland cattle. Simenowitz tells the story of how one of the younger steers,
when he was attempting to feed it an apple, "swiped" him. "I was grazed
slightly," he says, "but when I came home I was thrilled. My wife said,
'Why are you happy?' I said, 'As a kid, you learn in the Talmud about an
ox goring a cow and everything,' I said, 'finally here I am—48 years old, I
actually got gored by an ox. Who else in Yeshiva University actually got
gored by an ox?' It was a watershed moment." The Simenowitzes have also
developed a lucrative maple sugaring business. Like other Vermont farmers
before them, they have been conscious of every opportunity to work with
what has been put before them and have avoided boondoggles. "Where a
lot of people fail," he points out, "they go up with a preconceived notion of
what they are going to do, and they end up fighting the elements to make
it happen."

I found that unless you are salmon spawning, it's usually easier to float downstream. So we ended up through quite miraculous means with a homestead, sort of pre-Revolutionary. The house was built in 1780 and it had an incredible stand of mature maples. So in my mind I start thinking maples, horses, you know, maple sugaring. And we got the maple bug. You know, someone lent us a little pan, and we opened a trail, and we put in about 15 taps, and we boiled it in the house on the woodstove, and all the wallpaper started peeling off, and we steamed out the house. I remember we were sitting there in our *ghatkes*; it got so hot in the room, because we had the wood fire absolutely cranked to boil this down. And what did we make, a cupful or two? But that was it; we were hooked. Next year it was 125 taps and 250 and we've really never looked back. A sugarhouse, then a bigger sugarhouse, now an even more elaborate setup. So it was there, it suggested itself. You know, the Dubner Maggid once said, "It's always easier to, in a sense, shoot the hole and then paint the target around it." It's easier to hit a bullseye that way. We came to a mature sugar maple stand. It made sense to go into sugaring, as opposed to bulldozing everything and growing corn.

Such thinking seems intrinsic to life in rural New England, where economy of style has taken shape around a diverse set of agricultural prospects and a landscape that promises no kind of bounty but, instead, a humble sustainability.

For all of Simenowitz's apparent adoption of Yankee pragmatism, his farming is greatly informed by his practice of Orthodox Judaism.

I always had a nagging kind of roots back-to-the-land desire deep down. Much of Judaism and Torah is really agricultural. People tend to miss that point. They get so caught up in minutiae they don't realize that 50 years ago, 70 years ago, everybody had chickens. Today it's a novelty if a person has a chicken. It was just not that uncommon. Ask your grandparents; they used to bring live fish home for gefilte fish. And their parents? In those days, all the wagons were pulled by the horses. This radical technological explosion is really one and a half generations old. It's not ancient history. There are people today—many people's grandmothers know how to pluck a chicken.

Today, obviously, we've had this huge swoop of agribusiness and it has had the effect of disconnecting people from that way of life.

One of our reasons for leaving [the city] was to be reinvolved in the connection, which is an idea that has its roots in Hasidic philosophy as well. One of the central philosophies in Hasidism is that we're connected to godliness by two air hoses. Through one we draw down godliness from heaven. It's our job to take all the stuff on earth and plumb its depths for the godliness within [and] kind of send it back up the other hose. The worst thing that could happen to a scuba diver, someone steps on the hose or cuts it, right? Or you're on a space walk, connected to the capsule by that hose. The air hose gets cut, so too with society—it's also on a life support. And these hoses all get cut. Today the office places, I don't want to go into the whole corporate America thing, but they're certainly, by design, a movement to wean people away from a link with nature. You go into the supermarket or a casino, you don't know if it's day or night; in an office there are no windows. All these things really put people into an artificial place. What we were trying to do was bring out a more natural one, which is the way it always was.

Simenowitz is quick to point out that the Torah is primarily an agricultural text. "The laws of Shabbos are 70 percent agricultural," he explains.

People think it's just turning on a light. It really starts from all the acts which were done in pursuit of the construction of the *mishkan*, the tabernacle, in the wilderness. So it involved plowing and planting and harvesting and reaping and winnowing and threshing. You know all the acts involved in either baking bread or growing herbs from which they made dye to dye the wool. But you tell a kid about plowing or walking or running on the grass, that you might pluck out the grass and this, if they've never seen what a field looks like, and a plow looks like, they don't appreciate the whole dynamic of the cycle, dealing with animals. So much of Shabbos, once again, a hundred years ago, people had animals. So what do you do if your animal is sick on Shabbos? To people who live that way, these are common occurrences. But every kid who studied Talmud learned about the consequences of your bull getting out and damaging your neighbor's property, and the laws of chasing away a bird before taking the eggs, I'd say that the majority of it is really, has some base in agricultural pursuit. Certainly, the *shmitta* year, or the laws involving leaving the fields for the poor are obvious ones, but it goes beyond that a lot of them, most certainly the Sabbath laws. And not using produce the first, second, third year is consecrating the fourth year. And by the way, all the holidays themselves were really agricultural celebrations. This was the harvest; this was when the spring wheat came in; this was the end of the fall harvest. They were agricultural cycles, all of them. But living in the city you don't really appreciate that this is a time of the harvest. People to some degree sit in the *succah* and they make it more of an agricultural thing, but that's what it was; it was harvest time.

In still more down-to-earth terms, Simenowitz's farming practices are constantly being shaped by his Judaism. Once he and some local friends had collaborated on a threshing circle in which the farmers were to take turns assisting one another with plowing. Someone had a mule and was about to "throw [her] on the conga line with the horses." " 'You can't do that,' " Simenowitz recalls saying. "It says in the Torah, you can't work the different animals together."

A more striking illustration of the influence of Simenowitz's Judaic practice occurred in connection with his maple sugaring.

We don't sugar on Shabbos. Our horses are not allowed to work on Shabbos either. Animals can't work either. Obviously the defoamers we use have to be kosher. We have Passover certification, so as an added restriction, we never bring bread in the sugarhouse. And it's challenging when you're up all night sugaring and the wife wants to send up a couple sandwiches and everything, so minimally those are some of the things. We even had a minor miracle happen. One year we had a big sap run right before Pesach. As you know, sugaring season often runs right into Passover and all the buckets were overflowing. All my friends came and helped us collect, and then we went right to the seder. And all the sap got ruined over Pesach because it was already the end of the season and we couldn't boil on Yom Tov. We lost quite a bit and somebody in town passed a derogatory comment, like, "Gee, your God really helped you," something, some derogatory comment. And I said to them, "You don't get hurt doing the right thing."

About a half a year later I got a call from the Vermont Department of Agriculture asking if we were still doing an adopt-a-tree program we had started and I said we were. And it turns out they had gotten a call from Oprah Winfrey magazine and they were looking to do a little sidebar story on an adopt-a-tree, because they were doing a whole feature on the maple. They were doing recipes and stories, and a little sidebar, adopt your own maple tree. And sure enough, they've vetted us out over a few months and did a little story that ran on the last page. And the response was just thunderous; all over America, all of Oprah's fans, thank God, wanted to adopt a tree on our farm. So ultimately when we went to ship the syrup, the back of the truck was loaded with boxes. And I went, I saw the guy who passed the comment, and I said to him, "See, you don't get hurt." So there's the perfect example, if it's a question of sugaring or Yom Tov, there's no contest, Yom Tov always wins. And there's a certain attitude; we're not getting rich making maple syrup. To us the maple syrup is actually a metaphor of life. What is maple syrup? You take sap and you boil out 98 percent of it and you leave the essence. What is life? The same thing, boil away the 90 percent of superfluous stuff, what's left is really the essence. So it's an excuse for us to teach all the skills of sustainable living, our version of Torah through sustainable living. So there's a real God-consciousness to our sugaring. We're not just making a food.

Although such practices may occasionally bring raised eyebrows, it would appear that Simenowitz has gained more respect than disdain by virtue of his devotion to farming rural New England according to Jewish dictates. His practical sense—including his facility with farming tools and methods and his ease with animals—has served him well as he has worked to adjust to rural New England.

A more communally oriented Jewish farming endeavor, Adamah, has recently been established in nearby Falls Village, Connecticut, and has exceeded expectations for its first year. Shamu Fenyvesi coordinates Adamah as an organic farming internship for college-age Jewish students. Fenyvesi grew up hearing from his father about his paternal grandmother, who had been raised in northeastern Hungary. "Her family were observant Jews—Hasidim," says Fenyvesi, "followers of . . . Isaac Taub, a pretty famous chassidic rabbi from that area." The Hungarian ancestors set another example as well. "They were also farmers," Fenyvesi continues, and their American descendants, even though they lived in Washington D.C., retained their agricultural affinities. "We always had a big garden," Fenyvesi says, "and we composted, as long as I can remember. And because my parents grew up after the War, we obviously didn't waste any food; they had . . . sensitivities around wasting and around making stuff yourself rather than buying it, not eating processed foods." In Shamu Fenyvesi's view, Jewish heritage and subsistence farming go hand in hand. To be a committed Jew carries with it the obligation to live responsibly and to be a thoughtful steward of the earth.

Nonetheless, it was a long and circuitous route that brought Fenyvesi to the nexus of environmental and Jewish interests. Like Michael Docter's, his starting point was a fairly standard environmentalist background, on what he describes as "the wilderness model," in which the kids he worked with "played games . . . tried to understand the forest ecology and stream ecology, and how things interact." The path from "the wilderness model" to an involvement in Jewish-minded organic farming took shape as Fenyvesi was working in the Pacific Northwest, where the spotted owl controversy of the 1980s and 1990s led him to a new spiritual and political awareness.

We were living on the west end of the Olympic Peninsula, where it was highly polarized. . . . Often I'd take hikes in the park and then catch a ride, and the rides were usually with log-truck drivers, and there were some interesting conversations. . . . I just had the feeling that there was a lot that was lacking in the environmental movement at the time, in terms of understanding social issues, in terms of compassion for people, in terms of how science was used or wasn't used, and emotional/spiritual connection to the land. . . .

At the time, my father was doing research—he wrote a book on the family history—his mother's family, the farmers in northeastern Hungary . . . and got in touch with Shomrei Adamah—the keepers of the earth, the kind of original Jewish environmental organization in this country . . . and sent me some other literature that I started

looking at, and at the same time looking at the family stuff . . . and
that is how I started getting curious and interested in Jewish environ-
mentalism and just in Judaism in general as an adult. I hadn't done
anything Jewishly for a long time.

Jacob Fine, a rabbinical student who was also instrumental in the creation
of Adamah, shares a similar background, although in his case the Jewish
frame of reference pre-dated the environmental and agricultural orientation. Fine, who grew up in Indiana and in western Massachusetts, is the
son of a Judaic studies professor. He explains his journey toward Adamah.
Fine pursued environmental studies in college and "was interested in food
systems . . . and sustainable agriculture from a classroom study. After my
sophomore or junior year," he says, "I decided I wanted to give [farming]
a shot. . . . I fell in love with it. Even after I got beyond the romantic ideas
and realized that it's really hard work." Somehow on the path between the
suburban Jewish upbringing and their direct involvement in political and
environmental activism, in other words, Fenyvesi and Fine had managed
not to lose sight of a Jewish identity and spiritual connection that led them
directly into becoming participants in the Jewish farming revival in rural
New England. As is the case for Michael Docter, the legacy of parents and
grandparents seems to emerge as soon as soon as they begin to reflect on
such things.

Unlike the Food Bank Farm, however, Adamah, the program that
Fenyvesi helps to run, is a deliberately, self-consciously Jewish endeavor.
To begin with, the program is housed at the Isabella Freedman Center, a
camp that was established over a hundred years ago under Jewish auspices.
Fenyvesi tells the story of how the farm itself, which was only in its second
year of its existence when I visited there, came to be:

An old girl friend of mine at the same time found out about this program at Kibbutz Tarah in Israel—basically a kind of three months
program on Jewish perspectives on environmental ethics. So I went
out and did that. And had a great time, and it really made sense to
me, spending time in the desert there, working on the trees, working in the orchard, hiking through the desert, reading the Torah and
other Jewish texts; it all really came together for me in a big way in
terms of what Judaism had to say, and how the practice of saying

blessings can cultivate a sense of appreciation and so I wrote my master's thesis on Jewish environmental ethics in the book of Job, specifically kind of a wilderness ethic.

I taught for Tevah [a Jewish environmental education association] in its first season here and at Surprise Lake Camp, and we had a really great community here, figuring out how to teach Jewish environmental education—how to create Jewish community, how to get kids involved, how to get them excited about spending time outside and how to teach about composting from a Jewish perspective, and what to do with the *kashrut* issues . . . I'd always talked about with many people who taught here—young, ecologically oriented Jews—how this place could be more of a center, more sustainable for us. . . . [We] got some grant money together, and we talked about what it might mean here, and what we would want to do, Jewishly, agriculturally. . . . People have offered us land, and 12 fellows have wanted to come here and learn and work, and it's been really great.

Not the least of such successes has been the newcomers' apparent ability to apply their own distinct, Jewishly informed social philosophies and agricultural principles within the broader, pre-existing context of local agricultural practice. As ideology plays such a prominent role in endeavors like the Food Bank Farm and Adamah, a potential sticking point in the relationship between long-standing farmers in the area and younger, urban-educated newcomers of an agricultural bent is the issue of organic or non-organic cultivation, even where the farmers' Jewish connections may not figure prominently. Ironically, newcomers find themselves in the position of choosing to farm by means long-since discarded by local elders. Michael Docter describes his gradual evolution within Hadley's relatively large and long-standing commercial farming community.

I learned everything that I know from these farmers who preceded me. There were two or three people in the early years that I would constantly call for advice. There's one guy who died two weeks ago who would come by two or three times a week and just order me around in the early years. He was a fabulous guy, and that's where I really learned about how to cultivate. And I learned a lot of stuff from Carolyn who grew up across the street here, as well, in the early years. She really got me to the point where I could talk to somebody like Mike, another old Polish guy across the river who's a real good tractor mechanic. I learned a lot from him. So that was really what my friend Ricky taught me about life is to be collaborative, get information from people who know, ask questions.

A lot of growers that were moving into the organic movement when I was who had to learn how to farm organically really didn't know how to relate to some of these old-timers who had used pesticides. I mean, like Mike Telega, who just passed away—I went over to his farm years ago when I was first starting. I heard he'd used this particular tractor that I wanted to learn how to use. I said, "I hear you had an Alice G on your farm. I was wondering if you could teach me how to use it. We're not going to use herbicides. I need a tractor like that because we're not using any." And he came back the next day and said, "I'll teach you how to use that G; you just have to use herbicides." And I said, "OK," and I changed the subject. We became great friends. And so kind of having a moral and ideological compass has been real important to guide me through my life, but wearing it on my shoulder is something I've never tried to do, so that's enabled me to bring a lot of these old-timers in and become friends with them and learn a lot from them.

Docter's warm relationship with his fellow farmers sheds considerable light on how regional ties come to be formed in the process of visitation, collaboration, and mutual exchange. Docter's eagerness to learn from those who preceded him, coupled with his sensible tendency not to allow his organic, environmentally conscious principles to interfere with his good neighbor relations illustrates the long-term value of open-mindedness over ideology. No sacrifice of actual principles is called for; if anything, the cultivation of warm relations across the ideological newcomer/oldtimer divide leads to a healthy cross-fertilization in which regional norms, rather than simply adhering to some sort of bygone pattern, shift in accordance with every new arrival who takes the time to acquire knowledge of place and immersion in its patterns of cultural behavior.

In Shmuel Simenowitz's experience, the key to arriving at mutual respect is an awareness of and a willingness to be an active contributor to a "symbiotic" relationship with one's neighbors. "I bring certain things to the table that they don't have," he points out.

> Everyone up here knows to make maple syrup and they can't figure out how to give it away. I knew how to sell it, but I didn't know how to make it. So, hence, a good exchange was born. So I've learned everything from my neighbors and friends, but I've been now giving lectures for the Vermont Maple Syrup Makers at the annual meetings on ag-tourism and marketing. It's really been areas where I'm comfortable, so it's been an incredible exchange. . . . You know, as I said, I wasn't a city guy. But the reason God gave us two ears and one mouth is that we should listen twice as much as we speak. Just being out in the woods with loggers and foresters and being around organic farmers, that's how you learn to do it, teamsters. Mercifully I was a fairly competent teamster when I got up here, which gave me some credibility.

Adamah, whose farming project is brand new, has worked as well to forge a strong relationship with neighbors. For all of the apparent differences between the oldtmers and the recently arrived contingent of young, mostly urban-reared and self-consciously Jewish farm interns, a meaningful bond has already been established. Shamu Fenyvesi recounts the sequence of events that led to Adamah's large-scale vegetable-growing endeavor. It was the Jewish would-be farmers' commitment to a biblically inspired agriculture—their practice, for instance, of a Torah directive reserving the produce from the corners of their fields for donation to local food pantries—that figured prominently in that acceptance.

> We have a neighbor across the street, Allen, who's been a dairy farmer, and now he's shifted into grass-fed beef, and he does lots of other things. . . . He sets us up with things when we start asking . . . Where can we find a couple of acres to grow vegetables? He set us up with this land that *he* used to farm. . . Then Adam [Berman, the overall director of the project] met with the owner of the land, who I think was a religious person, which helped him to understand some of what we're trying to do, and he was happy to do it. . . . For this landowner it makes a difference that we're making some kind of

religious and biblical connection to agriculture. That's a positive for
this landowner.

Shared values across the religious divide appear in this case to have fore-
stalled potential social and political differences stemming from the typical
encounter between newcomers and oldtimers.

In certain respects, the ancestral values carried forward by younger rural
New England Jews come closest to matching the local mentality. Shmuel
Simenowitz tells a story that highlights how his adherence to keeping the
Sabbath may initially have earned him some quizzical looks and reactions
but, ultimately, stood him in good stead as a man of principle. When he
first came to southern Vermont, a neighbor

> went into the general store and said, "I hear there's some lawyer
> from New York moved up here, got himself a team of Percherons.
> Does he know what he's doing or are we going to read about him
> in the paper?" And my friend Tom says, "Well, you know, the guy
> plowed and disked his fields, got in all his firewood and sugared with
> them. I suspect he knows what he's doing." So that came in handy
> and actually bought me some credibility. But it was funny. One team-
> ster asked me if I'd be interested in driving horses for him as he had
> some overflow work, and I said I could drive for him whenever, but I
> could never drive Friday night sundown to Saturday night sundown
> because of Shabbos. And he looked at me and he said, "Not even for
> five hundred dollars?" And I said, "No, not even for five hundred
> thousand dollars." And he was amazed that I held to some principle
> that for five hundred dollars wouldn't go away. I figured if you're
> going to insult me, at least pick a bigger number, but he meant well.
> So we've made a lot of friends. I'm not naïve, I can't imagine every-
> one loves me, but I think they're at least civil enough that if they
> don't, they keep it to themselves.

Perhaps the most important articulated and esteemed value practiced by
small-town New Englanders is "hard work"—the belief that one distinguishes oneself through one's tireless devotion to leading a life dedicated
to hard labor and thrift in the service of family. We are reminded here of
Michael Docter's inherited farming bent, his mention of "hard labor" and

willingness to get dirty. He goes on to describe the survival mentality practiced by one of the neighboring farmers in his area, a man who recently died. Most of the farmers in Hadley, as Docter puts it, "just struggled to really survive. But one of the eulogies at Mike's funeral was he hated when people would come by and steal shit out of his jar or food off of his stand, but if anybody asked him for anything, he'd give it to him automatically. So these are all generous people but also people that struggled and didn't have a lot to give, but what they had was food, and food is pretty easy to give usually." That a native-born survival instinct should be matched as it is by a more outwardly "imported" sensibility should hardly be surprising. Neighborliness, after all, is in large part a product of radical relinquishment. Indeed, the recently deceased farmer of whom Docter speaks was not of Yankee extraction but, as is more often than not the case among the present-day farmers of the Connecticut River floodplain, of Polish heritage; when the Poles first came into the region at the turn of the century, they too were seen an outsiders. A few generations of hard work on their part proved otherwise.

Newcomers persevere and prove their worthiness by meeting or exceeding the unspoken "hard work" standard and self-sufficiency; people earn one another's respect by achieving and maintaining a certain amount of independence. In theory, anyway, any farmer who can manage to get by without imposing on his or her neighbors deserves respect. One of the first steps toward outgrowing outsider status would appear to be a willingness on the part of the newcomer to forgo ideology, and make the most of a concomitant spirit of tolerance on the part of oldtimers. Bob Rottenberg explains his gradual awareness of how neighborly relationships are formed in the country. His description goes a long way toward explaining just how commensurate a Jewish and a rural New England mindset can be:

> One of the things that makes it possible for Jews to live in rural New England is that the old time Yankees are very tolerant people, and what they look for . . . is your identification with place. Do you want to be here? Are you working to make this a better place for all of us to live? If the answer is, "Yes," they don't care what color you are, where you came from, what you're doing . . . Are you working to make this a better place to live? And that's a good idea environment to be in. Yankees are not particularly outgoing—"Y'all come on in

kind of thing." . . . It's the old concept of Yankee self-sufficiency; we
trust each other to be taking care of ourselves, so if somebody shows
up at your door, you know they've done everything they possibly can
to solve whatever the problem is, and you're their last bet. So you go
and you help them. And they'll go and help you. And that starts to
break down if they get the feeling that their house is the first place
you're going, and you haven't done a damn thing to help yourself to
take care of yourself.

Shmuel Simenowitz echoes the sentiment. In small-town New England,
he points out, "everyone carries chains in their pickups. The roads are icy
and the culverts are deep and you don't know which end of the tow chain
you're going to be on. One day you're in the ditch and you've got to wait
till a friend tows you out and the next day they're in a ditch and you're
towing them out." An ethic like this one, which also lies at the heart of just
about every Judaic sensibility, can't help but be intrinsic to a cultural and
religious tradition in which the goal is to live properly and constructively
in this world.

Native New Englanders too, for all their vaunted fealty to the Puritan
ideal of a city on a hill, have distinguished themselves in the national
mindset as the practitioners of an eminent practicality and a consistent
dedication to making do with the geography they have inherited. This
sort of versatility, which has so effectively contributed to their collective
longevity as farmers, has also served them well as they have pursued other
means of economic sustenance. Steve Steinberg, whose grandparents operated a farm in the hills of northern New Hampshire, gives voice to this
spirit of adaptability as he describes his grandfather's legacy. His succinct
pronouncement tells the story of total New England in the twentieth century and also previews the chapter to follow: "Whether you can survive on
a small hilltop farm just doing dairy farming, I'd doubt it. . . . So he was a
jack-of-all-trades. He supplemented his income by [his] garage, by trading
with the [other] farmers, by collecting rags, collecting scrap . . . that type
of thing." For viability's sake, small-town New England Jews—farmers and
non-farmers alike—have learned to turn the region's dynamic economic
and social conditions to their advantage.

CHAPTER 3

A Good Place for Jews to Live
Economic, Civic, and Community Life in Small-Town New England

o   o   o

Residents of rural New England have long prided themselves on their villages and small towns. Bastion of the town meeting form of government, the white church, the little red schoolhouse, and town common, small-town New England has long held a precious place in the American imagination as a model of civilized geography, John Winthrop's City on a Hill writ small. New England villages and towns bring about the ideal convergence of rural rusticity and civilized amenity. In theory, the centralizing geography of the New England town has been a major factor in shaping the region's cultural life. The small Congregational church long ago replaced religious pomp with a more egalitarian humility before God. The public school served the children of all economic classes equally. Such institutions appear to have contributed to New England's vaunted independent-thinking democratic impulse. In recent years, some of these seemingly indisputable aspects of New England village history have been revealed as nineteenth-century inventions, posited on nineteenth-century elites' often nostalgic projections onto the complex history of Puritanism. The town common, for instance, to the extent that it ever existed in colonial days, was never green during the earliest days of settlement. Like its English namesake, it was a sodden, muddy pasture, with none of the appeal of a pleasant park. Whether or not the accoutrements of New England town life are inventions, however, may not be of the greatest import. For our purposes, it is worth recognizing that by the time that the great majority of Jewish residents came to settle in these places, the church, schoolhouse, and common had evolved into the status of significant *mentifacts*, without which a separate New England cultural identity in the twentieth century would have been an impossibility.

Jews who came to rural New England starting at the end of the nineteenth century did their best to adapt to as many of the institutions of town life as they could without, of course, relinquishing their own sense of separate identity. The same can be said for more recent arrivals; the current-day Jewish residents of small-town New England, at least the ones I spoke with, value its tradition of neighborly engagement, political dialogue, and lively commerce and are often active and vocal participants in those endeavors. The earlier arrivals were perhaps more cautious; before entering the civic life of their respective towns, they labored long to establish economic viability and the respect that went along with it. Where Jews will not hesitate today to enter or initiate interfaith dialogues or political debates, the oral tradition suggests that their predecessors *built* toward such engagement more slowly and deliberately.

The underlying facts are rather plain: when Jews began to settle in rural New England, they had only just left places in Europe where both institutional and cultural anti-Semitism posed mortal dangers. Moreover, when they came to New England, although the mortal danger was gone, the region was still rife with suspicion and resentment of Jews (and other "outsiders"). Though small-town New England was worlds away from the pogrom-ridden *shtetl*, it didn't embrace Jews either. Several of the traditional-bearers with whom I spoke told me about the signs they grew up seeing, posted mostly outside certain hotels: "Jews and dogs not welcome." Still more tradition-bearers recount harassment and bullying that they suffered at the hands of hostile schoolmates and their families. Latter-day rural New England Jews still speak of isolated cases of anti-Semitism, but these incidents seem to emerge more from a general ignorance of Judaism than from any sort of hostility directed at them per se.

Not a few tradition-bearers, in anticipation of being asked to talk about their experiences of anti-Semitism, invoked their own lack of familiarity with it—a few even speculated ahead of time that I would probably not be interested in interviewing them *because they had no stories of anti-Semitic discrimination to tell me*. As my own inclination as a researcher was neither to emphasize nor to gloss over experiences of anti-Semitism, I tended to avoid asking direct questions like, "Did you ever feel discriminated against as a Jew living in small-town New England?" Reluctant to exercise an undue influence over the sorts of stories people told me, I instead learned which sorts of questions would naturally lead to frank recountings of unpleasant memories. The experience of a few interviews taught me that tradition-bearers' recollection of their school days were the most likely to evoke such recollections. Whether or not these stories represent a historically accurate picture of anti-Semitism in small-town New England is difficult to know; the mere passage of time might very well have dulled the edges of memory or at least of public recollection. Oral history interviews supply considerable insight into people's experiences of the past, but they take place in the present, and can't help but function as indices of contemporary conditions and desires. The relative lack of stories about anti-Semitism may tell us as much about tradition-bearers' eagerness to have done with a sometimes traumatic past as it does about the relatively hospitable and tolerant cultural atmosphere in which they grew up. If small-town New England, particularly before World War II, was anything like the rest of the nation, it would very often have been an arena for small-mindedness. "There is no question," Lee Shai Weissbach asserts in connection with the often well assimilated *German* Jews of the late nineteenth and early twentieth century, "that certain stereotypes about Jews persisted in small-town America . . . and that Jews continued to been seen as at least slightly out of place in an overwhelmingly Christian milieu."[1] My own field experience, in any case, taught me that recollections of youth and of school days in particular occasioned the most vivid—and often the only—memories of discrimination.

For all of these factors, nonetheless, small-town New England was and continues to be, by every account I collected, a good place for Jews to live. Historically, when rural New Englanders have shown themselves to be tolerant people, their magnanimity has been hard-earned, if not grudgingly bestowed. The standard of "hard work," which we have seen as having been operative as non-Jewish residents came to accept the handful of Jewish farmers with whom they might have been acquainted, was the central criterion of judgment that local people might apply in evaluating their neighbors. If newcomers, over a decent stint of time, could prove to their neighbors that they could both appreciate and cope with the local belief in self-sufficiency, honest trading, and plain dealing, they might eventually come to be treated perhaps not as natives, but as neighbors worthy of respect. "Economic exchange was the primary sphere and focus of the relations between Jewish and Gentile immigrant groups," writes Ewa Morawska about the area near Johnstown, Pennsylvania, in the early twentieth century.[2] In the area of business, where Jews had to overcome the centuries-old legacy of folk-based anti-Semitism, acceptance came after a period of informal—and often generation-long—probation. In today's shifting and often bifurcated social dynamic, such trial periods aren't viable. In many rural New England communities, newcomers and oldtimers lead increasingly parallel and, thus, non-intersecting lives, and are in less and less of a position to assess one another with any tools save those provided by obsolete stereotypes. Where Jews constitute newcomers in such communities, their Jewishness may very well be subsumed by their *newness*—a quality they share with countless other urban- and suburban-reared transplants. Since fewer residents of such places actually earn their money within the local community and economy, newcomers and oldtimers have a difficult time judging one another's adherence to the hard-work standard. Rather, the level of generous civic engagement, as well as the sense of proprietary commitment to place, would appear to be substitute qualities for those who might wish to impose a probationary period in either direction.

"Knocking Door to Door": Jewish Peddlers, Junk Dealers, and the Itinerant Trade

Most of the Jews who came to small-town New England at the turn of the twentieth century, as we have seen, tended toward one form or another of commerce. Among these, traveling peddlers and, later, junk or scrap-metal dealers, were predominant figures, and their story provides an appropriate starting point for an exploration of Jewish economic life in the area. Jewish peddlers, for all of their apparent transience, were highly visible elements within countless rural New England towns and villages well into the twentieth century. They were both outsiders and insiders, often enough. Foreign-born bearers of goods manufactured somewhere else, they were essentially emissaries from the outside world, mysterious men who were liable to be turned away at the door. Nonetheless, as the oral tradition represents their experience, these same peddlers were often enough offered at least some form of hospitality. Jack August, who was born in Northampton, Massachusetts, recounts a story that his father told him about one peddling venture in particular that took him into the hilltowns of western Hampshire County:

> He was up in West Chesterfield, and it was late, and it had rained
> something terribly, terrible all day. And it was cold, and it was getting
> dark, and of course that was a "sleep-over" trip to go to Chesterfield
> and peddle around. He had to sleep over. So he went to a farmhouse,
> and he rapped on the door. And he happened to be at the house of a
> John Curtiss. . . . He [Curtiss] said, "Come in. Come in." He [August]
> didn't know what he meant, but he [Curtiss] waved his arm. Father
> didn't know what he meant, but he made motions, and said he was
> hungry and he was cold, and would like to come in and stay the
> night. So he [Curtiss] said, "All right," and put him [August] up next
> to the fireplace and he took off his wet clothes and hung them up to
> dry and Mr. Curtiss said, "Now, you stay right here." And they boiled
> some eggs for him and gave him some milk and a cup of coffee. And
> Mr. Curtiss went out and put his [August's] horse up for him. And
> this began a very, very long friendship for him.

The inclusion of the reference to boiled eggs suggests that Curtiss was quite likely already familiar with traveling Jewish peddlers. Numerous anecdotes, from Jewish and non-Jewish sources alike, refer to the Jewish peddlers' preference for eggs as an alternative to non-kosher meats. In parts of the American West, according to this lore, Jews were referred to by local Indian tribes as "egg-eaters." Successful peddlers learned how to overcome their outsiderness or perhaps even to capitalize on it. "People didn't have transportation," points out Sonny Chertok. "You have to think back when people had no cars. If they had a horse, the horse was out working in the field. The peddler came by; the woman needed something. She needed needles, maybe . . . and he [the peddler] could sometimes take stuff in trade." In this respect, for all of their obvious origins in another world, peddlers came to be appreciated by and certainly knowledgeable about the communities they served. "In some ways," explains Bob August, whose uncles peddled, "the peddlers were providing services that the rural families would otherwise have had great difficulty achieving or reaching out and gaining on their own. They didn't have the mobility. They couldn't get in the car and go to the store. There was no store."

In her study of small-town Jews in Pennsylvania, Ewa Morawska found that the average length of time spent by one man in peddling was somewhere between 2 and 5 years.[5] Over time, peddling became less and less lucrative. Successful peddlers—men who had built up a large enough clientele and stock—settled in one town to become shopkeepers or, in a few instances, opened stores in more than one locale, as was the case for one Northampton, Massachusetts, merchant who, as Maurice Carlson remembers, actually operated several branches of the same business at the turn of the century. Itinerancy among Jewish merchants did not end with peddling, however. As we have seen in the previous chapter, Jews throughout rural New England worked as cattle and horse dealers; outfits like the Lipman family in Maine and the Sandler and Tablitz partnership worked as poultry truckers and salesmen. Outside the area of agriculture, several Jews who had once peddled dry goods began, after World War I, to go into the junk or scrap-metal business. Itinerant buyers and sellers of all goods were, by definition, familiar with the region; they could build their businesses only through frequent and sustained commerce within the surrounding non-Jewish communities to and within which they traveled. "Jewish immigrants," as Judith Goldstein writes, "knew how to move their human capital and activate the mechanics of adaptation. Intuitively, they sought ways to fit into the economic crevices of a new host society"[4] Itinerancy was an important means of doing so.

Peddling, more often than not, was the first economic enterprise that a Jewish newcomer would take on. Sometimes a peddler would require the initial assistance of a more well established Jewish merchant to get underway. Jack August explains that, in the early days of Jewish settlement in Northampton, a Mr. Cohen would routinely loan beginning peddlers $10.00 or so in order that the peddler, in this case, a man buying rags, "had enough to peddle all day." This, August says, was the principle of *gemlitchessen*, or charity, at work. Often enough, a peddler would go into business with a relative. Natalie Cohen's father was born in Poland and came to North America by way of Ellis Island. "He stayed with his uncle," Natalie Cohen explains, "and then this cousin from New Brunswick came and said, 'I need somebody to help me peddle.' So my father moved and then he peddled all these little towns." Pal Borofsky recounts a similar sequence. His father, who went on to found a successful Army and Navy outdoor clothing business that is currently in its third generation of continual operation in the same family with stores in Brattleboro and Bellows Falls, Vermont, and Keene, New Hampshire, got his start both in business and as a resident of small-town New England by peddling. "After World War I," Borofsky relates, as such things became regularly available in large quantities, his grandfather, father, and uncle "bought . . . clothing from the government and they went in front of the factories and peddled it on pushcarts and things of that nature . . ." Surplus and used items were a boon and offered just the right economic niche: "There was more money in that than selling new merchandise," Borofsky explains, "because they used to sell pants for a quarter or whatever, and the immigrants [i.e., factory-workers] couldn't afford to buy real new stuff . . ." In Greenfield, Massachusetts, the Kramer family got its start in the meat business as one man, Bob August's maternal grandfather, "outfitted basically a small truck. It was an enclosed truck . . . and he had shelves in it . . . and he had his customers and traveled through the countryside." Before settling down and establishing a more permanently situated meat and grocery business, Kramer peddled, as August describes it, "through western Franklin County, Greenfield, southern Vermont to New Hampshire." Peddling such items was a fitting means to earning a living in the context of New England's changing demographics and shifting economic fortunes. And it offered just the right sort of apprenticeship-stage endeavor. The low overhead of keeping up a pushcart or wagon or even automobile, as opposed to a storefront, minimized risk for people who, having just arrived from foreign shores, lacked capital.

In a 1976 interview, Jack August described the business that his uncles Mickel and Bennett operated upon first arriving in Northampton. "They had nothing else to do," August points out, "so they went into the junk business. They would buy a horse and wagon . . . and somebody would save goods for them. They went up the country and used to trade junk for pottery, tinware, brooms, pitchers, dippers, brushes, anything a woman would need in the kitchenware." Immigrant Jewish peddlers experienced the sort of immediate immersion in a foreign milieu that might lead to both a short-term awkwardness and a necessary initiation. August relates a story he had heard from his own father, who eventually worked as a cattle dealer but had gotten his start as a dry goods peddler. When Nyman August first came to Northampton, he worked for his uncle Bennett.

I remember father telling the story about how he worked for Uncle Bennett. . . . He went to Springfield with a horse and wagon one time and brought home a load of bananas. Well, he had never seen a banana in his life. And uncle Bennett had my father go to Springfield with the horse and wagon—this is a day's work, a day's chore, to drive to Springfield for these bananas. Well, on the way back, father got hungry, and he had heard they were good to eat, so he peeled the banana, threw it away and ate the peel.

Immigrant Jews would hardly have been the only people likely to have commemorated the commission of such an error. Upland Yankee tradition-bearers who grew up at the turn of the century tell a similar story of a venture to town resulting in the same surprise. What could all the fuss about bananas be if they tasted that bad? The story appears to tell us as much about the rural mentality as it does about the immigrant experience, and the contrast between the modernity of town exposures and homebound wit. For his own part, Jack August acknowledges the story's comic import and deliberate nature. "This is a story they tell as a joke," he says. "My father wasn't that much of a fool." In retaining such a story, the August family was expressing both its immigrant status and its allegiance to an old New England oral tradition in which the people of the backcountry quite self-consciously belie their worldliness by posing as provincial greenhorns.

On the same subject of peddlers getting their start in the business, another child of an early peddler, Maurice Carlson, told his 1976 interviewer a story that he marked as "the greatest story in the world." Somewhere on the road near Guilford, Connecticut, Carlson's father had "stopped in a farmhouse":

And this woman had many, many trees of apples. And he walked in, and he said, "I would like to buy your apples." And she said, "O.K., you can buy my apples—a dollar a barrel." You remember how apples used to come in barrels. Never saw them in baskets or bags or anything like that. So he said, "O.K., I will buy them for a dollar a barrel." She says, "There's only one way you can buy them from me. Every time you put a barrel on your wagon, I want a dollar from you." Maybe she couldn't count; maybe she wouldn't trust my father at all. So my father bought 150 barrels of apples; and every time a barrel of apples went on the wagon, he gave her a dollar!

Sonny Chertok of Laconia, New Hampshire, also grew up hearing his father tell him about his early days as a peddler. "My father used to call it canvassing," Chertok says, as he goes on to describe some of his father's adventures in the trade. Peddling was often a mixed bag of economic endeavors and often took shape as a partnership. When Chertok's father was young, he would go out and canvass, "knocking door to door," with a friend. "Look," he told Sonny, "I had to make a living as a boy."

At one point in his peddling career, the elder Chertok had seen some envelopes available for purchase in bulk. He recounted the enterprise to his son: "Talk about wise guys." He said, "I had a couple of dollars." Sonny asked,

> "How much are envelopes a gross?" He said, "The fellow quoted me so much a gross. Maybe they were $4 or $5 a gross." He said, "I had $2, so I said, 'I can't carry the whole gross with me now. I'll buy a gross. Why don't I take 3 dozen, that's all I can carry, and I'll give you the $2.'" He said, "I'd go out and go house to house, knock on the doors, and say to the woman, 'Do you need any envelopes to send a message to somebody?' And I'd sell the envelopes for maybe 2 cents a piece, and when I sold the 3 dozen, I had enough money so I could go back and get the rest of them." They [the peddlers] knew things.

A canvasser sold along various routes and, especially if he had not yet settled in one town with a family, he might travel quite far in his trade. Chertok's father was an inventive salesman, and he was evidently eager for his son, who had had greater advantages in life, to learn something about the art of peddling. The elder Chertok, according to his son,

> told stories of being an itinerant photographer. He and his friend Harry because he knew Block Island in Rhode Island; that was a recreation place for the wealthy in the summertime. Also, he'd been to the Mount Washington Hotel up in Bretton Woods. He said, "Harry and I would stand there with our camera, and as couples would stroll by, we'd snap a picture and then we'd give them a card, and then if they came back the next day, we'd sell them a picture." He also peddled furs. And these fellows knew how to knock on a door and sell most anything. They had to sell to make a living.

Even as peddlers like Chertok moved away from itinerancy as a way of life, they had evidently learned something so valuable from the experience that they never left it entirely behind. Although trading in this manner was—by the early twentieth century—a particularly Jewish enterprise, it was clearly suited to the mercurial economic atmosphere of the region. Jewish peddlers, like the Jewish farmers who chose specialization over an inefficient diversification, made a living and became acclimated to their communities through their public, and singularly unostentatious, displays of good business sense and honest values. In many communities, they functioned as relatively benign emissaries of changing times and of modernity itself. As Bob August explains with reference to his father's cattle dealing, they enabled the otherwise isolated residents of hilltowns to maintain both their independence and their connection to a rapidly centralizing economy. Though peddling is represented in the oral tradition as a temporary means to a more stable end, the lessons learned and habits gleaned from itinerant sales retained their importance through the generations.

Even once he had gotten underway as a store owner in Plaster Rock, New Brunswick, near the border with Aroostook County, Maine, Natalie Cohen's father Herbie Covin couldn't help but every now and then apply his peddling instincts as a means to earning some extra money, engaging his neighbors, and building his personal reputation. Initially, Natalie Cohen says, her father "peddled . . . by buggy . . . and then car. He peddled pants and shirts and stuff. After he opened his business, he was . . . an ardent fisherman. He loved to fish, and he had a special fishing hole, but he also had a store in Plaster Rock. So he would say, "Gee, John so-and-so hasn't been in for a while. I better stop. Maybe he needs a new pair of pants. And he would bring the pants, and these people were as honest as the day came, and when they would come to town, they would pay my father." A message implicit in Natalie Cohen's recounting of her father's pants peddling is that such work was a means of confirming all-around good will, both on the part of the peddler himself and of his customers. Whatever its practical function, peddling by Jews in rural New England served as well to increase Jewish visibility and solidity within the community. That the sons and daughters of peddlers grew up hearing accounts like this suggests that the peddlers themselves appreciated the psychic value of their experiences.

Indeed, as Sonny Chertok builds on his account of his father's adventures on the road, he recounts an experience he had once when his father decided that having an opportunity to apply peddling knowledge would impart some good business sense. "I graduated college," Chertok explains, distinguishing himself from his father who had not had the opportunity.

> I'd been working in my Dad's store off and on doing things ever since high school. I knew how to do the bookkeeping and stuff like that. One day I came in the store, and he said, "OK, you're coming to work fulltime now." He went and got a mattress sample. A mattress sample is a section of a mattress to show you how it's made opened up. He said, "Take this. Go out and do some canvassing. It's June now. The overnight cabins will be opening up. Go sell them some mattresses." Oh, Jesus. I didn't know how to sell. I went from place to place to place, knocked on the door. Nobody wanted them. You had to have a knack, and these guys had it. They could sell anything. . . . My dad, in the '20s as his business expanded, he bought two pickup trucks and had two men out on the road knocking door to door selling. The idea is you go up to the woman and say, "Here's an item. It's $9.95; all you need is $2 now. I'll be around every week to collect 50 cents." And that's the way they built their businesses.

Even if peddling constituted an apprenticing stage in one's business career, it was still more than a means to an end, as Chertok's story suggests. It appears to have been a form of exercise for some merchants, a tool for sharpening one's or one's children's sales acumen and business sense. For other Jews, peddling was a dead end. Charlotte Goos's grandfather, who eventually went on to found the Lipman Poultry Company, "had tried peddling, which his brother-in-law did, and it didn't work out for a living."

While many peddlers, including Natalie Cohen's father Herbie Covin, the elder Chertok, and Sam Borofsky, went from peddling to being store owners, others would enter another itinerant phase before finally settling down in one location. Jewish junk or scrap-metal dealers found a great deal to keep them busy in the period both preceding and during World War II. They operated in many communities throughout the region. In the area around Portsmouth, New Hampshire, for instance, as Sumner Winebaum puts it, "There were all kinds of dumps and junkyards owned by Jews." The scrap trade, like canvassing and cattle and poultry dealing, ensured a broad exposure on the part of its practitioners to the varying population groups and economic enterprises found throughout rural New England. Scrap dealers marketed a valuable commodity in an increasingly industrialized or industrializing region, and—like so many other economic enterprises in the region—their businesses took shape as dealers sought to take advantage of resources that were readily available. Where there were paper mills, as in Groveton, New Hampshire, and Erving, Massachusetts, the junk business often took the form of rag buying and selling; paper companies called for a constant supply of cloth. Today we would call it "recycling" and would most likely applaud its transformation of waste to economic advantage. Pre–World War II rural New Englanders may not have been motivated by environmental concerns, but the scrap dealers who traded among them practiced a frugality and resourceful innovation that had grown right out of the region's pre-existing value system.

Phyllis Nahman's father, Meyer Rubin, had settled in Turners Falls, Massachusetts, before World War I. He got his start as an ordinary dry goods peddler, and also—like Sam Goos—collected paper and rags for resale. He worked within about a twenty-five-mile range of his home. As with the other itinerants, his merchandising career evolved. In the tradition of small-town New England, he was a self-starter and an innovator.

He had a pretty wide circle, actually. He started doing that with a horse and buggy. And we have some very funny family stories about horse and buggy trips. And eventually of course he got a truck, then ended up with a whole bunch of trucks and people working for him. . . . He used to take things out of the paper mills here, and the tool companies, and made a very good business doing that. He did something very interesting: he started with no money. They were literally quite dirt poor—incredibly poor. He dropped out of school because he didn't have enough to eat. And—my dad was really smart—when he needed something and couldn't buy it . . . he went and looked at other people's and saw how they were built and how they worked and he built it himself. He was really amazing. He said he used to go to the engineers at places like Millers Falls Tool and various other places, and said, "Can you tell me how this works, and how can I connect that, or where I could get whatever," and he built his own.

One of Rubin's greatest qualities, as his daughter describes it, was his eagerness not just to learn from his neighbors, but to act upon his new knowledge and thereby become a valuable resource, in return, for them. Like many other itinerant, as well as store-owning Jews, he gained respect through his actions.

Rubin, like many other Jewish junk dealers, used his mastery of the metal trade as a jumping-off point to other ventures. In Maine, the Lipman family, as Charlotte Goos recalls, had done the same: "The junk business," she says, "was really what gave them the living in order to start in the poultry business." Customers that Meyer Rubin had acquired from dealing in scrap followed him into his and his family's later years. "These people who used to come to my dad's junkyard when he sold used cars," explains Phyllis Nahman, "all bought their cars there; the grandkids still tell stories about it, [and] their families too. And then we had the appliance business. . . . and the people came and bought furniture and appliances." Unlike some of the other junk dealers, however, Rubin stayed in scrap for several years, and became his community's resource not only in that trade but in developing a wrecking technology that provided the area with a much-needed service. He was self-taught in the enterprise. According to his daughter:

> He made a wrecker . . . with a huge boom. And he used part of it for hauling cars, because he always had a little side business with used cars. But he also had extensions and things so he could use it for pulling big machines and things. But he built it all himself. And it's astounding when I think about what he did. He took down some of the bridges after the big flood in '36 or '38. He took down the metal parts of some of those bridges. And when we would go for a ride as kids, he would point out, "This is where I took down this bridge or that bridge," and he would tell us stories about it—of himself and another man or two men doing whatever they did, and it's amazing that he knew how to do that. But he knew how to look for people who could give him information. And they were really helpful. So he made a living doing that, and we grew up in the midst of this business.

Timing, as well as personality, might have been a factor in Rubin's success. At any event, his story contrasts quite starkly with that of at least one other

New England Jewish scrap dealer. Evelyn Slome's grandfather "was about to make his fortune on and shipped out a hundred cars of scrap metal out of the train station [in Portsmouth, New Hampshire] and it all got shipped back because it was 1928 [*sic*] and the stock market crashed." A few years later, Max Schohan, of Laconia, New Hampshire, hit it big. Originally, according to Bob Selig, he "bought things and sold them in trucks. Of course, in World War II, that was a wonderful business, the junk business. People bought scrap metal and sold it for a lot of money and made a lot of money."

Great success in the junk business proved to be another man's means to acquiring both a fortune and a wide reputation as a town character in Laconia. Isaac Sakansky, either despite or because of being a recent Russian Jewish immigrant, was sufficiently eccentric as to attract the broad attention of Jews and non-Jews alike. The description that follows, which comprises Sonny Chertok's recollection of the man, is quite in keeping with a long-standing small-town New England tradition. Many communities besides Laconia were home to legendary characters.. Indeed, in their often ostentatious displays both of quirkiness and of sound, if obsessive business practice, men like Sakansky might be said to have *epitomized*, as opposed to defied, local standards of behavior. Junk dealing was just a small part of Sakansky's business repertoire, but junk dealing was what had gotten him started in Laconia.

> He was a super junk dealer, let's put it that way. He was here before my father. He came from a part of Russia, and he looked the part. He wore boots. He wore greasy looking clothes. He wore a cap that was like a black, almost miner's cap. It was always greasy. His features were real Semitic, a real hook nose. He had a lot of low price tenements. He had a lot of them. You might term him a slum landlord, but that is the wrong term because he took care of these people. If they needed wallpaper, he'd say to go buy wallpaper. They couldn't pay a week's rent, he'd let them stay. I was told by some of the older French people when he first had a house on one of the streets, he had his horse in the barn, and he had a window there, and when people would come in to buy something, the horse would stick his head through the window and be right in part of the house; it might have been part of the kitchen and the store where he sold stuff. Later on,

he bought another house in one of the ends of town; it was kind of at a fork in the road, and his neighbors all liked him.

Perhaps Sakansky's having allowed his horse to share his living quarters was an aspect of his having come to New Hampshire from a Russian *shtetl*, where such things were common, owing to limited available space. His expansive approach to business, however, seems to have been a New England innovation. Sakansky had apparently taken to heart the importance of maintaining good relations with one's clientele. His eccentricities only served to enhance his reputation, according to Chertok's recollection; they also gave him license, apparently, to be demonstrative when necessary.

Chertok tells a story about Sakansky once having gotten even with an exploitative Yankee. The account bears all the hallmarks of a traditional town character anecdote—the story one might be likely to hear not just about a Jewish eccentric, but about any man whose career and dealings brought him a larger-than-life status among his neighbors, and contributed to his having had an entire narrative tradition built around him. "There are many stories about Isaac," Chertok begins:

> One story was one told to me by a very prestigious real estate man who had once been the manager of the Laconia Foundry. When the Foundry went out of business after the car shop went out of business, this man, Ed Fitzgerald, became a real estate man, and he told me this story of Isaac years before that going to Laconia Savings Bank one day on a real estate deal. The Yankee came out ahead of time, and there were people standing out in front of the bank. You have to realize what life might have been like around 1912 or something like that. This fellow comes out and he has a fistful of money, and he opens his fist like he's opening up a deck of cards, and he announces to everybody out there, "Well, I just skun a Jew."
>
> "How come?"
>
> "Well, I sold that block across the street to Isaac Sakansky for $15,000 bucks," and he had the $15,000. Well, two weeks later, Isaac sold that particular piece of property—it was a chain outfit—for $35,000.

Whether Jewish Laconians took a special pride in such an outcome or whether they chose, on the basis of Sakansky's unusual deportment, to distance themselves from him is impossible to know solely on the basis of Chertok's account. Bob Selig, who grew up in Laconia as well, knew of Sakansky's reputation for one eccentric practice in particular: "he used to carry his money around in his high hat."

Sonny Chertok sheds some light on the eccentric behavior and on the money-in-the-hat story in particular. Among other things, he actually met the man once:

> He was a very shrewd man. He used to keep his money in his cap, and when he'd go to pay his bills, he'd take off his cap, and the cash was in there. His tenants would come into our store and buy wallpaper, and the first day of the month, he would come right in to pay. He paid all his bills very, very promptly. He and his wife didn't have any children. They lived in this particular house, and they kept it—well, by today's standards it wasn't attractive. He had a stove in the kitchen, and sometimes chickens would run around inside the house. But I met Isaac one night—it was a surprise—when I happened to become a Mason. Isaac did the same night. He was there, and that man was dressed to a tee. His clothing and everything was just so. The man was a wealthy man and evidently he used to go to Boston from time to time. He'd go to Brooks Brothers or some tailor and took care of things. But the man you saw on the street wasn't the same man you saw at a social gathering.

If Sakansky's legacy within Laconia's oral tradition is significant, perhaps it is so because the stories about him speak so directly to so many facts—not only of Jewish life, but of the regional culture itself. He was a dealer in junk, which is to say he made his initial living by trading in items no longer wanted; Jewish immigrants to the United States and residents of small-town New England alike could derive meaning and value from such resourcefulness. His outward eccentricities—particularly the cohabitation with horses and chickens—offers a possible window into what might have been a reluctance on his part to relinquish the legacy of life in the *shtetl*.

Even Sakansky's strange practice of concealing his money in his hat, as represented in both Chertok's and Selig's accounts, offers tantalizing possibilities for interpretation. The concealment was also an open display. If everyone in the community knew that he kept his money in his hat and

Sakansky was seen wearing a hat—and a high one at that—what was he really hiding? Economic life in small-town New England, and especially in small industrial centers like Laconia, was determined by all manner of unpredictable shifts in fortune. Wealth and deprivation lived in constant close proximity to one another; so too did oldtimer Yankees and a vast array of immigrants of diverse origins. Outward displays of impecuniousness like his wearing of greasy clothes and his disheveled living quarters, not to mention his "Semitic" physique, as features of Sakansky's storied reputation, suggest that he might readily have been identified as impoverished and alien—a quintessential outsider. His successes as a businessman, on the other hand, and his gradual amassing of a fortune offer insight into how very integral he was to the community and to its verbal repertoire, if nothing else. So too does the note upon which Chertok's account of Sakansky's life ends. Laconia was hardly the only town in New England to have harbored a hidden tycoon.

Local legends with similar surprise endings abound in the region, and shed interpretive light on how apparently divergent tendencies within a given small community can sometimes converge in the storied reputations of its oddest residents. At once rich and poor, native and alien, characters like Sakansky epitomize the culture of a place. No one ever knew the source of his wealth; rumors abounded. Likewise, Laconia itself could have seemed like an inexplicable place, a town in conflict with its own destiny. Chertok concludes his account of Sakansky's legacy with the following speculation:

> During World War I, Isaac, being a very shrewd man, under the table paid some of the managers or the executives in some of the local mills, and sometimes a carload of fresh cotton or something like that might be delivered to the mill, and Isaac might buy it and then sell it to somebody else for junk or something. I don't know what truth it was to it. But he did die a very, very wealthy man, and sure enough in his kitchen stove, was $175,000 in paper money inside the stove when the lawyer went over to examine all his things.

Clearly, Sakansky's enterprise had quite some time before his death outgrown its junk-dealing phase. Although he did not operate a storefront business, his entry into real estate and other buying and selling endeavors,

over time, made it possible for him to accumulate significant capital, and a
footing in the community's legendry.

Right up on Main Street:
Jewish Retailing, Manufacturing, and Hotel-Keeping

Retailing was a surer method, however, for accumulating a more stable
and visible prosperity. Junk dealing and other itinerant pursuits appear to
have been many families' means of gaining a business foothold. In Meyer
Rubin's case, a scrap-metal business metamorphosed into a much needed
wrecking business, which in turn branched off and helped fund a "cleaner"
furniture and appliance business. Sakansky's fortune went literally into his
stove. Even within a given Jewish community, the typical junk dealer may
not have enjoyed the status of a store owner. May Schell, recalling the only
Jewish presence in her hometown of Easthampton, Massachusetts, besides
that of her own family, remembers that one junk dealer's family seemed not
to have been on the same social plane with her own. The pioneering Jewish families were friendly to each other, "but not socially active [together]
because the father of the other family was a junk dealer." Store owners, on
the other hand, who traveled less and waited for business to come to them,
could gain both money and status more easily and were no less integral to
their surrounding communities. However they had gotten their start, Jewish families who became retailers had moved away from the margins of
town life and into a position of centrality.

Rural New England was hardly the only region of the United States in
which Jewish retailers attained high visibility. In the main, wherever the
peddlers had ventured—which was just about everywhere—Jewish retailing was likely to take root. Stella Suberman's recent popular book, *The Jew
Store*, which recounts her family's experience in the 1920s of running a
dry goods business in a small Tennessee community, offers useful insight
into both the ubiquity of such establishments throughout rural portions of
the United States and their evolution. In the South, places like her father's
Bronson's Low Priced Store were called "Jew stores," perhaps in the same
way that we might today refer to "convenience stores," "big boxes" and
so forth. It was "a modest establishment selling soft goods—clothing and
domestics . . . ——to the poorer people of the town—the farmers, the

sharecroppers, the blacks, the factory workers."[5] Lacking a population of blacks, rural New England nonetheless had more than its share of farmers and largely immigrant factory workers, and thus the Jewish families who ran stores hardly lacked for a market. The establishments themselves were frequent convergence points for Jews and non-Jews alike.

"Every retail store then [during the first decades of the twentieth century] was Jewish," Jack Pevzner recalls about Great Barrington, Massachusetts, which boasted a fairly large downtown. "Not all of them," says Irene Moskowitz, "but 99 percent—a lot of them." She continues: "Let's see, on Railroad Street there was . . . Harry Dakin's business, the Nagers had two businesses in town; he had a frozen food place—Sol Nager, also on Railroad Street. . . . Let's see, there was also Gans, on the left side of the street. On the right side of the street Leonard Cosberg had a dry cleaning establishment, and then eventually he bought Tommy Graham's bar, so he was running a bar, which was an unusual thing for a Jew to have, but he did."

Laconia, New Hampshire, had a great many Jewish retailers, though Bob and Joyce Selig are careful to clarify that "Jewish retailers were absolutely not in the majority." Nonetheless, they depict a townscape in which Jewish storefronts were clearly visible and integral.

> When Jews came to Laconia, they clustered together. They played bridge together, they socialized together. . . . Sam Achber . . . was a photographer. I forgot Ben Zulofski, and his father-in-law, Nathan Kaufman. Nathan was a tailor and Ben had a clothing store. They altered their own stuff. I forgot the Chertoks who ran a furniture store here. . . . In Plymouth . . . the Richelson family . . . ran a dry goods store which later became an athletic goods store. There was Sam Melnick who was shoe retailer and Louie Melnick who was a clerk at the Laconia Tavern Hotel.

Such stores offered both the premises upon which the members of a fledgling Jewish community might gather and a foothold for their proprietors within the surrounding gentile community. In addition, the stores created a physical trace, an identifiably Jewish space within the local geography. For many contemporary rural New England Jews, such places may feel like points of origin. Evelyn Slome speaks of her family having been "established in the Bangor area and the Lewiston-Auburn area[s of Maine] to make a living." She continues: "If you go into the small town of Richmond, you might still see the building where my grandfather and grandmother ran a mom and pop store, and that's where my father and his sister were born."

Contemporary tradition-bearers whose roots lie in such places can speak in detail about just how widespread Jewish stores once were. Their descriptions, especially in composite form, provide useful verbal portraits of the Jewish cultural landscape. Not restricting herself to one town, Natalie Cohen, in her recollection, draws a map that encompasses all of Maine's largest and most rural county, —Aroostook. The families she mentions all ran stores of one kind or another or—in one case—were potato brokers. "Green's was a big store, and they were merchants," she recalls. "Then there were the Weinbergs, and he's still there in Presque Isle. And in Fort Fairfield, there were the Greens and there were other [Jewish] families. There were two or three families. And even in Houlton, there were some potato brokers. And then these Etscovitz were car dealers. Every one of them." As Milt Adelman puts it, "Every town had a Jewish clothing store," and then he goes on to name the same towns that Cohen mentions. Saul Perlmutter, who grew up in Burlington, Vermont, in the 1950s and 1960s, offers a similarly wide-ranging depiction that extends beyond the confines of the town proper.

> There was a Harris family that owned a clothing store. There was Magram's, which was a clothing store. There was Pasacow, who owned a clothing store. I'm just thinking of some that I remember as a kid. . . . There was the junk shop. Samuelson family owned scrap metal. There were some grocery stores that were owned by Jews. Colodny owned a store. Saiger, I think, owned a store—a wholesale food or whatever. Sam Epstein had a little market in Winooski. Those are just some that come up.

Store-owning families built a Jewish geography throughout rural New England. Their economic endeavors brought them more than mere visibility within the larger community, however. Such stores instigated an energetic cultural as well as economic commerce, and brought about all manner of dynamic interactions.

The plethora of Jewish-owned stores also enabled Jews who were new in a given area to feel less alienated. When Amy Jo Montgomery moved from the Bronx to Bennington, Vermont, in 1960, she was 10 years old, and

quite unprepared for the culture shock of leaving the city for the countryside. The existence of so many Jewish stores may have eased the transition.
Montgomery offers another extended description of Jewish landmarks on
the Bennington streetscape. "All of them [the Jews in Bennington] had a
business."

> Every single one of them had some sort of a dress shop, or a cloth-
> ing shop or something around here. Right up on Main Street there
> were a lot of Jewish businesses. . . . Volgen Vanity was owned by the
> Greenbergs. And then there was Feenbergs—they had clothing. And
> then there was Schaffs Men's Store that was up front. It's still there
> and the son took it over, David. And there was Saul's. Saul's was a
> clothing store that you shopped at. There was a place called the Vil-
> lage Nook that was owned by the Butinskys. And Rose is still in the
> congregation. It was like an after school hangout for us. And that was
> really nice. What else was there? There was a jewelry store, Goulds
> Jewelry Store. So there were quite a few businesses right on the main
> street.

Montgomery mentions as well the television and radio store that her uncle
ran. Indeed, her own arrival in Bennington took place because she and her
mother had been invited by her aunt to leave the city in order to help run
a general store in Danby, a smaller village located a few miles north of
Bennington.

For several decades, Jewish economic life in small-town New England
was almost entirely a function of these sorts of enterprises. Retailing
enabled Jews to attain the sort of economic and social stability that they
had lacked in the Old Country and that in the bigger cities seemed only
to be attainable through higher education or participation in a far more
competitive marketplace. Indeed, as Bob August describes his own family's
integral participation in the economic life of Northampton, Massachusetts,
he suggests that in some ways, they had simply transported the close-
knit familial and economic life of the Lithuanian *shtetl* from which they
originated to New England: "The trades that they brought with them, not
unlike other Jewish communities . . . were the occupation[s] that their family pursued, in this case in Lithuania. In my family's case, many were in the
cattle business. Many were directly linked to what was a vocational pursuit
in Lithuania. There was a tailor. Again linked back, it was just that kind of

thing, so they kind of established themselves as a community within a community, but also moved out very rapidly to the bigger community." Jewish store owners in places like Bennington and Northampton were still, in some people's eyes, outsiders. But small-town New England was hardly stable or socially homogenous, and to the extent that the Jewish retailers who operated stores were helping their townspeople to become less isolated—by selling them televisions and radios, for instance—they were indispensable participants in the regional dynamic. The "insecure prosperity"—"now present, then threatened, then returning again"—of which Ewa Morawska speaks as she refers to the Jews of Johnstown, Pennsylvania,[6] was a condition shared by Jew and non-Jew alike in places like Bennington before and after World War II.

Despite the legacy of Jewish itinerants and the presence of Jewish farmers and professionals throughout the region, a great many non-Jewish New Englanders might very well not have seen or interacted with Jews in any setting other than a store. In this respect, the Jewish stores were significant points of encounter. Selma Mehrman, whose parents founded their first dry goods store in Ashland, New Hampshire, in 1922 and a department store in the mid-1930s, recounts a memory of her mother's, from the earliest days of the family's settlement in the area. "When they opened up the store," Mehrman says, "my father had gone off to do his peddling; nobody came in the store for two or three days. And one day, a woman walked in . . . and she looked at my mother and she walked all the way around her and she looked at her, and she says, 'I don't see any horns.' And my mother says, 'What?' " In her memoir *The Jew Store*, Stella Suberman recounts a similar occurrence. Great excitement had surrounded the opening of Bronson's Low Priced Store in northwestern Tennessee. On the day of the big event, a local boy had been brought into the new establishment by a cousin of his who already knew Suberman's family. The local boy had "never seen a Jew person in all his life." When he was finally introduced to the proprietor by his cousin, he exclaimed in exasperation at the man's lack of horns: "By golly, Mr. Bronson . . . You won't do at all." [7] Jewish families might eventually have achieved prosperity and relative acceptance, but they were hardly immune to countless encounters with ignorant and occasionally hostile non-Jewish townspeople. Selma Mehrman goes on to mention times when relatives of hers came to visit their family in New Hampshire. The Richelsons would take their urban cousins on drives up into the mountains, where signs outside various resort hotels would advertise rooms "for Gentiles only."

Store owning constituted a long-term rite of passage for rural Jewish families, and the initiation process tested their mettle. Another New Hampshire retailer, Max Chertok, learned valuable lessons about business, personal integrity, and the power of determination. His son, who recounts the experience, clearly derives a measure of pride in the telling. Sonny Chertok's father bought a store for a hundred dollars from an Irishman named Dustin, in Laconia:

And the agreement called that Dustin would stay with him for a week to teach him the business. The following day, they left Laconia early in the morning. In those days you took a train out of Laconia and went to Boston. They got to Boston, and Dustin took him around to introduce him to a few suppliers there in the North Station area. Years ago, there was Henry and Clark, Coleman Levin, a lot of supply houses sold stoves, carpets, bench ringers, crockery, things that people needed. And Dad went in, introduced himself, and said, "I'm starting in business. Could I get a little credit?" And he told me Waverly Stillpark gave him a $10 credit limit, somebody else gave him $15. He said after they'd visited four places, Dustin said, "I'm going out. I'll see you at the station tonight." Dustin left to go to a bar.

Dad said, "I continued going around all these different places—Prescott and Company, old established jobbers." Each place he got a little credit. Gave them his name, they gave him a little credit. He said, "When I got to the station, there's Dustin waiting for me with a big cigar, drunk. We got on the train and Dustin stretched himself out and starts to tell me, 'Young man, winter's coming on, and there's not going to be any business. You're going to get pretty discouraged this winter. I'm going to Florida at the end of this week, and I'll buy it back. I've done it many times before.' "

My dad said to me, "I was mad at that Irishman. I was never going to let him buy the business back. When he came in the next day, I told him to get the hell out." We cleaned up the place, and Dad ran the business from then on. He learned the business. Made a lot of mistakes, but he learned it. Of course, one thing he always prided himself on was his credit reputation because he paid his bills on time.

And when he wrote out a check, he had a big signature, and he had a nice Waterman fountain pen, and he was so proud of his reputation, and actually, establishing himself in the business.

Establishment in the business wasn't necessarily equivalent to full acceptance or establishment within the larger community. Small-town New England Jewish retailers had been trained by their Old Country experiences not to expect to be embraced. They were needed, however, and this circumstance, coupled with their determination to generate income and to better their circumstances, stood them in good stead.

Indeed, for all of trials they faced at the hands of occasionally anti-Semitic neighbors, Jewish storeowners and their families also experienced a large measure of acceptance and appreciation from their clientele. The descendants of these store owners retain the legacy of these positive encounters too, and commonly speak about the lengths to which their grandparents and parents would go to please customers. A good reputation could lead, naturally, to increased business opportunity and a gradual ascension of the ladder of success. Lillian Glickman, whose father owned a shoe store in North Adams, Massachusetts, describes one of his ordinary—and fabled—business practices—a practice that resulted, as she represents it, in significant business growth. "The story goes," she says,

> My father would look out the window, he'd see someone go in the store. He'd run down . . . at lunch time, and the guy wanted shoe strings or something else. So, from there, my sister tells me, that she remembers my father would have a horse . . . and he would tie it up in back of the shoe store. And a man would come along and see that horse and offer to buy it, and my father would sell him the horse . . . so, he'd buy another horse. And so he went into the shoe business and into the horse business . . . And so from there he went into the automobile business. So my brothers always joked that the natural procedure would be for them to go into the airplane business.

Jewish store owners, like Jewish farmers, gained success by virtue of their ambitious enterprise, their full-fledged embrace of the regional premium on innovation, and honest competition. The most important quality to be sought after, however, was neighborliness. Whether impelled by their Jewish background to enact *mitzvot* or simply out of ordinary human kindness, the Jewish store-owning families remembered today are represented by their descendants as having gone out of their way to act charitably.

Selma Mehrman recalls having recently had several former clients who spoke to her about their memories of her family's generosity. She had encountered these people at the funeral of one of her brothers, in 2001. "There were people there that stood up and they said they weren't Jewish," she says. "They came from Rumney, New Hampshire or Warren or whatever, and they said when there were times that [they] didn't have. . . . They said, '[Your family] never made me feel like I was on charity—that we needed to have clothes. We didn't have shoes to go to school.' And that's the meaning—the true meaning . . . You're taught to help others. So that's what we were taught." The level of trust that the Richelsons had achieved was enough, in one case, to have created a bit of a disturbance. Mehrman describes the scene in the store of a Saturday night, when "farmers and the people from the factories would come in . . . and the store was open until 10 o'clock."

> They'd come in and they'd do their shopping—whatever they needed; it could be the hardware store, the grocery store and clothing store. My brother was telling me . . . that there's like saloons . . . and very often they got paid (some of them got paid only once a month) and they'd come in with a bundle of cash. And a couple of them would come in and say to my father, "Here, will you hold this for me and if I come back and ask for it, don't give it to me. . . ."
>
> This one guy came in one night and he had come in early in the day and he came back and he wanted some money and my father said, "Now you had $50 . . ."
>
> "Yeah, but I want more. It's my money."
>
> [My father] said, "That's right, and you asked me to look out for it and that's all you're going to get."
>
> And this is the rapport he had with the, you can say, "goyim"— they loved him. I mean he could be tough but he was also a humanitarian.

In a region with diminished opportunities for large-scale social interaction, the busy environment of a small-town store was conducive to a spirit of conviviality, if not mutual accord.

Milt and Todd Adelman speak to this aspect of retailing as they describe the store that their family once ran in Mars Hill, Maine. Milt's father Hiram, who later went into potato growing and had completed a lengthy "apprenticeship" as a traveling peddler, had opened the store in 1903 on St. Patrick's Day. A 1996 article about Hiram Adelman's legacy describes the convivial atmosphere and indicates that he "tied a green ribbon onto every item." His customers "asked politely if he was an Irish Jew."[8] Decades later, the Adelmans' store in Mars Hill was still in operation, and still a lively point of encounter for the community's farmers and workers. Hiram's grandson Todd recalls hearing about his grandfather's sense of responsibility toward the townspeople. When Hiram

> was a storekeeper somewhere in the early 1900s, the entire town of Mars Hill burnt down, and we had fire departments without mechanical equipment. The town burned down, and when they rebuilt, I think it was Grampy that persuaded the town to move the stores further back in the event there was a fire both sides wouldn't burn. So it had this about four lanes wide main street, and it was before the Zayres came and before cable television, but every Friday and Saturday night all the Indians used to walk about, all the Canadians, everybody who had money in their pockets from harvest would come downtown and we'd double park.

The golden age of such downtowns ended in the 1970s when "Zayres and cable television" began their infiltration of rural Maine. In this respect, the demise of a multi-generational Jewish presence in small-town New England may be said to have occurred because of a combination of both Jews' and the region's shifting fortunes. Surveying the earlier history of another Maine community's Jewish retail district, Milt Adelman understands both constituencies to have arrived at a decline simultaneously. Old Town, Maine—adjacent to Augusta— "was Jewish merchants up and down the city, including my uncle who had a furniture store, and a hardware store and sporting goods store [and a] goldsmith's store there. There isn't a one now. Not a single one. That's rural America, nationwide . . ."

Although in the majority of circumstances, Jewish businessmen worked in retail, for the most part selling their goods to local farmers and factory workers, in a few instances Jews found roles as manufacturers as well. Sonny Chertok talks about how the Laconia Shoe Company, once owned by non-Jews, came to be purchased and then given a new lease on life. "About

1935 or '36," Chertok says, "a couple of Jewish fellows came in from Haver-
hill, Massachusetts, and started Laconia Shoe all over again. They had a
battle for a few years, ended up becoming very, very successful. . . . They
employed over 200, and they were a real good factory. . . . They contributed
a lot to Laconia; they were extremely successful in manufacturing." As Bob
Selig points out, the company, which was formally founded in 1937, eventually hired 475 workers in Laconia itself. Additional factories were established, in 1948 in Lowell, Massachusetts, and in 1977 in Sanford, Maine.
At the company's peak, it employed 1,100 workers. Moreover, the Laconia
Shoe Company's owners, the Brindises, were exceptions to a general rule
that manufacturers tended to be absentees. "Our philosophy," says Bob
Selig, whose father and uncles had founded the company and who served
as its CEO from 1972 to 1986, "was that the right thing to do was to live
where the factory was. Many [Jewish] people of that time had factories in
small towns, be they Rochester, New Hampshire; Sanford, Maine; Portsmouth, New Hampshire, but the owners and the chief executives lived in
the Boston area. We didn't do that."

In nearby Plymouth, New Hampshire, a family of Boston-based Jews
had opened up a factory as well. White Mountain Manufacturing produced
ski wear, which was just coming into demand in the 1930s. White Mountain Manufacturing evidently placed considerable emphasis on high style
in the face of a faltering local economy. Surrounded by a mountainous
topography, in other words, a company producing ski wear was a pioneering outfit. "They had these wonderful tailors," Selma Mehrman explains.
"I guess they would design . . . in Boston and the cloth would come up and
they would make these really . . . old-fashioned ski outfits but with real
class, that would have been considered pricey in those days." Small-town
New England was an ideal setting for such a business. By the 1930s, it had
a long- and well-established workforce of both native-born and immigrant
workers. In combination, the Jewish store owners and Jewish manufacturing families were instrumental in the development of Jewish communities
in the region.

The same tourist economy that created a market for ski clothing was
also a factor in the development of Jewish hostelries. New Hampshire, in
particular, was home to a few such places. Selma Mehrman describes a
small resort called Lake Tarleton, located in the town of Pike, which was
"all Jewish." The Lake Tarleton Club catered to vacationing city Jews, both

couples and singles, who wished to enjoy the comfortable company of other Jews in a remote and rustic setting. Vacationing Jews in the period preceding World War II were limited in their choice of places to stay. Indeed, as Selma Mehrman recounts her mother's story of having been examined for horns during her first few days of retail operations in 1922, she mentions the existing strictures that were in place. Aside from the exclusive colleges that applied quotas intended to limit Jewish enrollment, hotels and country clubs and real estate agents throughout the United States constituted the major practitioners of an organized and licensed anti-Semitism.

Two tradition-bearers, Selma Mehrman and Rhoda Sakowitz, cite the acclaimed Gregory Peck film *Gentleman's Agreement* as having turned the tide against the latter form of discrimination. The film may indeed have changed a few minds as it shed negative light upon such practices (it evidently had no parallel effect on Jim Crow laws or on segregationist practices in northern cities), but an even larger shift was put into effect by Jews who worked to create their own alternative vacationing venues. Before the 1940s, in any case, as Mehrman points out, posted discriminatory signs were hardly uncommon. If most anti-Semitism enacted silent, invisible discrimination, the posting of signs outside hotels spoke more volubly to the apparent "narrowmindedness," to use Mehrman's word, of some rural New England residents. Jews who sought summer accommodations outside New York City and Boston famously went to the Catskills, where dozens of Jewish-owned farms began to accommodate weekend and summer guests as a means of supplementing income. Several of these guest houses grew—especially in the aftermath of World War II—into the enormous resorts that we have long associated with the Borscht Belt. Small-town New England's Jewish guesthouses never achieved anything like resort status, but they were fairly numerous. Some of the Sandisfield farmers opened their places up for guests. Maxwell Pyenson, in adjacent Otis, Massachusetts, remembers his father's having remodeled the family's farmhouse and added a two-room cottage to accommodate vacationing urban Jews. Such establishments offered crowded and hardly luxurious accommodations, but the mutual benefits for housekeeper and guest were significant. For farmers in particular, guests yielded a captive market. According to the farm historian Herman Levine, they "would buy from the farmer whatever he produced, vegetables, eggs, [and] milk." [9]

On a larger scale than what one might encounter in the Berkshires, a unique sort of Jewish settlement was taking shape in and around the White Mountain town of Bethlehem, New Hampshire. The story behind Bethlehem's original settlement by urban Jews, which began in the 1920s and continues to this day, is one of rural New England's strangest-seeming Jewish narratives. Travelers who pass through the small town today during the peak summer months still see and may very well ask themselves how it happens that large groups of Hasidim can be seen strolling along the village's main street, evidently so far away from their homes in the city. For some Jewish families, although the Hasidim don't number among them, Bethlehem *is* home, or at least constitutes a second home, and has been such for well-nigh three quarters of a century.

The story of the town's Jewish presence is, in large part, a story of the hotel business. When Jews were first drawn to the town, they were greeted by large-scale discriminatory practices. Leslie Dreier, who began coming to the town from his earliest childhood, remembers hearing how his grandfather had gotten started in Bethlehem. "My grandfather came for his hay fever in the '30s, and he was in a hotel business in New York. And he was staying at some little hotel in Bethlehem and was taking a walk, and he was walking up toward Maplewood [another hotel] and there was a sign that did say, 'No Jews or dogs allowed beyond this point.' And he bought [the hotel]."

Despite the existence of such demoralizing signs and practices, Jewish families were drawn in large numbers to Bethlehem because its clear mountain air (the town sits at over 3,000 feet in elevation and claims to be the highest town east of the Mississippi) offered a haven for urban hay fever sufferers, many of whom were Jewish. An organization for this purpose, the Hay Fever Relief Association, was brought into existence in the 1930s, and—over the years—helped to sponsor dozens of needy Jewish families by subsidizing their stay in the town. Rhoda Sakowitz's family began coming to the town from her parents' home in Brooklyn in the 1940s. "My sister had hay fever and was suffering terribly," Sakowitz begins, "and there were no pills or drugs for it at that time. . . . She was just a wreck. . . . So when she was a little girl, the only place that was recommended to them was Bethlehem, New Hampshire, which was a hay fever relief area, so we came up here, and she was perfect. She was fine. So at that point, my father decided he'd have a business up here and a business at home and stay for the whole summer, which is what he did." Some sixty years later, Sakowitz still owns the house that her parents had bought in the center of town, right next door to the synagogue, which has been in existence since the early days as well.

Lee Bagdon, who is a full-time resident of Bethlehem today, first came to the town under similar circumstances. Her parents had first brought her to Bethlehem when she was 9 years old, in 1938, when her asthma became particularly severe. She describes her earliest memories of those visits. Refused entry into existing hotels and resorts in the area, Jewish families began to purchase and manage their own hotels and guest houses. They may not have ranged freely through the town, but their presence grew nonetheless. By the time that Bagdon began going there, many "Jewish families from the city whose kids or themselves had hay fever and asthma were coming up there. That was the going thing," she suggests. "I don't know how large the Jewish population was, but I think it was well in the hundreds for the summer." The numbers were sufficiently large, in any case, for the vacationing Jews to have raised the necessary money to purchase, in 1924, the former church that continues, to the present day, to house the town's synagogue, the Bethlehem Hebrew Congregation.

The other major purchases necessary for the formation of Bethlehem's seasonal Jewish presence involved the "takeover" of several hotels in the town. Leslie Dreier, whose father was a participant in the endeavor, describes how it took shape. As mentioned above, the elder Dreier first bought the Maplewood. That hotel had been in existence since 1875, when an earlier wave of elite Anglo urban New Englanders had begun visiting the mountains in order to escape, among other things, the teeming masses of immigrant factory workers who were filling the region's urban areas. The elder Dreier bought the hotel, which had fallen on hard times anyway, in the 1940s, and continued to run it for the next twenty years. Other hotels, as Rhoda Sakowitz explains, had begun "deteriorating a little bit, and people were coming, and they started being bought out by Jewish merchants." In the surrounding area, Sakowitz indicates, many hotels continued to discriminate against Jews, "but Bethlehem became a little enclave of Jewish people." The business takeover was the only means of making this happen. As Sakowitz explains, Jews "couldn't have gotten into the hotels if they [the hotels] weren't Jewish."

If the Jews didn't own these hotels, they weren't allowed in, and people were coming at that time for the whole summer, so they said, "Boy, that's a good thing." I mean, it's not like they came for a couple of days like most hotels today. In those days people would come for the entire summer because it was a big ride up here. Of course, they would come by trains. There were a lot of big trains coming. When I was growing up here, there were three trains a day that came into Littleton [a neighboring town].

Over the succeeding decades, the town's seasonal Jewish population grew and more and more hotels became Jewish. The synagogue was seasonal as well and held services, with visiting rabbis officiating, from June through the High Holidays or even Sukkot in early autumn. In fact, as Lee Bagdon explains it, in the early years of the Jewish presence in Bethlehem, the synagogue and the Hay Fever Relief Society were interchangeable. "It's all the same bunch of people running both operations," Bagdon notes, based on her perusal of the two organizations' minutes.

As Jews filled the town, they purchased more and more hotels. Rhoda Sakowitz enumerates the hotels that, at one time, operated under Jewish auspices and served kosher food—the Sinclair, the Park View, the Perry House, Strawberry Hill, and the Howard House. In the service of the increasing Jewish clientele, rabbis would be brought to the town to inspect food and ensure that it was kosher. "We even had a kosher butcher in town when I was growing up," Sakowitz indicates. "He was from Boston, and he would come up for the whole summer." By way of seasonal Jewish retailers in Bethlehem, Sakowitz mentions as well "a fish store that catered to Jewish tastes" and a delicatessen.

In at least one instance, the Bethlehem Jewish hotel phenomenon can be said to have spread to an adjacent community. Steve Steinberg, whose grandparents ran a small dairy farm in nearby Whitefield, New Hampshire, recalls hearing the following story as he was growing up. Jews suffering with hay fever came up to Bethlehem "in droves," Steinberg remarks.

One guy was coming up from New York and he was very sick. He couldn't breathe so they put him off the train in Whitefield and since he was Jewish they called my grandfather and he came down and picked him up. He nursed him back to health and he said, "Could I stay here for the summer instead of going back to

Bethlehem?" . . . And my grandmother, who was a motherly type said, "Yeah, you can." Well, he wanted to come back the next summer with some friends or relatives, so they turned the farm into a resort of sorts, which is called the Kimble View House. And my grandmother cooked and the children helped and people didn't do much. They built a couple cabins for the guests. My grandfather built a tennis court himself—carried the clay out of the mountainside. And various relatives would come there and stay and you could have some guests, and they ran that off and on for ten, fifteen years.

The extra income provided by such an enterprise made it all the more possible for Jews to maintain their presence in rural districts. Kimble View House also kept a sort of Jewish connection alive, perhaps an important consideration in a place like Whitefield, where—aside from one of the resident school teachers—the Blumenthalls were the only Jews around.

Along with the synagogue itself, which was the most obvious source for Jewish cultural activity in the town of Bethlehem, the hotels themselves served as cluster points as well. Leslie Dreier, who continues on as a seasonal resident of the town and also works in the hostelry business himself, describes what went on. His family's hotel, the Maplewood, "was very self-sufficient. It even had its own post office," he points out, "so there was never any reason to leave." Indeed, the family was so absorbed in the operation of its hotel that even though it was only a mile from town, the Dreiers rarely left it to go into Bethlehem village. The Jewish life in the hotel was distinctly "cultural," as opposed to religious. Like its much larger counterparts in the Catskills, it catered to an overwhelmingly Jewish clientele without necessarily supplying any sort of religious experience. The hotel was run, as Dreier puts it, "Jewish *style*."

Jews who wished to attend religious services, in other words, had a perfectly commodious synagogue that they could attend. Much of the temple's support came, in fact, directly from the Hay Fever Relief Association. The hotel, on the other hand, was a business venture whose primary purpose was to entertain. Leslie Dreier describes the typical fare from his earliest days of watching the family conduct business at the Maplewood:

So you had this nice Shabbat meal on Friday night, but on Saturday you had lobster. And they had very good comedy acts and dancing and singing and that sort of thing. Harry Belafonte and Alan King and all these guys used to show up there, and half the jokes were in Yiddish. So obviously the clientele was Jewish. And in my time, when I was really aware of it, like in the '50s and '60s, there were a lot of weekend visits. A week would have been a long stay because people were driving. The streets were all lined up with cars at the time.

Places like the Maplewood continued on in this vein until the 1960s, by which time more and more urban Jews, having succeeded economically, had begun to purchase their own second homes and no longer had any need to stay at such hotels.

A notable exception to this trend could be found, beginning in the 1970s, when—by dint of the town's already formidable reputation as a Jewish destination—large groups of vacationing Hasidim began to arrive and, in several cases, bought the existing Jewish hotels and transformed them into venues for Orthodox families. Today, Bethlehem continues on with a significant Jewish population, not only during the summer, but— increasingly—year-round. The synagogue continues to be a mainstay for the non-Orthodox elements in the town. Like shuls throughout rural New England, it caters to a mixed population of "older" families—in this case, those whose families started coming to the town in the hay fever relief days, as well as a more recent influx of arrivals, largely professional, artistic, or retirement-age urban and suburban Jews who have chosen to make their homes there. The earliest influx of the latter began in the 1970s. As Rhoda Sakowitz explains, a nearby college, Franconia, began in that period to attract a disparate crowd of young ex-urbanites, several of them Jewish. As had been the case in many other sections of rural New England, this sort of new influx coincided exactly with the waning of the older Jewish families who, in this case, weren't only thinning numerically but were also seasonal in their residency. The new arrivals began the gradual revival of the local synagogue, which led eventually to the formation of a *havurah*, and they continue to populate Bethlehem.

Describing the current-day Jewish demography, Lee Bagdon cites as well the more recent arrivals as a major factor behind the Bethlehem Jewish community's relative longevity. Services at the synagogue may attract as many as 40 regular attendees, who number among them, as Bagdon puts it, "a tremendous mix. Almost everything . . . a number of professionals, a number of people who did not a have a professional life. Nurses, doctors, people who are not college graduates. It's a fairly intellectual group that lives here that come, but it's very much a mix." Notwithstanding the traces of the "old" Bethlehem, including the visibility of the Orthodox summer visitors, the Jewish community of Bethlehem resembles that of many other rural New England communities. Its membership is comprised in large part of "transplants," each of whom came to the area as a result of what Howard Cohen, of Bennington, Vermont, refers to as a "self-actualizing" lifestyle choice.

"Doctors, Dentists, Lawyers, Teachers":
Small-Town New England Jews in the Professions

Jews continue throughout the United States to comprise an ethnic group with one of the highest rates of college attendance; as of 2000, approximately 85 percent of Jewish high school graduates went on to higher education. Many first-generation Eastern European Jews, most of whom were employed as laborers or traders or small-time merchants, worked to ensure that their American-born children would have higher education and a way to earn money that would rely less on market conditions and more on the qualifications formal education afforded. While this trend tended for the most part to reinforce the "traditional" American Jewish attachment to cities and, later on, to suburbs, it also spawned a small countercurrent, beginning with the idealistic 1960s generation, of Jewish affinity for the perceived tranquilities of rural life. Today, Jewish communities throughout rural New England still include the owners and operators of small businesses, but they also number among them, in larger proportions, doctors, lawyers, dentists, school teachers, college professors, artists, and other professionals. In the region's ever-changing economy, people who can generate income in such ways can be at an advantage; their level of education, though it might qualify them to be earning larger incomes in cities, can also predispose them to being "independent thinkers" with sufficient gumption to leave urban life behind. This phenomenon is hardly restricted to Jews. Throughout rural New England, where the influence of higher education, the arts, and the counterculture may be at peak operation, latter-day rural transplants derive from myriad ethnic and religious backgrounds.

It was not always this way, of course. In the early days of the settled Jewish presence in the region, as we have seen, peddling, retailing, and, to a lesser extent, agriculture were viable means to income. Eastern European Jews, if they were educated when they first came to America, were non-native speakers of English and tended not to enter careers in which flawless English was a requirement. Restricted access to colleges and universities contributed to this general pattern and, as a result, the more intrepid Jews who comprised the earliest settlers gravitated toward work in which they could make their own way. While college attendance among Jews began to soar in the 1930s in New York, Jews in smaller towns and rural districts were slower to change their attitudes toward professional life. In what Ewa Morawska refers to as "the ethnic entrepreneurial niche"[10] of small-town Jewish life, retailing offered sufficiently steady income and social stability to enable Jewish families—even in the face of the Depression—to live with relative comfort in small-town New England. The professional life, from the standpoint of small-town Jews, was not as enticing or realistic a prospect as it would later prove to be. The obstacles faced by Dr. Nathan Brody, of Belmont, New Hampshire, shed light on this phenomenon. Brody came to Belmont in the 1930s, upon graduating from medical school. As his nephew Bob Selig describes it, "He came to Belmont because that was a place where he could establish a practice. He was a general practitioner, and when he first came to Belmont, he did not have hospital privileges. It took a long time for him to get hospital privileges at Laconia Hospital as it was called in those days . . . Uncle Nathan was denied privileges at Laconia Hospital for many years because he was Jewish." As Joyce Selig remembers it, Brody had been invited to set up his practice in the area in the first place because the locals who had contacted him believed, on the basis of his name, that he was Irish. When he was found out to be Jewish, he was kept out of the hospital and made to fend entirely for himself.

Brody was kept out, according to Sonny Chertok, because the Franco-Americans who ran the hospital in those days harbored anti-Semitic views. It is an apparent testament to his resilience and to Jewish longevity in the region in general that his story, over time, unfolded. Like the early generation of Jewish peddlers, store owners, and the like, Brody paved the way for rural Jewish New Englanders to come. Denied access to the hospital, Chertok says, Brody "opened up in Belmont in a house. He became so successful and so outstanding compared to those others that now there's a part of the hospital named after Doctor Brody. Today I don't know how many Jewish doctors there are in the community," says Chertok. "Doctors, dentists, lawyers, teachers, the professions. This is the change, the second and third generation." Today, Jews throughout the region practice all manner of professions, and in large numbers. Most of the small retail stores are gone. Sonny Chertok claims that when he was growing up, Laconia had twenty Jewish-owned stores. Only one remains, according to Bob Selig—Sawyer's Jewelry. On the other hand, the ranks of medical offices, hospitals, law firms, and grade-school and college faculty currently abound with Jewish members.

Taking into account the equally significant presence of artists and assorted counterculturally oriented Jewish residents, most communities feature, to use Lee Bagdon's term, "mixed" constituencies, where money is not scarce but hardly abundant either. As Pal Borofsky, an old-time retailer in Brattleboro, Vermont, puts it, "There seem . . . to be some people [in the Jewish community] who are financially sound—very well off, and there seem to be others that are far more dependent on a daily basis for jobs." Mainer Natalie Cohen, another relative oldtimer, marks a similar trend. In the area around Augusta where she lives, most of the Jews, she says, "are either working for the state, working for the university, working for the hospitals, either in computers or some of that stuff. We have some doctors and stuff. But the people with money are dying off. There is some old money still in the area, but not like it was even when we came here." The trend toward professional life among Jews, in the last several decades, may or may not contribute to their broader participation as a thoroughly regionalized population. On the one hand, as more and more generations of Jews and non-Jews alike seek medical treatment from small-town Jewish doctors, for instance, the broader impact of a Jewish presence becomes more evident. Looking over the last several decades of change in the Jewish community in Bennington, Vermont, Amy Jo Montgomery speaks to the shift toward professionalism. When she first came to southern Vermont in 1960, every Jewish family she knew operated or worked in one small business or another. Now, however, the situation is entirely different. "I would think most of [the Jews in Bennington] are professionals," she says.

> They don't just come up here to buy a house and work in a factory. They're going to be doctors; they're going to be lawyers; they're going to be psychiatrists; they're going to be eye doctors. I mean they're all professionals. I don't see just Joe Shmoe moving up here without

something to come to, because let's face it, they don't pay you much in Vermont. We're very low paid here. And if you're going to make a change, you better have something to come to and have something to bring with you. And if you have a profession, then you're going be OK here; you're going get paid more than anyone else here in this community. I think . . . a lot of the people that come here are from the city, want to get away from the city, raise a family and be safer here than living in the city, even though they may not make enough money here as they would in the city. I think that's a good trade-off for them. I see a lot of Jewish people in my practice. I'm a dental hygienist, work for a dentist. And a lot of Jewish people I see, if they're older, they've come up here for retirement. If they're younger, they've come up here to settle to live, to have a business, or like I say, a professional and to have children and be in a safer community. That's what I'm seeing.

Amy Jo Montgomery's husband Bob remarks that the growing professionalization of southern Vermont Jews has had a positive effect on Bennington's synagogue community. In the heyday of Jewish retailing, few congregants could afford to close up shop on Shabbat. The synagogue was an on-again, off-again phenomenon that relied, in his words, on "rental rabbis" coming to the town for the High Holidays. "It's a pretty strongly rooted community now," he says.

On the other hand, professional life, unlike retail and agriculture, for instance, tends not to lend itself to a multigenerational presence. For all of its obvious expansive virtues, in other words, higher education enacts a dispersal of the population. Howard Cohen, the rabbi of the Bennington Jewish congregation, has had recent pause to think about how careerism, whether it takes shape in a rural or an urban community, often detracts from the sort of multigenerational family life that would seem to lie at the heart of any thriving local culture.

I've been thinking about the fact that most adult Jews don't live in the town where they grew up. They pursue their career opportunities elsewhere, and in this community, lots of adults [were] born and raised here. And the more I'm involved in other aspects outside of the Jewish community, the more I'm meeting people who are living

around grandparents and parents in the same community. So I've
just been wondering about the Jewish value that was really esteemed
career goals versus . . . family orientation. We've seen the Jewish
community seem to say, "extended family is not a value, not a high
priority—pursuing goals and professional goals is more important."

Whether the Jewish population of small-town New England, or any rural
American community will ever, like the various other ethnic communities
in the region, become a sustained, multigenerational presence or, instead,
perpetuate itself through a sequence of not altogether contiguous revivals
remains, of course, to be seen. A vibrant and apparently "strongly rooted"
cultural life today is no guarantee, of course, of any continuation into per-
petuity.

"There Is Nothing Like an Education": The Legacy of Schoolroom Experience

The first generation of Jews, whose members arrived in rural New England
communities as intact adult citizens, for the most part, set about the task of
earning a living and raising families. In many instances, in other words, it
was quite enough to be establishing a business and building a clientele. By
the end of his or her life, as we have seen in the case of Louis Richelson,
for instance, it was quite conceivable that a first-generation immigrant
might have earned not a few admirers within the wider community. Or,
as was the case for Isaac Sakansky in Laconia, if admirers were not one's
only legacy, one might at least have gained a recognizable status as a town
character of sorts, a person whose reputation preceded him. It was not until
the second generation of American-born rural New England Jewish residents had come on the scene, however, that a more direct civic engagement
might have been viable. Absorption into the public schools constituted one
obvious means of bringing about this result. In actual adulthood, moreover,
second-generation rural Jews were participating openly and abundantly in
various publicly visible endeavors. Successive generations continued in this
vein. Indeed, the current generation of transplanted rural Jews may constitute the most civically involved Jewish constituency of all.

At any level, from early participation in the school system to a mature involvement in village and town affairs, engagement in the wider community represents a rather obvious form of immersion in and shaping influence over the local culture. Rural New England cultural life, as we have seen, has long been a village affair, and a family's level of participation within that village life would represent a key component of its commitment to locale. Whether Jews have always been "accepted" as full-fledged locals in such communities may be beside the point, since their degree of involvement in and influence over the culture derive not from one or another constituency's *approval* but from the essentially inadvertent facts represented by their activities. Embraced, resented, or simply tolerated by their non-Jewish neighbors, Jews in rural New England have been actors in the cultural development of their hometowns. The legacy of the group's oral traditions speaks directly to this sustained involvement.

Public school, for many Jewish children growing up in small-town New England, offered the earliest exposure to local culture. If children grew up feeling relatively accepted as Jews living in their communities, their experiences in school played a significant contributing role. On the other hand, to the extent that Jewish children growing up in rural New England ever felt the sting of anti-Semitism, even of a relatively mild variety, an encounter with schoolmates was quite likely to have been the initial source of that sting. Unlike any other local institution, in other words, public school ensured a sustained mutual exposure, an often unfiltered encounter of cultures under one roof. Often enough, the school experience, for whatever trials it might have imposed on them, comprised an environment in which young small-town Jews might actually gain acceptance, or at least the respect of their teachers. Sonny Chertok describes the experiences of Jewish children who grew up in his native Laconia. "As far as school was concerned," he says, "the teachers liked the Jewish kids because the Jewish kids knew their lessons; they worked at it, and they didn't need the discipline that many of the rough other boys did." In Great Barrington, Massachusetts, the rabbi of the local synagogue earned points for the entire Jewish community, as Irene Moskowitz describes it, by always advocating for educational interests in the town. "A lot of people in [the Jewish] community," she says, "didn't like him because he didn't speak English. The teachers in the town loved him. He was always for the teachers, for anything . . . the teachers wanted . . . in the public schools." Indeed, in an article published in 1904, Emelyn Peck noted the centrality of education among the Russian Jewish immigrants in New England. Schools represented "the open highway" for Jewish "ambition."[11] "According to the Jewish law of life," as Jack August puts it, "there is nothing like an education."

School offered an extended opportunity for Jewish children to interact with non-Jews, and the early relationships formed in such a context would often continue on long after one grew up. "Most of our friends," Bob Selig remembers about his attendance at the Laconia schools, "were non-Jews." As he explains: "It was significant at that time to blend in with the community. . . . Certainly, all the Jewish kids I know wanted to be part of what went on in the entire community. Many of them played baseball. They tried to cut out of Hebrew school to go play baseball. Their mothers found them on the field and brought them back to the religious school sometimes." Lillian Glickman, of North Adams, Massachusetts, recalls having been absorbed into an after-school social club. She did engage with her family in the social life that centered around the synagogue. But, she says, "in grammar school and high school I belonged to the Lingernaut Girls Club. There was a group of eight of us, and I was the only Jewish girl in the group."

For all of the opportunities that school offered for second- and third-generation Jews to become active and lifelong participants in the local culture, its culturally majoritarian atmosphere could also be a source of trauma. In the entire body of interviews that I collected in the course of my fieldwork, stories about school yield the largest measure of references to anti-Semitism. To be fair, no tradition-bearer I spoke with regrets having grown up in or moved to rural New England. A significant number of the people I interviewed who can date their families' presence in the region to the period before World War II, however, speak quite forthrightly of their encounters with intolerant fellow pupils. It may be that the therapeutic passage of time has dulled the edges; despite the obvious trauma conveyed by these accounts of cruelty and taunting suffered at the hands of anti-Semitic classmates, tradition-bearers seem for the most part eager to downplay the long-term effects of these exposures. Anti-Semitic harassment is represented, in several instances, as a test that one simply had to endure. Indeed, as field interviews among numbers of other ethnic groups who grew up in the first part of the twentieth century in small-town New England show, a significant amount of inter-ethnic rivalry was quite common whether or not Jews were present. In the first half of the twentieth century, many of the area's small industrial towns mimicked cities in their multiplicity of ethnic "gangs" continually feuding for neighborhood influence.

Sumner Winebaum describes a fairly spectacular experience of anti-Semitism; but his account is presented within an overall context that seems intended to suggest that acceptance was almost an intended result of the trauma, as if the harassment he received was a sort of initiation rite. Winebaum's initial overlay suggests that an ease within both Jewish and non-Jewish circles has been his general experience. He suggests as well that a certain amount of class solidarity and athletic camaraderie served to overcome any early sense of alienation, so that the harassment he experienced at the hands of his tormentors served a long-term positive role.

I live very comfortably in both worlds, Christian and Jewish . . . I don't know [about] *very* comfortably, but I lived in both worlds. I clearly remember my good friend Eddie Tauber, [a] Jewish kid, and myself walking to grammar school each day which meant we had to pass the St. Patrick School, which meant we had to go through a cordon, which meant sometimes we had to fight. But the most unique fight was one time when the cordon sort of stopped us and somebody said something like, "The Jews don't know how to fight anyway," and I don't know how it happened exactly, but the next thing I knew Eddie Tauber and I were fist-fighting each other, surrounded by all the Irish kids, and I do remember that I hit Eddie on the nose a couple of times, [and] he had a very big nose. And then I think I finally stopped the fight and picked up our stuff [and] we went on. But I'll never forget, as I was moving through I heard one of the Irish kids say, "Well, of course, no wonder Winebaum's such a good fighter, his father gives him boxing lessons." Not true, of course.

We had to go through the cordon. But the other half of the story was that I was very taken by the Christian kids particularly in the south end, the poorer part of town. Because they were great athletes and I would for years as a teenager and just before I guess, I would ride my bicycle down to the south end—I'd be alone, I'd be the only Jewish kid. And I'd play baseball, football, pick up games that we had.

In general, anti-Semitic taunting in school was taken for granted by small-town New England Jews. Their parents, who had obviously known much worse in the Old Country, had prepared them to face whatever came their way, boxing lessons or no.

Other tradition-bearers speak of having undergone similar ordeals. In Steve Pyenson's case, the sufferers were both himself and his children who, at the end of the school days when they could be picked up early to attend Hebrew school, —would be harassed. Nonetheless, the Pyensons resisted the temptation to restrict their children's Jewish education to what could be accomplished in the home. "If you're all alone with non-Jewish children," Pyenson suggests, "there's animosity; there's picking on them." Presumably, having had the benefit of knowing his grandfather, who had come to the Berkshires from Russia, Pyenson was able to maintain perspective. "There was always something going on, nothing really terrible, but there was always some animosity." In some communities, the church's teachings might account for the persecution. "Any given weekend," Todd Adelman recalls about his schooling in Mars Hill, Maine, "You['d] come back to school on a Monday and [someone would say] 'Oh, I learned this weekend that Jews did this or the Jews did that, and you're Jewish, so you must be blah, blah, blah.' " Amy Jo Montgomery recalls baiting in school around Jewish holidays. "All the chairs out empty on a [Jewish] holiday when we didn't go to school: 'It must be one of the Jew holidays.' " Montgomery remembers having suffered more at the hands of other children's disapproving parents than at the hands of her classmates.

A greater degree of animosity, or perhaps more properly a larger legacy of animosity, was what Selma Mehrman came away with from her growing up days. She was showing me an old photograph of herself with her eighth grade classmates, in 1945, and I asked if any among the children had been Jewish: "No, no, no," she indicated. "I was the only Jew in town and I was beat up practically every day I went to school. It got to the point that my father used to take me there and the store was only like a half a block down the hill but someone was there to pick me up. It was really ridiculous." For all of their appreciation of having grown up in small-town New England, not one of my tradition-bearers claims to have been raised in a Jewish paradise or to have been entirely unscarred by anti-Jewish sentiment. Exposure to this sort of harassment, however, is often represented in the oral tradition as an aspect of one's maturation process. It may have imparted a more profound sense for these tradition-bearers of what it meant to be a Jew and a small-town New Englander simultaneously. When she felt most persecuted, Amy Jo Montgomery, as she recalls, "would seek out some of the Jewish kids to be friends with because it was safer to be with them."

In one case, an intended snub that one rural New England Jew experienced ended up solidifying her relationship with a sympathetic school teacher. Charlotte Goos, whose family ran a poultry business in Maine, speaks positively about the outcome.

> When I went to school, there may have been a few [anti-Semitic] people, but basically . . . maybe I ignored it, but I didn't feel it. One of my teachers who liked me wanted me to get the DAR medal and she submitted my name. I was . . . one of the class officers, and I did well in school and she was fond of me. I did not get the DAR medal, and she came to me afterwards and she said, "Isn't it too bad because somebody isn't a certain religion they can't receive this medal?" But she was a transplant from Skowhegan. And the teacher that would not let me get the medal happened to be one of my favorite teachers because she was the algebra/geometry teacher, and math was my subject. But that's the way life was, and there are still certain societies that if you're Jewish, you don't belong.

Again, in comparison to the often fatal expressions of anti-Semitism from which their parents had fled, such injustices may have seemed at least tolerable. As Todd Adelman describes it, the name calling to which he was occasionally subject while growing up in Mars Hill, Maine, cut both ways. "It was never harsh," he says. "There was nothing brutal about any of that." In a way, the occasional ignorance or even malice on the part of his schoolmates "just affirmed that I'm unique, or I'm special, so I'm here."

Current-day Jewish residents of the region rarely speak of any sort of overt expressions of anti-Semitism either in or out of school. Nonetheless, in sending their children to small rural schools, where they may be the only Jewish students in attendance, they do occasionally speak of encounters fraught with at least a measure of awkwardness. Gen Uris, who teaches grade school in north central Vermont, often finds herself explaining Jewish culture and religion to her students.

> . . . My kids ask me a lot, or they'll say, "You know a lot about this. How do you know all of this?"
>
> "Well, I'm Jewish." And I feel that rather than saying my father's

Jewish, I have to say I'm Jewish because it's the closest that they may come for a long time. . . . There are some odd, I don't know if it's anti-Semitic as much as just ignorant things that happen where I'll have kids refer to phrases like "someone Jewed you down." And I say, "You can't say that." And I don't think it's even occurred to them, and they think about it, and the other kids next to them say, "Yeah, that's really not OK. You can't say that." And they think, and say, "Oh, it never even occurred to me." So there are definitely a few instances like that.

Ignorance—benign or otherwise—explains a great deal, and current-day rural New England Jews speak of their willingness (occasionally of a somewhat grudging variety) to straighten out their neighbors. The educational mission of the public schools, in other words, is interpreted as offering a unique opportunity for a sort of grassroots sensitivity training.

In Bennington, Vermont, for instance, Rabbi Howard Cohen often finds himself having to advocate for Jewish interests in the same way; he places frequent calls to the school district supervisor's office:

There has always been a Jewish presence in the Bennington schools for 75 years. The public schools here and in the community in general show indifference to anybody's religious practices, Jewish or otherwise. So I can't say that it's particularly evident that they are indifferent or insensitive to the Jewish rhythms anymore than they are to anything else, but you know every year they schedule tests on Yom Kippur and I have to contact the superintendent's office and say, "They did it again," and he's like, "I can't believe they've done it again; let me call the principal." But it's the problem of just being a minority and . . . people just default to what they know and what's the majority and what's the easiest. . . . And the town is so stratified that it's really hard to know what people know. . . . It's hard to know how much people know about Judaism and Jewish life and for that matter anything.

Not far from Bennington, in the neighboring town of Pownal, Julie Chamay speaks with some frustration about the surrounding lack of knowledge that infiltrates the local school. This broader closed-mindedness, which in her view was what underlay the general ignorance about Judaism, caused her to take her son out of the public school system. "I don't get the impression that they have that sort of respect and regard for other beliefs," she says. "I know that the fifth grade was doing a Santa's Workshop, which I guess is okay if you're doing everything, but I don't get the impression that they do everything."

Naturally, holiday celebrations bring the most frequent frustrations, inviting as they do both disappointment and disillusionment. Elizabeth Lerner, who grew up in White River Junction, Vermont, learned to dread the Christmas season for this reason and built up a measure of resentment.

In my school around Christmas time we always sang so many Christmas carols, and I always used to get in trouble for not singing them. And I wouldn't know what to do. Some of the Christmas carols I'd just sing, but then, "Silent Night"—do you say "Christ"? Do you not say "Christ"? So maybe I'd mouth it and sing the rest. So I'd always get kicked out of the music class for mouthing along, and get sent to the principal's office. So every year my parents would have a talk with the principal and say, "Well, it's no wonder she doesn't want to sing Christmas songs." And then every year my school would take a whole day off and go caroling, to all of the nursing homes and the hospital, and I hated that, the one year I did it. And after that I made my parents keep me out of school that day. But I did not like it at all.

The school made a perfunctory effort to equalize by including a Hanukkah song in its music curriculum, but Lerner was only more frustrated by this token gesture. "We used to sing . . . the one Hanukkah song," she says, "but I hated that song more than anything, because it's such a stupid song."

On other side of the coin, the willingness to learn on the part of school teachers and neighbors pleases some small-town Jews. Joe Kurland, whose children attend the elementary school in Colrain, Massachusetts, embraces the opportunity to educate. "From the time that Aaron [his son] was in preschool, the teachers stressed values of inclusiveness and the sort of rainbow of people that make up America," he says. Cale Weissman, who has attended public and private schools in western Massachusetts, finds spiritual value in the opportunity to impart his knowledge and experience of Judaism in school. "I believe it's nice there are Jews here to teach the non-Jews about other cultures, and I believe we need to teach people about other cultures everywhere," he says.

"It's Nice to Know Your Neighbor":
Jewish Civic and Community Involvement

Many "early" Jewish families, as we have seen, sent children away to college, and if and when those rural offspring returned to their hometowns, they were quick to engage fully in civic enterprises. As local stakeholders, they were able to appreciate the importance of participating in, as opposed to simply being witnesses to, the community life of their respective towns. Business or professional endeavors laid the foundation for their having come to and settled in small New England communities in the first place. School provided a testing ground of sorts, a place where young Jews would first encounter the surrounding majority and learn—often enough the hard way—about just how dissimilar and similar they were to the majority culture. But Jewish involvement in civic and cultural activity was perhaps the surest means of gaining broad acceptance and appreciation. Such involvement might possibly ensure mutual respect, but it most certainly brought about visibility. Once they were engaged in their respective towns' social and political activities, Jews could no longer live anonymously, even if they desired to do so.

Based in part on their successes as retailers, farmers, or in other areas of the economic life of their communities, Jews often found themselves being offered membership in various groups whose activities, well into the 1950s at least, often defined a given town's social life. Jews in small New England towns were quite routinely admitted to Rotary clubs and Masonic lodges. On the other hand, when they were restricted from joining such groups, they knew that they had just taken the measure of their outsideness. As Todd Adelman describes it, the involvement of Jewish families in Aroostook County's civic life was marred when, on occasion, Jews were made to feel like outsiders. Such treatment felt especially unjust, he says: "We weren't the only Jewish family up there that was to some degree considered successful or willing to contribute leadership in forms of community giving. That was always the undercurrent, so it was really kind of hard. It would be one thing if we were destructive or divisive, but most of the Jews up there were the ones that were heavily involved in Rotary, heavily involved with the school boards, heavily involved with the hospitals." As she was growing up in Ashland, New Hampshire, Selma Mehrman's family was active in the Grange. She herself was a member of the Rainbow Girls, which was the girls' equivalent of the Eastern Star. Her father was a Mason. Bob and Joyce Selig, Evelyn Slome, and May Schell, from Laconia, New Hampshire, Portsmouth, New Hampshire, and Easthampton, Massachusetts, respectively, all speak to wide involvement on the part of Jews in their hometowns' club affairs. On the basis of their long-standing and wide-ranging involvement in the economic life of Northampton, Massachusetts, Bob August suggests that his family "move[d] very quickly. . . . They were representatives of those organizations that made up the community in later years, the Masons to Kiwanis, you name it—Rotary . . . as well as other community civic organizations." In Orange, Massachusetts, as Louis Plotkin recalled in a 1976 interview, Jews were "connected with . . . your Masonic Lodges and your Knights of Pythias and your Odd Fellows and all of those organizations." Such groups had not always been so tolerant and inviting. In Plotkin's earlier days, he steered clear of those same groups for fear of being humiliated or blackballed.

Based in part on his stature among his neighbors, Louis Richelson was offered opportunities that rarely came to Jews. Selma Mehrman tells the story of how her father was given a chance to make an individual investment and ended up relinquishing the opportunity because of his commitment to what he took to be the greater good of the community.

In Ashland, there's a Squam Lake—Big Squam, Little Squam, and the town wanted [the land]. . . . After a few years they decided he [my father] wasn't such a bad person after all, even if he was Jewish—and there was property that came for sale. Now Big Squam, and Little Squam, to this day in 2004, is a closed place. The only way you're going to get a piece of property is if somebody says, "I got this for sale." They want to make sure who is going to buy. They offered my father this lovely piece of property on Little Squam, and this is the way he was brought up and what do they call it—doing a good deed—a mitzvah. . . .

He liked the people of Ashland; he really loved them. And he said it was wonderful, and he said he wanted to buy this piece of property, and they said fine. But when he told them what he was going to do with it; he was going to make a public beach for the people of Ashland, they said no way you do that, you don't. Because these people were . . . from Boston and from wealthy homes and families, and they were real snobs, and the people of Ashland were beneath them. And so [they said,] "No way, you're not going to have it.

In Selma Mehrman's representation of the Squam Lake dealings, it is the absentee landowners—the Bostonians "from wealthy homes and families" who stood in the way preventing her father from benefiting his fellow Ashlanders. Solidarity with local interests—an old small-town New England theme—was what made Richelson's gesture a proper mitzvah. If his neighbors wished to take the Jewish store owner's measure as a locally identified man, in other words, they could see the evidence in his efforts in their behalf.

Civic activity might take the form of informal or social endeavors, like Richelson's attempt to purchase land for the town of Ashland. It might also, in the years to come, evolve into Jewish involvement in local and state politics. Occasionally, a first-generation immigrant would jump into the fray, accent and all. Steve Steinberg recalls hearing that his grandfather showed no hesitation to speak out in his adoptive home of Whitefield, New Hampshire. "He was always speaking out in town meetings and so on," Steinberg says. There's no question that a lot of people knew him and liked him. No question a lot of people would shun him maybe." More often, earlier generations would follow a more tempered, strategic approach. In Laconia, Max Chertok, as his son reports, became involved in civic life early on. The combination of his economic and social influence was sufficient to help bring about some major changes in the life of the town.

My father would go to important council meetings. There was a time when Laconia Shoe Company was having a rough time at the beginning, and they needed to get some fuel for winter, and they didn't have the money. And the City Council had a meeting; my father went, and he wasn't particularly friendly with the Brindises [the owners of the shoe company], but he went, and he said that they had to be helped out at that particular time. During the Depression years . . . the car shops went broke. . . . The city took all those buildings for taxes, and they formed Laconia Industrial Corporation. I didn't realize it until later on, 30 years later—I was the president, and I looked back in the history, and there's my father's name as one of the original settlers. But they [Jews] stayed out of politics.

Members of the first generation did, for the most part, avoid politics, or at least playing too visible a role in political life. But behind the scenes, a man like Max Chertok might occasionally pull some strings.

Chertok explains that, despite his avoidance of too bold an involvement, his father "understood the value of politics."

> Of course, he was very friendly with Stiles Bridges because Bridges was a Kiwanian, became a U.S. senator. The war came on, and all of a sudden our supplier of coal, the mine, was exhausted and the fellow that sold us the coal said, "Max, I can't sell you any more coal. I don't have it." And we needed a carload of coal. Dad sent me right to Stiles Bridges. I wrote to Senator Bridges—and this was during the war years—and said, "We're out of coal." A flyer came back the next day, "A carload of coal on the way. Signed, Stiles." He was one of the overseers of United Mine Workers, in cahoots with John L. Lewis. So the political connection was good.

As it happens, another Jewish New Hampshirite had the ear of Stiles Bridges at the same time. Sumner Winebaum tells of the time when his old neighborhood in Portsmouth was about to be "made into urban renewal housing."

> My father and [a] historic preservation guy went down to Washington, D.C. and they went down to Stiles Bridges' office—he was the Minority Whip of the Senate [and] from New Hampshire. Very, very conservative, I mean rabid . . . I mean, [he] couldn't have been more right wing. My father [and two companions] went down and they made their case to Bridges that it should be historic preservation [rather] than housing, and the senator said, "Gosh, you know, that makes good sense, I want that to happen." Whereupon, the aide to the senator said, "Senator, you can't do that. The law says this is title eight," or whatever it is, "and it has to be urban renewal, the money's been put forth, you can't change the law." Whereupon Bridges said, "These people have made a very good case, number one; number two, I'm the minority whip; number three, I'm from a small state—I get practically nothing compared to other states. I want this to happen. Make it happen." And it did happen; it was the only time when they had ever changed urban renewal to historic preservation.

To heritage-minded "native" New Englanders, such political action on Winebaum's part might only have helped to gain him greater stature as a local.

The work of pioneering men like Max Chertok and Harry Winebaum also paved the way for a second generation of small-town Jews. After a long and successful business career as a furniture retailer, Sonny Chertok went on to become the mayor of Laconia. He points out that in 1974, when he was elected, three other Jews (all of them, like himself, happened to have been furniture retailers) were the mayors, respectively, of Claremont, New Hampshire, Bellows Falls and Rutland, Vermont. Bob Selig, a younger member of the Laconia Jewish community, points out as well that Bernard Snierson, a lawyer of long standing and a member of Laconia's Jewish community, was a district judge.

More recently, the state of Vermont has witnessed a relative upsurge in Jewish political involvement. Rabbi Max Wall of Burlington describes how he came into first-hand awareness of their influence.

We've had prominent attorneys who were appointed for temporary service as judges. Of course, we've had a Jewish governor, Madeline Kunin. An interesting story: We had a former governor, Governor Richard Snelling, who died in office, a heart attack, and I got a call from a very close friend of mine who's a lawyer, and he says, "Mrs. Snelling wants you to officiate at the memorial service at the House in Montpelier." I said, "They're not Jewish." He said, "Well, you can call her . . ." I called Barbara Snelling, and she said, "Yes, I want you to officiate at the memorial service at the House Chambers." Very odd thing. So I did. I ran the service, and I spoke words about him. As I was going out of the House onto the lawn—they were going to plant a tree in memory of Governor Snelling—I overhead two legislators talking. One says to the other, "I didn't know that Governor Snelling was Jewish." So they started inviting rabbis for opening prayers at every legislative session, and governor installation. I was appointed to various committees. I sound like a telephone pole, but I don't mean that, but I was the only rabbi around for many, many years. So they used me. I was the official rabbi for the hospital system in Vermont, including the mental hospital. I was the official rabbi for the prison system.

Indeed, the current-day political scene throughout rural New England places Jews in increasingly visible roles. One of Vermont's most notable political figures today, Bernie Sanders, is Jewish. Howard Dean, himself a Protestant, is married to a Jewish woman and is father to Jewish children. Small scale has something to do with this, as well as what appears to be a Jewish predilection for participatory democracy and social change movements.

Elizabeth Lerner, whose parents moved to Vermont shortly before she was born, grew up valuing the accessibility afforded by such a small scale.

> When I was in high school I was very appreciative of Vermont's more progressive politics. And I really liked that the size of the state meant that even as a high school student it was really easy to be involved in statewide politics. I loved that our state senator and representative had to come door-to-door. And that my dad would end up talking to them for a couple of hours and dragging them around to see the garden out back. One of my state representatives was the person who gave me drama lessons as a kid and was also involved in keeping our local opera house running. . . . The things that I like best about Vermont are when that kind of close-knit community actually works and when people really have that sense of place. And I think that's what draws me back to living in Vermont as an adult is having that kind of community where you're important and you're necessary and it's so small that you need to be involved in different areas of the community.

Beyond the realm of politics itself, the endless opportunities for volunteerism enable any interested parties to become engaged on a daily basis. Rabbi Howard Cohen is often called upon to lend his participation to various endeavors in Bennington, Vermont.

> If . . . an organization in the community wants something done, they call me. . . . The Homeless Coalition wants me on their board and the Jewish community that I have access to is recognized as a community of people who act, who do, who support, who are involved with things happening. There is a strong desire for there to be a liberal presence in the community—a liberal energy, although it's not a particularly liberal community, but the clergy force in general is pretty

conservative to the point of being largely fundamentalists. So that's important to community members who want to have a clergy presence at any level, whether it's a board of a business association or a hospital association where they want someone who values pluralism and who's going to be a religious voice and presence but not shove it down your throat. . . .

I am part of the community. I think my personality makes it easier for ordinary people to relate to me as a person than a lot of the other clergy. I was asked to be the chaplain of the fire department after September 11, so I'm chaplain of the fire department . . . they have not had a chaplain as long as they can remember, but when you ask the local people who had been around for a while and they say, "The rabbi's a chaplain of the fire department," they can't believe it because it's the barrier that's been broken. . . . If you walked down to one of the churches and said, "I'm homeless and I need a place to stay," they would send you down here to me here. I just recently turned over the responsibilities to that to a new clergy person in town, but obviously she is working out of our office and we still have an involvement with that. . . . That's one of the nice things about being a rabbi in a small town.

Bill and Mary Markle of Randolph, Vermont, have long been involved in a litany of volunteer endeavors. Bill describes some of this activity. His work is inspired, as he tells it, by his sense of Jewish ethics:

I've worked in organizing a not-for-profit corporation to deal with a homeless situation here and in the central Vermont area which we got going so that we could help the local clergy deal with people who didn't have a place to live. . . .

We each try to give at least 200 hours a year of our discretionary time to community undertakings. And now that I'm retired I give them even more hours than that and so does she [his wife]. And as we do this, we try to do it from a Jewish orientation which we're right on the table with. . . . I was always an advocate of the fact that the hospital would take care of everybody who came regardless of their ability to pay or whether they had insurance. That wasn't necessarily original with me . . . but I was comfortably able to be an advocate of that. Also [we] believe strongly in *tikkun olam*—repairing the world, and people know that I work from that frame of reference. I've been invited by several churches to speak about *tikkun olam* and my view of it in terms of why I involve myself in community affairs and why Mary does.

In the interests of enabling neighbors to appreciate "a Jewish view," formal political or social involvement may not necessarily be the only or most effective means, however.

Being an accepted participant in the local culture may also, in other words, derive from what one does in one's private social life and—traditionally—it is just such involvement that tends to be more difficult both to break into and to document. To the extent that local culture tends to be just the sort of thing that develops underneath the surface of ordinary life, at the level of folklife and friendship, however, such subterranean involvement is key. When such acceptance was achieved in the early days, it might very well have occurred inadvertently. Natalie Cohen describes how one regular event that her father ran brought about an unanticipated result. "He had a bridge club," Cohen says, whose members included the school principal and the local monsignor. This connection, in turn, led to Cohen being adopted as Santa Claus for the yearly town parade. The Pyensons of Otis, Massachusetts, remained on the margins of their town's social life until a few decades had passed after their initial settlement there in 1902. I had asked Maxwell Pyenson how his mother, who had come to live in a the small farming community as an adult who had grown up in the city, learned to make cheese.

> She knew how to make all of these things . . . how to make butter, cream and cheese and so forth. I never questioned it. . . . [My parents] probably learn[ed] different ways of doing things from the various farmers in the neighborhood. . . . We were finally accepted into this neighborhood with all of the Christian farmers. We used to have a sewing circle here, where all of the neighbors would get together and sew. They would sew blankets, and comforters and everything else. And the men would come to this house that was selected for this month, to eat in the evening. So we were finally accepted into this sewing circle. And we would go around to the various houses and have supper. Women would come in the afternoon and sew. And we'd also take our turn to have the neighbors come

to our house and eat in the evening and have a sewing circle in the afternoon.

Other folk pastimes provided venues for Jewish residents to become acclimated to local culture. Gen Uris, Selma Mehrman, Milt Adelman, and Steve Pyenson all indicate that their fathers hunted and fished with Jewish and non-Jewish friends alike. Uris wasn't a particularly avid hunter, as his daughter explains; "He just [liked] being outside walking around with his fellow people in town and felt like he was really a part of this." For his own part, Steve Pyenson did some hunting for partridges and pheasants while growing up in the Berkshires, but "never enjoyed it." His father, he says, was more of an enthusiast and shot a few deer in his time.

One's comfort with the local culture might also take the form of something as simple as a gesture of greeting. When I asked Saul Perlmutter what sorts of New England traits he felt himself to have inherited, he ended up telling me about something he learned early on from visiting a friend whose family owned a cabin in Lincoln, Vermont. "People in Lincoln," Perlmutter explains, "if you're driving and you say hello, you just sort of lift a finger off the steering wheel and put it back; that's saying hello. It's this kind of understated Vermont kind of stuff. . . . I know if I were in Lincoln if I want to wave to someone I know, I know how to wave to someone, which would be very different than how I would wave to someone in a different city. So there are just pieces of me that know this Vermont stuff and feel comfortable around the Vermont twang and this kind of thing." Acceptance is a two-way street. That Jews came to be accepted as locals is, in this regard, no more surprising than their having chosen to accept rural New England. As Charlotte Goos describes her and her husband's experience, she offers the following insight:

> We've been well accepted, Julius and I. Maine's been good to us. We've worked hard for what we have, but we're very fortunate. As my husband said, we educated three children in private colleges. They've all gone on. They make a living. They're good citizens. I think part of it is being in Maine. Even though they all have moved away from Maine, two of three of our children send their children to summer camp here in Maine, and the other one always comes with his family and spends time here. We're not city people, so it's nice to know your neighbor. We go into the grocery store, and we're greeted by people.

Whether or not there is something inherent in Jewish culture that causes some of its adherents to feel comfortable in a rural New England environment is difficult to know. But we may find nonetheless that a historical Jewish openness to diverse experience—the quality that may, for instance, have led to the Bennington firefighters feeling more comfortable with Rabbi Cohen than with any other of the town clergy—makes such an existence more palatable.

Bob Rottenberg refers to a teaching of Reb Schacter Shalome as he tries to explain the attraction that Jews like himself have to life in small-town New England. Schacter Shalome speaks of triumphalism and post-triumphalism, the latter being a mode of thinking in which the adherents of the various religions each do their part, like the cooperating organs of a body, to keep the world alive:

> The Jews need to make sure the other religions are able to function well. We need to support them; we need to encourage them, because then the planet—the whole ecosystem—can do its thing. And that's all stuff in Deuteronomy—if you take care of your piece of the world, then the world will be okay. And you'll be able to stay there and everything will be fine. And it's fascinating—in its own way I think it's a very New England sort of way of looking at things. You know, we acknowledge that there are people who are different, and we let them be different. And we let them do their thing, and we don't bother them. And they don't bother us, and if we need to do things together, then we'll do them together. But meanwhile we'll go and do our thing. . . . The small towns . . . are really the bastions of that kind of New England ethic.

Whatever the case may be, those rural Jewish New Englanders who have thrived—economically, culturally, and socially—have done so because both they and their neighbors managed to transcend their hesitation and cultivate interaction with each other.

"They Spoke Russian, They Spoke Polish, They Spoke Lithuanian":
The Jewish Experience of Ethnic Diversity

Jews who began moving to rural New England at the turn of the century were not occupying space in a monolithic regional culture. Even the remotest sections of New England, at least by the mid-nineteenth century, were already populated by a mixed constituency of ethnicities. Although the area was most certainly dominated, well into the post–World War II period, by people of Anglo stock who began coming with the Puritan Great Migration of the 1600s, their settlements were hardly impervious to people of non-Anglo, non—-Puritan backgrounds. Though the preponderance of the Scotch-Irish who began coming to America in large numbers in the mid-1700s went to the Middle Atlantic region and the highland South, a significant number settled in upland New England. The mid-nineteenth century saw the region's large influx of Irish immigrants. Though many of these went to New England's burgeoning urban and industrial settlements, small towns drew Irish immigrants as well, especially inasmuch as they too were often built around industrial enterprises that could hire broadly. French Canadians began coming in large numbers in the 1870s and 1880s, and the same was true shortly afterwards of Italians and Eastern Europeans of various nationalities. The Jews who began settling in rural New England around 1900, then, were taking their places within a dynamic interplay of cultures. The same is true, of course, of latter-day Jewish newcomers. New England is now as diverse as it ever was, and given the new climate of self-conscious cultural diversity, traditionally "outside" groups now tend to be more visible and deliberate participants in the regional culture.

When Jews first came to Laconia, New Hampshire, they may not have been welcomed with open arms, but Sonny Chertok recalls hearing that the settlement of David Snierson, the town's first Jewish arrival, was cause for at least a measure of interest. Snierson's son, Bernard, told Chertok about his father's experience: "[He] told me that some of the Old Yankees in the town used to come over and sit with his father at night," Chertok says. "They would discuss the Old Testament. And the children's names of these Yankees, they used Isaac, Isaiah, and biblical names, and they would discuss the similarities. They got along very, very well. There was a lot of respect between these people." Yet whatever admiration may have existed between Yankees and Jews seems mostly a matter of speculation. Despite apparent ideological and theological parallels, Chertok's recollection constitutes one of only two references I found in the oral tradition to any sort of Jewish/Yankee mutual admiration society. The other story, nonetheless, offers a remarkable corroboration. In a 1976 interview, Jack August, who ran a fish restaurant in Northampton, Massachusetts, recalled meeting a non-Jewish woman once who had known his uncle in his peddling days. The woman spoke to August as follows one day when she came to eat at his restaurant:

> "Mr. August, I am from Shutesbury[, Massachusetts], and when I was a little girl, there was a man who used to come to Shutesbury, and he used to buy rags and rubbers and bottles—stuff like that. And he ran a tin cart, and in turn he would trade enamel pots and clay pots and tin pots to the farmers . . . and I remember as well as it though it were today," she said, "when Mr. [Bennett] August used to come to our house, he would write my father a note, a postcard, and say, Mr. So-and-So"—I can't remember the name—" 'I will be in Shutesbury on Tuesday next.' My father knew he would be there on Tuesday." Well, Uncle Bennett—it happened to be my uncle Bennett—he was a very learned man; he had gone to the Yeshiva. Well, as soon as he got that postcard, this man would call all the neighbors, and he would say, "Now, Mr. August will be here Tuesday night. You all come to our house, and we will have a bible lesson." Well, Uncle Bennett, as I said, graduated from Yeshiva, and he could translate and of course he was pretty good in English. And so he translated the Old Testament into English for these people. . . . She said this was the highlight of their lives. And she said, "Mr. August used to come to our house, and he used to bring his own pot, in which he boiled his eggs, or cooked his milk or cereal or brewed his tea." But the thing I got a thrill out of, I got a big thrill out of, was the fact that she said Mr. August's coming to our house was an event. Everybody came!

That the peddler was admired for more than his pots, pans, and other sundries suggests that tolerance and even appreciation of Jews could, at least in some circles, derive from more than mere economic or social convenience.

On the other side of the Jewish-Yankee relationship, one amusing story, offered by Sumner Winebaum, constitutes the only direct reference collected to any specific Jewish admiration of Yankee culture or heritage. I had asked Sumner Winebaum about his intriguing name, and his response to the question offered insight into whatever influence, real or imagined, that the Old Yankee mentality had over recently arrived Jews in the early twentieth century.

Yes, my name Sumner is in no way, shape, manner or form a family name having anything to do with any dead relatives. However, we had an aunt in Boston—my father's side—who had certain ideas about New England and her family and what they were or what they weren't. And she convinced my mother to give me this name. But, more importantly, I had—I have—two first cousins who have the same name, Sumner. There are three Sumners in our family. It has nothing to do with Charles Sumner. It has nothing to do—. The name, though, she thought was a very fancy, Brahmin name. It turns out that when I went to college and I studied Chaucer, one of the most despicable characters in Chaucer is the Summoner, who you could buy off, you know, you'd come for your atonements and you could say to him, "Look, here's some dough and whatever." And he'd say, "Well, you only have to do six, rather than sixty 'Hail Mary's," or whatever it was—your indulgence was.

So the name was always an embarrassment to me. I hated the name, I always found it a heavy burden. As a matter of fact, when I went to college in California, I decided this is a great moment, my middle name is Joseph. So I introduced myself as Joseph Winebaum. And all the guys [said], "Hey, Joe, how're you doing?—Hey!" And then the first letter came from my folks or whoever, saying "Sumner." And they said, "Sumner!—What a name! Where'd you ever get a name like that?" So I was Sumner after to everybody. I hated that name. I really hated it. I still hate it. But it was an idea of one of my aunts that it was a real New England, Brahmin name, and we should have it.

Yankees and Jews certainly interacted in the early days of Jewish settlement, as they continue to do now. Notwithstanding whatever cultural influences may have existed, the bare facts of commercial and civic engagement explain a great deal. Ewa Morawska notes that Eastern European Jews, in their every-day expression, followed a tendency not uncommon among the ruling Anglo power elite to look down upon other immigrant groups—especially the Slavs, with whom they had a long-standing Old Country familiarity. "In the eyes of the *shtetl*," Morawska writes, "the goyim—peasants—represented everything a Jew . . . did not want to and should not be." [12] Yankees of Puritan stock—at least the educated among them—might perhaps have merited a greater degree of admiration in such a worldview.

For what it might be worth, however, I found far more references (nearly all positive) to the interactions between Jewish settlers and their non-Anglo neighbors than I did to Jews and Yankees. As simultaneous participants in the massive immigrant influx in the region that began at the turn of the century, Jews and the various Irish, Polish, Italian, and French Canadian newcomers with whom they shared the status of outsiders thought quite bit about each other. May Schell, of Easthampton, Massachusetts, suggests that in her growing up, "There was no anti-Semitism that we were conscious of." Her parents were welcomed, for instance, into a German social club in the town, the Turn Verein. Pal Borofsky, of Brattleboro, Vermont, remembers that his parents were "very, very friendly with a group of Italian people in town." Selma Mehrman remembers a mixed population in her hometown of Ashland, New Hampshire, of French Canadian, Irish, and Syrian settlers. Her best friend growing up was the daughter of one of the Syrian families. In general, she recalls having felt, as the daughter of a store owner, that she enjoyed advantages that many of her less fortunate neighbors lacked.

Especially in their capacity as retailers to factory and farm workers, Jewish settlers in small towns often found themselves reaching out to their less fortunate neighbors. Sonny Chertok's father, who ran a small business in Laconia, apparently went out of his way to be equitable, if not downright philanthropic, in his dealings with non-Jewish customers.

My father had a way of relating to people, and he treated everybody with respect whereas the Yankees tended to look down on the French. And there were two furniture stores in Laconia at the time, one big one, a big, big, store—Lougee Robinson Company, one of the most important stores on the Eastern Seaboard. . . . The French didn't get along with the Irish, so these people would come into my dad's store, and he would treat the French people with dignity, extend credit to them, and his business grew, and it grew fast. And he got along with these people, and many of the French people were his buddies. Some he'd go fishing with and so forth. They knew him . . . and they got along. He had a way of doing well with people, so he didn't have the problems. And you'll find that I speak of my father—this goes for most of the Jewish people who came to Laconia, they're all warm people for the most part. They got along with their neighbors.

Such attitudes would naturally have been conducive to an atmosphere of trust. No matter the degree of mutual suspicion—the Old World's legacy of anti-Semitism could hardly have been vanquished in a single generation— the oral tradition among rural New England Jews suggests that a spirit of openness prevailed, or preserves the memory of one, at least. In describing his family's early days in Orange, Massachusetts, Louis Plotkin remembers a preponderance of Swedes in town, but speaks as well to the presence of French Canadians, Poles, Lithuanians, and Italians. "The general feeling amongst the people," he said in a 1976 interview, "is good."

Selma Mehrman remembers that her parents, largely owing to their multilingual abilities, were held in high esteem by many neighbors. Louis Richelson's facility with communication, as well as his apparent generosity, quite endeared him to his customers. "They spoke English, Russian, Yiddish, and some Polish. And, of course, there's a lot of Polish immigrants working up in the mills up in Lincoln." Life in small-town New England mirrored conditions in the Old Country. In both places, as in Johnstown, Pennsylvania, writes Morawska, "the primary form of interdependence was between Eastern European Jews as commercial dealers and Slavs and Hungarians as their customers." [13] If Jews had constituted the only ethnic group in a position to lend a helping hand, of course, their doing so might have been conducive to creating a sense of dependence and disequilibrium. Commercial and civic activities were two-way affairs, however, and the divisive economy kept every constituency on its toes.

As long as ethnic groups could see and experience each other not as rivals but, in the spirit of cooperation, with mutual respect, tensions might be held at a minimum. In the context of early twentieth-century small-town New England, a great many people had to be paying attention to one another. If they could perceive their own struggles and successes in the doings of others, presumably, they could maintain harmony. As Jack August reflects broadly on the changing ethnic dynamic in the Connecticut Valley of Massachusetts, he suggests that Jews as a whole benefited from being one of several ethnic groups in the region. Their participation in a multilingual, inter-ethnic exchange, instead of marking them as outsiders, might easily be argued to have formed a basis of their gradual acceptance within this dynamic milieu.

> The Jewish people and the Polish people got along . . . very well. My father spoke Yiddish, he spoke German, he spoke Lithuanian. He spoke Russian, he spoke Polish fluently. My father talked Polish better than some Polish people. But he had to learn for his business. He had to learn. And the two of us, the Polish community and the Jewish community, grew. . . . The Polish came and they bought their land. There are still a lot of rich Yankees and still a lot of rich Irish. But the majority of the rich farmers in the Connecticut Valley are Poles, whose sons have worked in the tobacco fields, whose sons have gone to college, whose sons are now lawyers and doctors and judges. These Polish people. The Jewish people, it's the same thing.

Jack's nephew Bob comes to a similar conclusion. Again, that the Jews spoke the same languages as their customers seems to have helped to ensure their relative ease with one another. Interactions between Jewish merchants and East European customers could recreate for both constituencies the cultural sureties of the Old Country in the more expansive economic and social realm of rural America. "They spoke Russian; they spoke Polish; they spoke Lithuanian; they spoke a lot of the Slavic [languages]," Bob August says.

> That made it probably fairly easy to relate to a lot of the people who were here. And even extending up the valley. I remember going to my grandmother and grandfather Kramer and rather late in his life as a peddler. He was still peddling and we were driving around and we stopped at one of his customers' homes in Nashua, New Hampshire, I think it was. And it was a Russian family, Russian, Polish, I don't remember which. And they were conversing in Polish or Russian. I think there was a sort of an identity with a common experience and a common language which probably made it a more comfortable business experience and a relationship as a vendor of goods and services. . . . I suspect the same applied with my grandfather and his brothers who were in the cattle business in the early days. They had the Yankee customers, but they also had people who were from Ukraine, Poland, other countries, who were farmers in the valley,

that they were dealing with. And not only speaking perfect English, I'm sure, they were using the languages that came up.

In addition, of course, to linguistic facility, a stable economy appears to be a requisite aspect of this sort of mutual admiration. When all groups could maintain their own integrity and work toward the realization of their American success stories, the life of the region could prosper. Rivalries only got out of hand when people lost their place or, to use Jack August's phrase, one group or another "got too big for their britches."

Phyllis Nahman remembers hearing from her father about some of the Polish families in the area around Turners Falls, Massachusetts, with whom he had a lifelong relationship.

> There were a lot of families who we're still connected with today; they still remember who I am; they know my brothers and my dad from their businesses. . . . My dad said that his family wouldn't ever have survived had it not been for . . . some of the Polish people in the area. Which is interesting to me, because as I've done a lot of reading about what happened in Poland during the Holocaust, and you know, it makes it very clear that you can't paint with a broad brush because we hear stories about some of the horrible things that happened with some of the Polish towns that helped the Nazis, but there were also wonderful Polish people.

At one stage in their family's early settlement in the area, their connection to one Polish family in particular proved pivotal both from the point of view of the Rubins' day-to-day survival and to their overall status in the community's life of inter-ethnic interdependence.

> My dad told a story about a woman in the Patch [a section of Turners Falls] who—they were all working people, frugal people—and this woman saved her family's money. My dad described her as a woman with big breasts and a long dress . . . and cotton stockings. . . . That woman stored money between her breasts, inside of her bosom there, and in the knees of her stockings. . . . And my dad said that if his family didn't have enough money for food, but when they needed to make a payment on a horse or a wagon or something, my grandfather would send my father, a little boy, down to the Patch, to one of these

women. . . . and tell him to borrow ten dollars or something, which
at that time was a lot of money. And my dad remembers as a little
boy being amazed to see this woman reach into her blouse and from
between her breasts pull out this roll of bills—they might have been
dollar bills, I don't know—and peel off and count them. And he could
say this with an approximation of a Polish accent—"You shure dat's
enough, Sonny? You father, he need more? Maybe twenty dollars?"
And my dad said, no, he was told to just get ten. And he said they
did this back and forth; he would repay the money, and occasionally
they'd have to borrow again. And he said she hauled up her skirt one
time, and unrolled her garter, and there was some more money. He
said if it weren't for those people he wouldn't have survived. And he
taught all of us from a really early age, using stories such as that,
nobody can get along without everybody else. And even though there
may be some ways in which people disagree . . . —some of these people, they would spit when they walked in front of the synagogue—
and the Jewish kids would spit towards the church—those kinds of
things went on, but at the same time, on a level of human being to
human being, they helped each other out a lot. I walked with my
grandmother to some of these houses to deliver soup when somebody
was sick; they used to cook things and take them to each other, and
they took care of each other when they were sick, the women. There
was an incredible level of cooperation, which was really nice.

Mutual respect of this kind had, of course, to be posited on fair dealings
on everyone's part, especially in business and farm endeavors. Maxwell
Pyenson speaks to this condition as well as he recalls his family's eventual
acceptance within the broader social life of their community in Otis, Massachusetts. "I think they found out we were relatively honest people," he
indicates, "and good neighbors." Economics was key: "We didn't interfere
with their markets," he adds.

Able to sustain themselves without exacting a price from everyone
else, small-town Jewish New Englanders were model practitioners of
the regional ideal of resourceful self-sufficiency. They may also have
scored points, in the early days, by going out of their way to avoid calling attention to themselves. In the tiny town where Natalie Cohen grew

up, Catholics made up the majority. "There was a town meeting once," recalls Cohen, "and the Catholic people wanted all the stores closed on the Catholic . . . holidays." The example of her father, an unobtrusive Jewish store owner, was invoked and the proposal was dismissed: "One man got up and said, 'Herbie Covin closes his store four times a year, and he never asks us to close ours. What right do we have to ask him?'"

Latter-day Jewish residents of the same districts experience a different order of relationships with non-Jewish neighbors. In part owing to their more visible status not so much as Jews but as transplants, the recent arrivals may be noticed as Jews only when some sort of religious discussion or display is underway. Gen Uris, who grew up in the area around Waitsfield, Vermont, was raised at a time when the entire area was being transformed, demographically speaking: "There were almost 50/50 people from Europe, people from cities, people from different areas who came to the ski area [Sugarbush] and kids whose families had been here for generations. And it was a fairly obvious distinction in many ways—economic, cultural. We're not a generation of people from this area." Saul Perlmutter mentions that his "friendship group" as he grew up in Vermont in the 1960s was "a mixed group of Jews and non-Jews." In 1967, during the Six Day War, he recalls conversations with non-Jewish friends who expressed interest in and sympathy for the Israeli cause.

Jewish visibility, which tends in the current era to be intentional, brings a certain amount of consciously inter-ethnic or inter-religious dialogue. Suzie Laskin, whose radio announcement in the early 1990 helped to create a White Mountain region *havurah*, mentions one such highly visible undertaking.

> I guess we're becoming a little more known in the area because we have . . . an ad in the newspaper now on the church page and the church page had a banner across it with a cross and we asked them to take that out and then we would put an ad in. So they took the cross out and then we have an ad in the paper that says we meet once a month and gives our phone number so they can call us if they're interested, and so we get some phone calls from that. I guess we're starting to become more visible and people are starting to become aware that there are some Jews here.

Visibility, once avoided by Jews who wanted to find their place within American communities, now seems to be a desirable end.

Bob Rottenberg of Colrain, Massachusetts, notices this trend.

What's been fascinating to me is that over the years I have allowed my Jewishness to become more and more public, which I didn't always. But as I became more and more involved in the synagogue, and my name started being associated more publicly with Jewish life, Jewish ritual, what I've noticed is that people give me that space and almost expect it. Like I'll walk into a place around Christmas time, and . . . if they know me, it will start the automatic "Merry Christmas, have you done your shopping," kind of thing, and then they'll stop; they'll say, "How's *your* season going?" Like that. Perhaps it's the circles that I navigate through, where there are people with perhaps a slightly higher level of awareness, consciousness. . . . But I've found that around here there is a greater receptivity to other paths, and that the more I do it, the more receptive people seem to be; it's fascinating to me. I've had groups from other churches come to talk about Judaism, and one of the ministers said to me afterwards . . . "That was a great session we had; the only problem is everybody wants to become Jewish now."

Jewish residents of small-town New England may not necessarily find themselves the center of attention, but their involvement in the life of such places, noticed or not, figures in as part of a larger Jewish participation in the lives of non-Jews—a testing ground, as it were, for the Jewish culture and faith itself.

Joe Kurland, who lives as well in Colrain, Massachusetts, undertakes a self-appointed role as an emissary of sorts, whose life is lent more meaning as he, through both ordinary and deliberate interactions with non-Jews, helps to build a better world.

I sort of feel that Judaism has a role in the world and that involves being everywhere in the world. . . . I think that as a Jew I'm involved in political things, as a Jew I'm involved in community things. The ideals that I have learned as a Jew apply to the larger society. In the Torah, it says—God says to Abraham, "You shall be a blessing to the peoples of the world," you know, "the people of the world shall be blessed through you." And how does that mean? It means the moral teachings that we have need to be applied to the world to be a blessing to the world and that means standing up for the poor and the orphan and the widow and the stranger and it means standing up for justice and peace, and it means doing it anywhere, And if there's a purpose in being Jewish, in retaining Judaism in spite of all the difficulties of being a Jew and all the prejudice against Jews, it means doing that work wherever you are.

Economic and civic life in small-town New England, from the turn of the century to the present, offered ideal opportunities for such engagement. The religious life of Jewish residents brought about another set of rich exchanges, as well as a continual reinvention of Jewish identity itself.

CHAPTER 4

"Just Enough to Make a Minyan"
Religious Practice among Small-Town New England Jews

o   o   o

The practice of Judaism has been both a stabilizing factor and a bell-wether of changes for the Jewish residents of rural New England. Often the growth, dispersal, and reformation of Jewish communities throughout the region have matched the general trends found among Jewish communities throughout the United States. The area's first Jewish settlers were thoroughly Jewish by inheritance; their folklife—a re-creation, to varying degrees, of the Eastern European *shtetl*'s folklife—was inseparable from their theology. Generations of sustained exposure to the vernacular and civic culture of their respective New England communities, as well as to larger changes affecting the evolution of Jewish practice throughout the United States in the twentieth century, had a tremendous reshaping impact on Judaism in the region, however. Jewish congregations—many of which were Orthodox in their formative stages in small New England towns—gradually evolved toward affiliations with the more Americanized Conservative, Reform, and, more recently, Reconstructionist movements. Rituals followed suit; where bar mitzvahs were once restricted rites of passage for male children only—and those few who might have access to sustained formal study with a rabbi—the bat mitzvah has become a mainstay for young Jewish women; the first one was performed in 1922.[1] As early as the 1950s, fully half of the nation's Conservative congregations had adopted the practice. Likewise, Orthodox Jewish weddings and courtship practices were once the only means by which Jewish communities marked the entrance of new families. Recent years, by contrast, have seen an upsurge both of less traditional ceremonies and of interfaith families and rituals. The oral traditions of small-town New England Jews bear evidence of an adaptability to change and a certain reluctance to relinquish difference. Where Jews are so few in number, they can ill afford to be divided over sectarian concerns; formal affiliations with the various movements in American Judaism seem often to have been more a matter of convenience than of ideology. By the same token, where Jews who live in more densely Jewish areas can "feel" Jewish by crossing the street to buy a bagel at a neighborhood deli, tradition-bearers from small-town New England have almost uniformly spoken of the extra measure of intentionality required of them; traditional Jewish practices, in this regard, take on an added significance. The mixture of traditional and adaptive practice appears to mirror the culture of small-town New England, in which the legacy of past practice is counterbalanced by a tendency to overlook merely ideological differences in the interest of an enhanced neighborliness.

Where Orthodox practice has waned, Judaism can hardly be said to have lost its connection to tradition, however. In their own communities and in dialogue with one another, as well as with other Jewish religious groups in the region, small-town New England Jews have revitalized Judaism's tie to the past. A unifying force in this simultaneous retention and rebirth has been the *cultural life* of Jews—their immersion in *Yiddishkeit*, their dietary adaptations, oral traditions, and other customary practices. In all these areas, the conditions of life in rural New England have both tested and rewarded the efforts of Jewish residents to be both good Jews and properly acclimatized New Englanders.

Jewish rural New Englanders have long benefited from an atmosphere of relative tolerance. Even if facts might not always be commensurate with reputations—and the area's considerable legacy of anti-Semitism, especially in the pre–World War II days, suggests that tolerance was an ideal embraced and practiced by far too few people to make being Jewish *easy*—the existence of an ideological and folk legacy of openness could operate as a powerful incentive, and many tradition-bearers emphasize the positive treatment they have received from the non-Jewish majority, either omitting altogether or minimizing the impact of any anti-Semitism upon them or their parents and grandparents. The linchpin for this folk emphasis on tolerance would appear to have been its confluence with another vaunted regional tradition—that of unostentatious and quiet behavior, or—to use Dona Brown's formulation—the "abstemious life of hard work and simplicity."[2] This may be why the *idea* of Jews as integral small-town New Englanders *seems* strange; another set of folk beliefs, both imposed upon Jews and self-touted—describes them as inherently outspoken, argumentative, and conflicted. Where both mythologies—that of quiet New Englanders and loud Jews—begin to fall apart is precisely where the idea of Jews being *at home* in New England begins to make sense. Nowhere has this been more true than in their actual practice of Judaism.

No region of the United States has a more recognizable theological pedigree than New England. Although the outlying colonies of New Hampshire and Rhode Island did not share Massachusetts Bay's or Connecticut's direct derivation as specifically Puritan plantations, the region as a whole was settled and often governed by a singularly theocratic body until the Revolutionary Era. From the Mayflower Compact of 1620 to the Halfway Covenant of 1662, the region's ideological underpinnings manifested a religious set of convictions. Even long after the waning of Puritanism per se, in the mid-nineteenth century, for instance, the region's most influential personages invoked its religious heritage. Transcendentalists knew how to be iconoclasts because New England's dissenting Protestant heritage showed them how to break convention; Abolitionists drew much of their rhetorical fire from the same originating pulpit. Jews were hardly welcome participants in—or even eyewitnesses to—the Puritan experiment that yielded New England. By the late nineteenth and early twentieth centuries, however, when they began to settle in larger numbers in small New England towns, Jews were inheritors, nonetheless, of a regional culture whose origins lay not only in the economic vicissitudes of rural life but in the social and cultural pastimes of the town church.

The earliest New England Jews—those intrepid pioneers who threaded their way up and down country roads and, even as outsiders, knew its geography first hand—could hardly avail themselves of any synagogue. Their practice of Judaism, therefore, if they were inclined to maintain it at all, was wholly private; the need for a minyan precluded any casual performance of synagogue rituals. Only when these same peddlers, perhaps complemented by a contingent of Jewish farmers, actually settled permanently in a given town or village, could they *establish* Judaism in any way analogous to the preexisting establishment of the region's churches. Generally, this began to occur in the period between 1900 and 1930. Many of the tradition-bearers for this study are currently members of synagogues founded during this pioneering age of Jewish settlement in the region—Augusta, Rockland, and Presque Isle, Maine; Bennington and Burlington, Vermont; Great Barrington, Greenfield, Northampton, and North Adams, Massachusetts; and Laconia and Bethlehem, New Hampshire. Where synagogues exist, of course, so too do denominational affiliations, and so our initial exploration of the practice of Judaism in small-town New England also tells the story of how the region's Jewish communities have evolved from Orthodoxy into and through various non-Orthodox affiliations.

"Our Synagogue Was the Center of Everything": Jewish Congregations in Small-Town New England

New England's earliest synagogues were urban institutions. Colonial Newport and mid-nineteenth-century Boston, Hartford, and Bangor saw the development of small but viable congregations whose constituency was either Sephardic or predominantly German in derivation and whose members formed part of those respective cities' mercantile life. Rural sections and smaller towns, where Jewish populations took shape in the wake of the larger Eastern European migrations of the late nineteenth and early twentieth centuries, could only develop their own Jewish institutions once the Jewish residents had first established an economic foothold. Where urban congregations throughout the United States had largely split into Orthodox or Reform factions by the turn of the century, the smaller shuls of small-town New England all began with Orthodox congregations. Old Country origins had everything to do with this development. Where Reform-leaning congregations tended to be comprised in large part of urban-born German Jews whose theology didn't shy away from a certain assimilationism or by East European Jews who had adapted to such modernized practices, the more Orthodox congregations tended to be populated by founders who had grown up in the *shtetl* and for whom Judaism was equivalent to strict adherence to established non-assimilationist practice. The earliest synagogues in small-town New England were formed by men who knew only one Judaic practice. Though they might in their economic and even social lives seek if not to assimilate at least to participate in the larger surrounding culture, to the extent that they adhered to Judaism they did so by sticking to the existing template. As their children and grandchildren tell it, at any rate, the official religious undertakings of the earliest rural New England Jews avoided innovation in favor of the old ways. Current-day small-town New England Jews may in large part have replaced Orthodoxy with various shades of a more inclusive Judaism, but they seem universally to value the stalwart efforts of their predecessors to forge ahead according to East European precedent.

Aside from the money necessary to establish a house of worship, the first steps of course in building toward the permanent establishment of a congregation are the formation of a minyan and the purchase of a Torah. Phyllis Nahman describes the synagogue in Turners Falls, Massachusetts, that she attended as a child. Her account emphasizes the potential pitfalls of having an established congregation with only ten member families.

> There was a little Jewish community. There was a little synagogue . . . it was a church—a small wonderful building, that in my memory still smells of the women baking downstairs in the little tiny hall, baking honey cake and *rugelach* for Rosh Hashanah. And there were just ten families, and just enough to make a minyan. . . . The building was quite beautiful. It had all that vertical beaded wood on the inside, and over time it got darker and darker. . . . I have a picture somewhere of the ark that was there: simple but really lovely. And it was just the right size for our community. There were these ten families, and everybody knew that when it was the holidays everybody had to go to shul because they needed ten men—it was only the men that counted then. And my grandfather, who lived next door to us, used to come over to our house, and he would bang on the door or kitchen window, and he would yell to my father, "Meyer! Come to shul!" And he'd say what time it was in Yiddish and they would walk to shul; they did not drive. And folks, of course, were Orthodox; they'd come from an Orthodox tradition in Europe and they maintained that.

In the immediate aftermath of their arrival from foreign shores, Jewish families sought one another's company as a matter of survival. Whatever their religious convictions, the psychic benefits of sustaining old ties to a synagogue-centered life were sufficient to promote such a drive. Lillian Glickman, who grew up in North Adams, Massachusetts, describes the synagogue that her family attended as the absolute center of Jewish social life in the area. "Our synagogue . . . was the center of everything," she indicates. "We all belonged to it. . . . We all went to synagogue on the high holidays. . . . It was the center of our life. And even when I got married, it was the social center of our life to a great extent. We had the bridge parties, the dances, we ran everything. Today's there's nothing, but we used to have a huge social life attached to the synagogue." The synagogue was key to the continuance of Jewish tradition among otherwise isolated rural New England Jews. Most of the earlier families attended one, and were willing to travel some long distance to get there.

The early years of many Jewish communities are represented by the oral tradition as having inspired people to heights of communal giving. A congregation or synagogue could not simply materialize, and since few of the pioneering Jews in the region were particularly wealthy, acts of charity had to come from all quarters. Formative years saw Jewish services taking place in people's homes. "Jews can have a synagogue anywhere," says Louis Plotkin. "Any meeting room is a synagogue." In Northampton, it took the large-scale arrival of several East European Jewish families to bring about the formation of a synagogue. German Jews had been living in the area since the 1850s. According to Jack August, whose father had come in that 1880s wave, the Germans had already been "hungry" for the formation of a formal synagogue. Beforehand, the Germans "used to have services in individual homes." In Augusta, Maine, the Lipman family witnessed and helped to usher in the growth of a small but active religious community. As was the case elsewhere, the first Jewish families had to do without an integral worship space.

> They used to have their services in a room downtown that a Jewish merchant allowed them. It was above his store, and that's where they had their room. My uncle's oldest son was bar mitzvahed there, and my Uncle Frank said, "It's time for us to have our own building." And the Lipmans had a lot of connections, and I have to tell you the Jews of the state of Maine were generous; everybody gave something, whether it was an I-beam or lumber or light fixtures. And people bought the Eternal Light. And this building was built, and there was not one cent owed on it.

Synagogues in rural New England materialized as a result of joint endeavors such as this one. Community—or minyan, at least—had to come first. Ruben Tablitz, a poultry trucker and dealer who was a part of the Sandisfield, Massachusetts, group that was started in 1924, didn't have time for the work of founding a synagogue. "I give the money," he says; "I didn't care. I give them the money. I didn't have time to establish. I let them establish themselves. I helped them."

In Laconia, New Hampshire, as Sonny Chertok recounts it, the Jews went through a succession of public meeting places before they set up their own house of worship. "In Laconia in 1915 to 1925," he says, "the Jewish population was completely Orthodox. It was an Orthodox type service, and they had enough families, about 20 families, so that one very wealthy man named Isaac Sakansky had bought a Torah. They kept it in one of the houses, and they would get together for services. And in the early '20s there were enough people so they would hire a hall for Rosh Hashanah and Yom Kippur." An actual synagogue for the Laconia Jews didn't come along until 1937, when, as Bob Selig describes it, "They put together enough money to actually build their own building."

The Jews of Northampton underwent a similar progress toward synagogue formation. Jack August recounts three stages. In the aftermath of the East European influx, "They started a community, used to hold services in the homes. They got a little bit bigger so the homes became too small and they rented a hall. Then they rented a different hall because it was a little bit bigger." Finally, in 1905, the Northampton Jews bought a church for $5,000: "They all pitched in their nickels and dimes and they remodeled the inside. Put in some stained glass windows. . . . Put up a *bima* . . ." The church, August explained in a separate interview, had been sold at a discount by an elder of the Episcopal church. August's father had appealed to him: "Mr. Clark, you know, we buy a little coal from you; but we are just coming into this country, and we need a place of worship." In Orange, Massachusetts, the founding of the first synagogue in 1911 occasioned a large-scale celebration, as Louis Plotkin recalls. The founding of congregations in towns like Laconia, Northampton, and Orange was an indication of permanence; in each case, Jews had been present as peddlers and even shopkeepers for some time, but had held off on establishing synagogues, perhaps for fear that their presence in those places might prove to be a fleeting one.

Jewish communities in more remote areas, such as Aroostook County, Maine, often took turns visiting other communities in order to build a broader sense of connection and to save expense. Milt Adelman tells about how his father, who first arrived in northernmost Maine as a peddler, participated in this gradual evolution.

> He went straight up there [to Maine], and he walked with a pack on his back. He was one of the first Jews up there, but not *the* first because there were other families up there. One time we had a pretty good Jewish population between Canada [and Aroostook County]. We're right on the Canadian border, and we have a synagogue that my dad was instrumental in getting the building up. We used to meet wherever we could for holidays. Sometimes we'd go to Canada and join a group and sometimes we'd rent a place over there, but we celebrated holidays and then they decided to put up a synagogue in Presque Isle[, Maine], which they did.

"My kid brother was the first boy to be bar mitzvahed in that synagogue," says Natalie Cohen of the synagogue in Presque Isle. As she describes it, the temple came to be built largely as the result of one man's efforts. It "was built by one of the potato growers," she says, "because he was getting mad because nobody would make up their mind to make it, so he just built it." Jewish life in the region was sustained by people's willingness to travel long distances in order to complete a minyan. Alternatively, a family would forgo synagogue attendance almost entirely because of the prohibitive distances involved in getting to one. Such was the case for the Pyenson family, who ran a large farm in southwestern Berkshire County, Massachusetts. "We never went to synagogue," says Maxwell Pyenson. "My father was quite versed in Judaism, I guess probably my mother was too, but being out here and not having a synagogue within walking distance or within relatively few miles, why we never went to shul and we never got bar mitzvahed. So even though we were brought up Jewish and we adhered to the Jewish principles and everything else, this was the situation which we had to endure."

Where other families may well have failed to maintain their Judaism in the face of such isolation, the Pyensons persevered. Maxwell Pyenson's grandchildren grew up attending synagogue services and Hebrew school, and his grown son—who still maintains the family farm and business—is now making up for lost time and enrolled in the adult religious school at a synagogue in Great Barrington.

Orthodoxy was the dominant trend for early rural New England Jews because as first-generation immigrants from Eastern Europe, Orthodoxy was what they knew. Julius Goos, who was raised in Bangor, Maine, describes the choices available to the local Jewish population. "There were three synagogues in the area," he points out: "the Orthodox and not-so-Orthodox." The same pattern held in many communities until well after World War II. Bob Selig, of Laconia, New Hampshire, mentions his father's example as indicative of the general level of observation to be found in that community. "My father had gone to Hebrew Teacher's College," he says, "and was fluent in Hebrew—not spoken Hebrew as a language, but prayerbook Hebrew. . . . We certainly went to synagogue and were practicing Jews, but we certainly did not observe all 613 commandments as they pertained to food."

The congregation in Burlington, Vermont, according to Max Wall, who led it upon his arrival there in the late 1940s, had been founded in 1885.

> So they were pretty old. They came basically from Lithuania. Lithuanian Jews. And they had all the services. They had a rabbi, they had a couple of *shochten*, a couple of kosher butchers, they had a *talmud torah* for education. But it was falling apart because it changed radically. When the Jewish kids who were my contemporaries and joined me in that premise were kids, they used to have to gather together to walk to school because if they walked separately, chances are they would be assaulted because they were Jewish. That was the kind of community I came to. Most of the Jews at that time were what I would call non-observant Orthodox. In other words, they wanted their rabbi to be a very punctilious, strict observer of all the rituals and traditions. For me, I remember laughing to myself when I'd take a walk on Shabbat, and I would see members of the congregation beginning to look very furtive and holding their hands behind their back because they were smoking cigarettes, and they didn't want the rabbi to see they were smoking. It was that kind of community. But that was the way a good part of American Jewry was at the time.

Orthodox practice clearly set Jews apart from their non-Jewish neighbors. In the more densely populated centers of Jewish life, the Reform Judaism that had arisen first among the German Jewish immigrants of the mid-nineteenth century was growing in popularity among East European Jews both before and after World War II. In 1952, a study was released indicating that "only twenty-three percent of the children of the Orthodox intend to remain Orthodox."[3] In small-town New England, however, Eastern European Jews, whose *shtetl* background and rural existence in America might have insulated them from such trends, tended to retain their Orthodox affiliations. "Evidently," as Rabbi Wall puts it, "they still felt guilty about the things they [were] supposed to do, but they still [didn't] do them." Bob Selig acknowledges that the Orthodoxy of the first generation was somewhat compromised by their need to put good business practice and economic survival ahead of strict synagogue attendance. The Jews of Laconia, as reverent as they were, didn't close their shops on Shabbat. Despite their official affiliation, Selig offers the following pronouncement about the first-generation Jews: "I don't believe that there were that many people who were really Orthodox."

Notwithstanding such qualifications, current-day descendants of the founding generation point to the older Orthodox synagogues of their parents' and grandparents' generations as strongholds of an Old World holdover of gender separation in worship. Evelyn Slome's description of her congregation highlights this attribute. "In my grandfather's day, the women sat upstairs when they first got here," she says, setting the practice in her use of the phrase "grandfather's day" far apart from that of her own time. Phyllis Nahman paints a more vivid picture. Her grandfather's day in tiny Turners Falls, Massachusetts, coincided with her own childhood.

The men sat in the front. The rabbi came in and read only Hebrew. They talked to each other in Yiddish, but the service was in Hebrew. It became interesting to me only when I was 16 and went to Israel and learned a little Hebrew and came back and studied Hebrew in Greenfield, and then it became really interesting. Before that, it was just sort of went on in the background. It's interesting: the men sat in the front and were davening up there, or at least moving back and forth, and the women sat up in the back, dressed to a fare-the-well; it was when women dressed to the teeth, like what kind of hat are you going to wear, you know? And in the back, since none of the women knew how to read Hebrew, they sat up in the back and talked. They visited, they gossiped, they talked about their children and that's what happened. The women would come and go, but the men, they had to stay because there had to be a minyan in there. And the kids were up in the back with the women until they were old enough; when the boys got bar mitzvahed they sat in front . . . there was no such thing as a bat mitzvah in that synagogue at that time. I don't know if there was anywhere around here. I don't think so. So that's what went on in that shul . . . It was a pretty close-knit community.

No other single change in Judaic practice compares, within the oral tradition of rural New England Jews, to the evolution away from a strictly male-oriented synagogue worship toward a more inclusive and, ultimately, egalitarian approach. The Jewish congregation of Great Barrington, Massachusetts, which was founded in 1926, was no exception. "You had to have a minyan with ten people," says Jack Pevzner. "If he [Rabbi David Axelrod] had nine men and a hundred women, he . . . didn't have enough. It has to be ten men. Now you go to a shul, and the women are running the whole thing. The women [in the old days] weren't allowed to go up to the Torah." In some communities, gender separation continued on well after World War II. Amy Jo Montgomery, who moved from the Bronx to Bennington, Vermont, in 1960, recalls separate seating in the synagogue that was located 50 miles north of her home, in Manchester, Vermont. "The women used to sit on one side," she recalls, "the men, of course, sat on the other side. It was a whole gender division."

For all of the strictures imposed by the Orthodox tradition, however, it seems as well to have engendered a wistful admiration on the part of those who grew up in it. Even as Phyllis Nahman depicts the separate seating for men and women in Turners Falls, she describes a lively feeling of community among the women and children upstairs. She speaks quite fondly now, in any case, of her early days attending services in the Turners Falls shul. As she explains, the congregation didn't have a fulltime rabbi, but hired an itinerant to conduct high holiday services.

That's the one time of the year we knew the synagogue would be open. Although they used to be open on Simchat Torah, and maybe there were some things on Purim from time to time, but that was organized by people in town, usually by the women, who wanted to have events for their children. We'd march around the shul with paper Israeli flags and sing and carry the Torahs around and all that. . . . I have very fine memories of events that that synagogue. We used to walk downtown; we lived a little over a mile away. My mom used to push a baby carriage down for the high holidays. And tucked in the baby carriage she used to have little bags of food for the kids, even on Yom Kippur. She'd say, "But you have to sit outside to eat it; you can't eat it in the shul.". . . . It was a fun thing.

Bob August tells a similar story. The Jews of the founding generation in his hometown of Northampton, Massachusetts, "were Orthodox. They kept kosher homes." August clarifies: "They were also pragmatic. I say that because I remember my father often telling the story that at Rosh Hashanah, Yom Kippur, being sent to the synagogue by my grandmother with a bag of boiled eggs. You can't send the kids to sit in the shul all day and not eat. You've got to eat, you know, not fast. So I think they were pragmatic, but they personally maintained an Orthodox and kosher lifestyle." Natalie Cohen, who grew up Orthodox but is now affiliated with Augusta, Maine's Reform temple, speaks of how grateful she is to have raised her children in a different town. "I'm glad my children were brought up in Bangor and not here in Augusta," says Cohen, "because they're too loose here as far as religion goes. They're not giving the children the Orthodox way; they're teaching them Reform, and some of the Reform is, 'Well, if you don't want to do it today, you can do it tomorrow.' And I feel that there should be more strictness because we're going to lose them." Orthodoxy, she says, is valuable as a set of core teachings. "I still feel the Orthodox," Cohen says, "even though you may go into other phases, you should have the Orthodox as a base and then go from there. If you don't want to do this, fine, but at least you learn that this is the core." Natalie Cohen is hardly the only representative of this latter-day, philo-Orthodox sentiment.

Regardless, in any case, of how they view the movement away from Orthodoxy, those congregants who can remember the days when Orthodoxy represented the norm offer a unique perspective. The retrospective view can be quite telling. As Amy Jo Montgomery explains it, the changes have been sweeping and not entirely uncontroversial. Speaking of the synagogue in her hometown of Bennington, Vermont, where she has been attending for several decades, she observes:

Some of the older people that come here say it's not religious enough. I've heard that complaint and we had opened our arms to gays and lesbians here, which is not a big deal, and we have a woman that's African American that was the president of this temple. It's very much changed. You never would have seen that in the old days, in past times. I think that a lot of the religious part of it, it's still religious but not the Orthodox. You don't see them walking around on Friday nights and not driving, not answering your phone, you know, not using lights, not that I see. I don't think it's as religious as it used to be, know what I'm saying? I think it's really a lot more homey here. . . . We used to always dress up when we went to temple. You see rabbis walking around in jeans, it's very different. [For] some of the older people . . . it's hard . . . because maybe they feel it's not respectful.

Whether this type of lament over the decline of Orthodox practice among small-town New England Jews constitutes a commentary on a perceived loss of religiosity or a pronouncement on the apparent decentralization of Jewish life in the region is difficult to know. Indeed, some would argue that the religious or spiritual quality of Jewish life has only improved since the early days. Such a view is represented by Rabbi Max Wall, whose sense of the early synagogue life in Burlington, Vermont, was that it was painfully restrictive. "When I first came . . . you had to belong if you [were] a small-town [Jew]; otherwise, you [felt] really lost. Maybe 95 percent of the Jews in the area were associated," he points out. "They didn't like it; they didn't like the rabbi; they didn't like whatever it was, but what can you do? You still have to be buried as a Jew. So we had control: 'No matter what else we do, we're going to get ya!' " Regardless of the restrictions it imposed, however, Orthodoxy gave early small-town New England Jews a structure for their religious life, and—at least according to their children and grandchildren—it guaranteed the survival of their Jewish identity.

Founding a Jewish congregation in a rural New England community was hardly an easy undertaking. The same Great Barrington, Massachusetts, congregation of which Jack Pevzner speaks had to overcome a certain amount of resistance on the part of non-Jews in the town who were opposed to its existence. Toby Axelrod, the granddaughter of the synagogue's European-born rabbi David Axelrod, recalls having heard the following story when she was growing up. Townspeople had rejected the idea of a synagogue being built. A local Jewish junk dealer, Ike Broverman, as the story goes, bought an old house on State Street "for use as a junk shop." As Axelrod explains, "Little did the townspeople know his true intention—to turn the building into a synagogue." In close-knit outlying New England towns, the founding and maintenance of a synagogue congregation was an intrinsically tenuous prospect. Such congregations' anchoring in Orthodoxy may have seemed to give it a sure footing, but the broader context of rural New England life and culture made even the most committed traditional congregations all the more susceptible to a waning of influence.

Rural New England congregations began to move away from Orthodoxy as a second generation of American-born Jews came along, preferring English to Yiddish, wishing for a broader inclusion of women and girls within worship and for a more open policy with regard to girls' education. As first-generation Yiddish speakers aged and passed the mantle of local Jewish practice onto their English-speaking, much more thoroughly assimilated children, the attractions of both the Reform and the Conservative movements were considerable. "I think as children at home," says Bob August, the second and third generation of small-town New England Jews "followed the household rules. . . . [But] when they moved out of the house, they moved away from those kind of family customs, basically." As if to underscore how much more tidily such practices fit the preexisting worship patterns of small-town New England, Evelyn Slome, when she refers to the current incarnation of Portsmouth, New Hampshire's Temple Israel (which was Orthodox in its founding) somewhat self-consciously slips: "I want to say—what is it?—the United Conservative; I want to say it's like the United Church of Christ—the United Synagogue thing. It's a Conservative synagogue." Summing up the generational transition as he experienced it in Burlington, Vermont, Saul Perlmutter offers the following explanation, which sounds formulaic even though it isn't necessarily meant to be: "So my grandfather belonged to the Orthodox shul. My family went to the Conservative shul." The generational differences which evolved a changing congregational allegiance were largely cultural, it seems, as opposed to strictly theological. In the old days, as Perlmutter describes it, "Yiddish was around. My grandparents spoke Yiddish most of the time. I heard Yiddish. . . . This is an age thing."

The transition away from Orthodoxy, at least as it is remembered within the oral tradition, seems to have occurred with a minimum of strain. As Louis Plotkin describes it, the shift was fairly uncontroversial in Orange, Massachusetts: "Eventually, even in the old synagogue, it finally got to the women and men were sitting together. . . . Some of the older people resented it, but they had to yield. . . . The younger people came along and wanted it that way." In one instance, the rabbi himself was apparently the source of a set of institutional changes that ushered in a new era. Rabbi Max Wall, who was hired to lead a synagogue in Burlington after his term of service as a World War II Army chaplain came to an end, worked to shape his congregation in accordance with a more contemporary Judaic practice. When he first arrived, as he puts it, "Everything was small-townish." He effected first small- and then later large-scale changes.

> We started singing in the service, teaching them all kinds of traditional melodies. It was an exciting change for everybody. Pretty soon we had a sisterhood going; we had a men's club going in addition to supporting the actual ongoing work of the congregation. I came in 1946, and by 1948, I started to murmur about—this is old fashioned. They had a balcony for the women upstairs. When I came, we joined the congregation for Friday night services, men and women together on Friday nights. But on Shabbat morning, men still sat downstairs and women upstairs, and same for the holidays. I didn't want that. I wanted an integrated kind of service, so eventually we got it on in maybe the third year.

Over time, similar changes occurred in synagogues throughout the region. Particularly as second- and third-generation rural Jews tended to leave the area for college and professional careers, Jewish congregations had to reach out and be attractive to a new constituency—one which was more likely to have been reared in a Reform or Conservative urban context and was also ripe for a spiritualized, as opposed to merely traditional, Judaism. "When the old-timers died," says Jack August, "and the young people came to town . . . we wanted to know more about what we were doing." August compares the evolution away from Orthodoxy and its attendant exclusion of English from services to what his peers in the Catholic church were demanding: "they discontinued a lot of the Latin because the average layman didn't understand what it was all about."

When I asked Charlotte Goos, a native Mainer, how the membership of her home congregation had recovered from the exodus of her contemporaries and their children in the 1950s and 1960s, her answer echoed any number of similar pronouncements by members of pioneering rural Jewish generations: "Ever hear of the hippies?" she asked. "There were a group of them that came to Maine; many of them were Jewish. And they've come back to religion. Our rabbi brought them in from the woods." Gradually, across the whole region, congregations shifted not only their formal affiliations but their actual constituencies. Rabbi Howard Cohen, who led Bennington's once Orthodox and now Reconstructionist temple, describes the evolution of his community in detail. He notes the gradual turnover in leadership, some of which he was witness to on his arrival.

There are different migratory rings on the tree here at Bennington. There are a couple of families, people who were born and raised here and whose parents—they're first-generation Americans but their parents came here to Bennington when they were young—when their parents were young. There are some people like that. Lots of those people who are still around like that, or I should say a number of those families like that, have largely intermarried and have virtually nothing to do with the Jewish community anymore. There are some who still have something to do with the community. But each ring of arrivals sees themselves as the old guard, so the current sort of manifestation of the congregation is such that there are a lot of people who moved into the area in the last ten to fifteen years who have become involved and the people who might have moved in fifteen to twenty years ago are less involved. . . .

I'm the first fulltime rabbi the congregation had since 1970. That's when a fellow named Hyam Gross died and then for a period of time they had a series of itinerant and part-time rabbis; one of whom lived here but was a rabbinical student in New York. And I noticed that these people weren't around. They'd seemed to sort of fade away, and so we were at a board retreat and I made this observation, and I said, "Am I doing something wrong? Have I driven away the people who were involved?" And one of them said, "Oh, absolutely not; you've done what we've been waiting so long to happen is that you've brought new people in so that we can let go and let other people do it."

Though such changes could hardly have occurred without any tension, rural New England Jews have tended to be more realistic than ideological on such matters. Time and time again, both rabbis and congregants of all generations and observational backgrounds have emphasized the need, in

an area with so few Jews to begin with, for an open spirit of compromise
and non-sectarianism. In certain respects, the apparent tolerance that man-
ifests itself in multiple approaches to the practice of Judaism seems also to
derive from, or at least mirror, the sort of compromises that characterize
neighborly relations among small-town New England residents, Jew and
non-Jew alike.

Joe Kurland, whose family actively attends Temple Israel in Greenfield,
Massachusetts, offers insight into the need for tolerance: "The synagogue
in Greenfield is the only synagogue in Franklin County," Kurland points
out, "and it has to serve everybody, and there are more observant people,
and there are less observant people, and there are people who are more
traditional in their observance, and there are people who are more modern
in their observance. This community has to make room for everybody. And
it does. The older families weren't necessarily more observant, but they
may have been traditional in their observance." Julie Chamay, whose family participates in the Bennington, Vermont, temple, speaks as well about
the absence of sectarianism that characterizes current-day Jewish practice
in small-town New England. Her sense is that her community's affiliation
with Reconstructionism derives from the fact that its rabbi, Howard Cohen,
was ordained in that tradition.

> The synagogue in Bennington is more inclusive and it's much smaller
> and they expect people to participate and there's a lot of women who
> wear *tallitot* and you're expected to wear a *tallis* if you go up on the
> *bimah* to read from Torah. . . . I talked to one woman who said it
> brought tears to her eyes to see that. Because it's true that when I was
> growing up to be a woman who was involved in the synagogue, you
> put the cookies out for the *oneg*. . . . You know, the Brotherhood sat
> up on the *bimah* and the Brotherhood held the power and made the
> decisions and the *rebbitzen* and other women . . . didn't call the shots.
> They weren't on the Board. Their role was very small and peripheral.

A spirit of openness seems to preside, at least in the accounts of the Jewish
congregants throughout rural New England with whom I spoke. Freedom
of choice seems to be an operative principle. In describing her hometown
of Bethlehem, New Hampshire, Lee Bagdon emphasizes this quality.
"There's currently no animosity," she says, referring to the relationship
between the town's significant population of Hasidim and other Orthodox

Jews and those who attend the town's Conservative synagogue. "We have
the Hasidim," she explains, "the Modern Orthodox, and us. People have a
choice if they want to come move here." The Jews who "came out of the
woods," to use Charlotte Goos's expression, encountered some resistance,
but their numbers—as we have also seen in previous chapters—have precluded them from being held at bay for any length of time.

Small-town synagogues seem in the current day to be undergoing a
revival of sorts. A new demographic, though small in number, infuses new
energy and practice. The revival goes back, in some areas, to the 1970s. Bob
Selig, a Laconia, New Hampshire, oldtimer, also ascribes Laconia's good
fortune to its status as a one-synagogue small town.

> As I read more and see more of what happens, I find that a lot of
> Jews that grew up in New York are unaffiliated with a religious orga-
> nization. Some are, but many, many are not. I think that being in
> a small town, the identity as part of a Jewish community is a more
> significant part. When one lives in New York and grows up eating
> Jewish food—you can find it every place—one sometimes considers
> that eating Jewish is being Jewish. Well, I don't think that's the case
> when you grow up in a small town. I think that one understands that
> being Jewish involves being involved in a community, helping to sus-
> tain it, making sure that it grows and that it will be there for future
> generations to come. I think there's more of a sense of responsibility.

Saul Perlmutter, who grew up in Burlington, Vermont, makes a similar pronouncement. Growing up Jewish in Vermont may sound as though it would
have been an isolating experience, he suggests, but because the synagogue
life in such a place was so crucial a node for one's socialization, Perlmutter
views it as an unmixed blessing.

> Ironically, because I grew up in a smaller place but with a decent
> number of Jews, I had a very rich Jewish youth group experience
> and even a semi-decent Jewish education, especially for the boonies.
> I think sometimes people who grow up, say, in Newton or someplace
> where there are a lot of Jews, maybe their parents don't send them
> to Jewish education or make as much of a big deal about them being
> part of a youth group because their peer group is largely Jewish.
> I'm talking about from large Jewish neighborhoods—Brookline or

something like that. So ironically, we may have had a stronger youth group in Burlington, Vermont, than they have in some places at least today in some cities where there are more Jews. I think that's one maybe unanticipated differences.

Multigenerational families who remained in the region reaped multiple benefits of small-town synagogue life. More inclined to welcome newcomers than to turn them away, they often saw reform, their oral testimony suggests, not as a threat to the traditional fabric of Jewish life but as a potential means to its revival.

Elizabeth Lerner, who grew up and continues her affiliation with the synagogue in Montpelier, Vermont, has noticed an atmosphere of growth that has taken shape since her childhood. The enlargement of the synagogue community, ironically, has ushered in some less than ideal changes, from her point of view.

> For rural New England it's actually very large—about 200 families. But it's also more of a suburban mentality than a lot of rural communities . . . Because people didn't necessarily have a hand in founding it, or because they're affiliated with Dartmouth, and don't really care that much one way or the other. . . . There are people who are members who are twice-a-year Jews to a larger rate than I think happens in really small communities. Until we got our new rabbi and he kind of changed things around, there was a struggle to make minyan on Shabbos morning. Now there may be 40 people there sometimes. And it's crazy, because I remember when we didn't have services during the summer because the rabbi would go away, and if the rabbi would go away how could we have services? So now every week of the year, obviously, there are services, and it's a much larger community now. . . . I don't know if the actual enrollment has risen or if people have just started coming to things, but it feels much bigger.

Leslie Dreier, who returned to the (summering) Jewish community of Bethlehem, New Hampshire, as an adult, speaks appreciatively of the oldtimers' and newcomers' collective spirit of goodwill. He and his wife walked into the Bethlehem temple one evening and found themselves embraced. "We were not temple goers," he explains, "and we walked in with two three-year-old twins on a Friday night; it was full of people. The lights were on; it was very warm and welcoming, and everybody lit up when they saw them." Dreier contrasts the small-town experience with what he knew as a resident of Miami. While living there, he once asked someone, "Do you ever go to the synagogue?" The person he asked responded, "I don't go there because you can't go on a Friday night if your wife doesn't have a mink coat." Dreier's Friday night experience in Bethlehem, he indicates, "was the exact opposite of that." Located in a historically summering community whose current percentage of Jewish part-time residents consists of Hasidim, the congregation of the Bethlehem synagogue makes do in a fashion similar to some of the region's earliest congregations. As Lee Bagdon explains, it hires visiting rabbis, student rabbis, and cantors, and hopes for the best. Current-day synagogues' relative openness to change and diversity in worship styles derives in part from the influx of a somewhat countercultural constituency, whose first comers arrived in the 1970s and continue to be a visible presence.

Bob Rottenberg, who came to Colrain, Massachusetts, in 1974, recalls that elements in Greenfield's old guard resisted the influence of newcomers. "The rabbi . . . routinely threw people out," he says, and then offers an illustrative anecdote.

> Once, several of us actually went to synagogue—it was Purim—so we came down for the *megillah*—figured this would be a good time, you know? And after the *megillah*, he [the rabbi] said, "What's going on out there [in the hilltowns]? I've heard there's stuff going on." And I said, "Well, you know, we get together on Friday night; we light candles and we drink wine, we eat *challah*, and we sing songs." And he was incredibly threatened by that. He actually said to me, "Wine and bread—you know, that's Christian. That's not Jewish." And I said, "Well, I guess we've got nothing to talk about," and left, and didn't go back there until he had left and a new rabbi . . . showed up . . . in the late '70s, early '80s, and he was far more receptive to and less threatened by what you might call the counterculture of Judaism.

The receptivity to new approaches has as much to do with the countercultural Jews' investment in reinvigorating tradition as it does with a spirit of experimentation. On his family's homestead in Readsboro, Vermont, Shmuel Simenowitz has undertaken a project which seeks to combine an aspect of traditional New England agriculture with a Jewish notion of "sacred space."

> We've expanded our sugarhouse and this is very consistent with my own involvement in the Jewish environmental movement. There's a big push now towards what you call the greening of sacred space. . . . It says in the Torah that God says, "Build me a sanctuary and I will dwell *b'sochum*." *B'sochum* means in them. The building is just an excuse for the godliness to come down. The godliness ultimately resides within every person. That's the sacred space, so in a sense, we're part of this dialogue.
>
> Our statement towards sacred space is a sugarhouse because it's a place that Jews live and work and spend time and learn Torah and sing and eat and sleep. So it's kind of like a *succah. Succah*'s the mitzvah that you even bring the mud in your boots on; it's all encompassing. So we spend a lot of hours in the sugarhouse, so I thought that would be a good metaphor for saying what is sacred space.
>
> . . . We've got a guy named Ed Levin doing the design; and it's being actually modeled after the Polish wooden synagogue architecture of the eighteenth century. You'll notice the rooflines, the gable on the hip, and we want to make a statement that way. And I know there were movements to rebuild these wooden Polish synagogues, but then they find there are no Jews. And personally I don't really want to be part of an effort to build a museum to the dead Jew. I'm into the museum of the living, working, breathing, sleeping, eating, reproducing Jew. So this is our tribute.

This combination of an experiential orientation with an interest in the promotion of spiritual practice is a mark of distinction for several Jewish religious endeavors in small-town New England. The sugarhouse/synagogue, however, appears to epitomize the melding of religious and regional styles in a way that few other small-town New England Jews have approached.

Often, informality, a frequent behavioral attribute of baby boomers, figures in as part of the formulation. As Rabbi Cohen of Bennington, Vermont, describes it, "countercultural" may or may not be the right word. "But we're definitely not like your typical suburban synagogue," he says. "In fact, if you would take a template of what a typical synagogue looks like and put it on top of us, we'd look like we were dead in the water because we operate very differently. And we are informal. Tomorrow, because there's a bar mitzvah, I'll be wearing a tie. But I never wear a tie—I mean funerals and weddings—that's about it. And people come in; they take their shoes off. So in that way, it's informal and the culture is different." Among other things, actual temple membership, while still a requisite aspect of Jewish life, need not be a stumbling block in the participation of new community members.

When he first came to western Massachusetts, klezmer musician Joe Kurland found his way into the Greenfield temple as a result of a series of unanticipated convergences. He explains: "About 20 years ago; I'm sort of not sure what happened first but sometime around that time there was a Hiroshima Day . . . vigil on the Greenfield Town Common and I came down and I blew the *shofar* there, and I think I had met Rabbi Rieser once or twice before that. But a couple of days later I got a phone call from him saying, 'I heard you blow a mean *shofar*, would you like to come blow *shofar* for us at Rosh Hashanah?' " Even a self-described nonobservant Jew can find a welcoming home in the context of rural New England Judaism. "I'm a simple guy," Michael Docter says: "OK, so I'm a Jew, big deal, what . . . does that mean? I don't know. We do Shabbat dinner on Friday nights when we get around to it as often as we can, and it's really nice. Do I enjoy going to synagogue? Absolutely not. Do I believe *anything* I've ever read in synagogue? No way. Do I like some of the people who go there? Yeah." With such a range of affiliations and levels of belief, Judaism in small New England towns has learned to build itself out of a seemingly unmanageable diversity toward what looks to be a largely unanticipated but thriving communal life.

"Our Home Was Jewish": Ritual, Family Life, Life-Cycle

Jews have maintained their traditions over the millennia in large part owing to the centrality of ritual. At every stage of life and at every calendrical point, ritual reifies Judaism. Observance of Shabbat, of the High Holy Days, and of numerous festivals brings Jews together to pray, to read the Torah, to sing, and to discuss and debate over ethical matters. Within Judaism, one's entire life is punctuated by ritual. The bris, or circumcision ceremony, marks the beginning of life for Jewish boys; bar or bat mitzvah ushers Jewish children into adulthood. Marriage and funereal rituals mark

other life passages. Whether these rituals are to be observed in the synagogue as public occasions or in the home as familial ceremonies, Jews assert
their Jewishness by participating in them. Many Jews who may identify
themselves as nonbelievers nonetheless acknowledge the integral role that
Jewish ritual occupies in the Jewish culture. They may practice without, in
fact, "believing."

Rural New England Jews, like all American Jews, have anglified many
of their ritual practices, but, in the spirit of their ancestors, have meticu-
lously maintained integral elements such as the use of Hebrew, the chanting of age-old prayers, and the reading of sacred text. A spirit of innovation
and dynamism, combined with an adherence to core practices and beliefs,
has allowed Jews to be both adherent to old ways and open to new practices.
The rituals of Judaism are markers of both modernity and tradition. So too
is the cultural life of small-town New England, in which old patterns of
land use, human interaction, and cultural practices have been continually
reinvented and reshaped to fit the fluctuational economic and social patterns of life in the region. Small-town New Englanders of all backgrounds
have survived and, occasionally, prospered as a result of their facility with
change.

No Jewish ritual is as central or as holy as the keeping of the Sabbath.
In the mid-nineteenth century, the German Jewish peddler Abraham
Kahn walked the byways of rural New England and, in the diary he kept
of his travels, agonized over his inability to keep the Sabbath; for him, this
relinquishment was equivalent to a relinquishment of Judaism itself. Kahn
usually found it impossible to observe the Sabbath and, on many occasions, even felt compelled to violate it by selling his goods on Saturdays. In
small-town New England, Judaism was a practical impossibility before the
end of the nineteenth century. Indeed, even in the heyday of larger-scale
Jewish settlement in the area, in the mid-twentieth century, full-fledged
observance of the Sabbath was quite rare. Jewish merchants who once ran
hundreds of stores in dozens of small New England towns rarely closed on
Saturday, as doing so would have shut essential customers out on the most
important buying and selling day of the week. "In those days," says Louis
Plotkin, "if you did not work on the Sabbath, it was practically impossible
to make a living." Indeed, even in urban areas where much larger numbers
of Jews clustered, such practice was, by necessity, commonplace. "Numerous jobs in the clothing trade, the cigar trade and even on farms and ped-

dling," writes Jonathan Sarna, "made working on the Jewish Sabbath a condition of employment." The presiding dictum, as Sarna suggests, was "That 'if you don't come in on Saturday, don't bother coming in on Monday.'"[4] Within the oral tradition I found only one reference to full-fledged Sabbath-keeping among Jews of the earliest generation. In Northampton, Massachusetts, according to Jack August, the German Jews who had arrived first "didn't care." But the East European Jews, at least initially, went out of their way and hired help in their shops for Saturday.

> When the Sabbath came . . . these Jews would come down the street to the synagogue with their silk top hats, long velvet coats to synagogue dressed as this was [a] holiday. The Sabbath meant something. It meant an awfully lot to these people. . . . My father would say, "Mindell," to my mother, "today I'm going to bring home the men of the synagogue. We're going to have a *kibba*, we're going to have a little party." My mother would make chopped herring, chopped liver, a *cholent*. . . . We used to take it across the street to the bakery and put it in that oven overnight because the bakery was closed. . . . This *kibba* would last an hour or two. They had their whiskey and their wine and their beer and talked and sang.

Notwithstanding the somewhat public display of Sabbath-keeping on the part of the East European Jews of Northampton, Shabbat was experienced for the most part by the early generations of small-town New England Jews as a compromise—practiced in the home, as business dictates might allow.

Although Jewish store owners quite frequently closed their doors on the High Holy Days, Sabbath closings were more or less impossible since the farmers and factory workers who formed the customer base had to do most of their shopping on that one day of the week. "This was economically important," Irene Moskowitz of Great Barrington, Massachusetts, asserts. "If you had a shop you didn't close the shop Friday night or Saturday. You kept the place open." Indeed, as Moskowitz's friend Beala Schiffman recalls, this practice scandalized at least one party of visiting Jews from the city. "They were outraged," Schiffman remembers, "when they came here and saw all the stores that Jews had were open." To the extent that settlement-generation Jews were able to maintain the Sabbath, they had to do so in an accommodating spirit. One kept the store open and went home to one's family when possible at the end of the evening.

Business and family life were separate spheres for early rural New England Jews. Again, perhaps in accordance with the regionally sanctioned mode of privacy and tolerance, one could, in this respect, lead two lives. Judaic practice was adapted to fit some very odd circumstances. In New Brunswick and Maine, where Natalie Cohen grew up, deer hunting was part of an age-old way of life. Cohen's father Herbie Covin owned a restaurant, in fact, where he prepared and served venison, both for his own family and for his customers. "It was good," his daughter recalls approvingly, even as she acknowledges the violation of *kashrut*. The restaurant was a public setting in which such things could be allowed. The home was another sort of environment. "Our home was kosher," Cohen asserts. "Our home was Jewish. Friday nights we had a Shabbat meal, and we were home Friday nights. We didn't go anywhere. We had a meal together. The rest of the nights we went back and forth, but Friday night was our night. Then we did things afterwards. But my mother always had Shabbat meal for us Friday night." The same was true in May Schell's home in Easthampton, Massachusetts. Schell's mother "had a regular Friday night dinner," but, she acknowledges, her "father must have worked on Saturday—had the [shoe] store open." Only when her family relocated to the more urban setting of Springfield, Massachusetts, did it become possible for May Schell's family to observe Shabbat without interruption. In Springfield, she says, "it was different because . . . we were surrounded by Jews."

Other Jewish holidays—Rosh Hashanah and Yom Kippur, in particular—were occasions for a less divided celebration. Families who attended synagogues would travel back and forth from shul to home; if they lived close enough by, they could also observe the traditional stricture against any means of travel besides walking. Even a family who almost never attended a synagogue, like the Pyensons of Otis, Massachusetts, took time out to observe important Jewish holidays and were sure to excuse their children from school. Maxwell Pyenson remembers that in his growing up, "we observed the holidays." His mother and father, both of whom were versed in the Orthodoxy and *yiddishkeit* of the day, knew enough to carry on old practices.

In the current day, as all residents of the region lead much more divergent lives and as individual choices abound, Jews who wish to can and do observe the Sabbath without encountering the same diversions that once made such observance a practical impossibility. While such observance may still be largely invisible to anyone else in the surrounding community, it nonetheless assures a greater degree of deliberate Judaic practice than was ever possible in earlier days. Current-day Jewish residents of the region live in a context in which individual or familial choice is perhaps the primary operative factor. Because synagogue communities are open to diverse perspectives and approaches to the practice of Judaism, the overall atmosphere tends not only to allow for but to encourage a revival in spirituality. As tradition-bearers point out, for instance, a casual atmosphere predominates in many instances. On Shabbat and on high holidays, as Joe Kurland describes it, one is assured of being able to participate in uninhibited practice.

> I grew up feeling that I was perhaps one of the less knowledgeable people about Jewish studies, Jewish learning—Torah, synagogue skills. When I came here, I felt like "Uh oh, I'm one of the more knowledgeable people." And I think that it sort of propelled me into doing more, and more, and more, because I sort of missed a lot of the things that I grew up with and felt that if I want to have them I have to do them, and that includes singing; you know, being a prayer leader singing in the synagogue. I just really missed the sounds that I heard as a kid, and if I wanted to hear that particular type of sound, I had to provide it.

In Bethlehem, New Hampshire, Lee Bagdon describes a similar spirit of openness and inclusion. Compared to the urban synagogues that she had grown up in, she finds that the small-town temple is

> much less formal. The first thing that you would see if you came here on a Shabbat is that the people are dressed in everything to what they might have worn in a New York synagogue to people who just came in from a hike and came in and sat down. We don't care, and we tell people we don't care. The first time that happened—the couple had come in on the way home from a hike—they sort of peeked in. They wanted to see the synagogue, they were new in the area, and I told them to come in and sit down. It was Yom Kippur. I told them to come in and sit down, and they said, "Oh, you mean we can come in dressed like this?" I said, "You bet! You certainly can. Come in."

Jewish ritual, at once rendered less formal and more fully integrated into ordinary life, seems widely incorporated into the lives of present-day small-town New England Jews. Suzie Laskin, who lives at a considerable distance from any synagogue, nonetheless makes the trip whenever she can to temples in Bethlehem or Dover, New Hampshire, or to Portland, Maine. Her own Jewish community is the *havurah* she started in the White Mountain Region. "When I go to shul now, it feels good," she says. "When I hear Hebrew, it feels good. It just brings me back to my roots." Even the journey to the synagogue fits into this scheme. Laskin and her husband and friends occasionally go to Bethlehem, an hour and a half from their home on circuitous mountain roads. "We'll go up there a couple of times a year for the high holidays," she says, "and it's a beautiful drive through the mountains, especially in the fall, and that feels sort of exciting or it's sort of the journey of getting from here to the shul as sort of part of the experience because it's such a long, beautiful journey to get there." Laskin's is clearly an adaptive practice—a Shabbat ritual born of rural removal and automobile transport. Where in the Orthodox practice of her predecessors (and some more urban contemporaries) walking to shul is the only proper means of getting there, she has learned to incorporate the lengthy trip over the mountains into her experience of the day's holiness. Of course, automobile transport to shul on Shabbat and high holidays has long been a mainstay of life in most American Jewish communities, going back to the post–World War II period of Jewish settlement in suburbia.[5]

Sabbath-keeping in a contemporary rural context may occasionally be complicated in ways that practically minded first-generation Jewish settlers would not have anticipated. Like the Jews who peddled or sold from their retail stores on Saturdays because they could not afford to forgo the biggest shopping day of the week, the earlier Jewish farmers in the region would most likely not have considered not performing necessary chores on Shabbat. At least one group of their current-day counterparts, however, has devoted serious consideration to the question of whether or not it is acceptable to milk dairy goats on Shabbat. During the summer of 2004, the farming interns at Adamah, the Jewish organic farm in Falls Village, Connecticut, engaged in a lengthy debate on the subject. Although the outcome of the debate was a somewhat uneasy decision that, *halachah* or no *halachah*, the goats *had* to be milked, the discussion itself, according to Jacob Fine, was conducive to an overall consideration on the part of the interns of what it means to be a Jewish farmer.

Granted, this sort of debate over the Shabbat-related implications of farm work is not likely to affect Jewish ritual behavior in more than an instance or two. Jews growing up in the country today are also increasingly likely, however, to encounter Jewish ritual in places other than the temple setting—in the outdoors, for instance. Jacob Fine, whose father was a professor of Jewish studies at a sequence of small New England colleges while he was growing up, recalls having attended holiday celebrations in a unique setting. "We went to Middlebury[, Vermont] a couple of years," says Fine. "I think there must have been some *havurah* that got together with the university community for the *chagim*. And there was some family that was active that had a farm, and a bunch of land and they would get together for meals or celebrations over the *chagim* at this farm, and a lot of this seemed very sweet. I have images of everyone kind of standing in a big circle towards sunset, singing or sharing, and it was very beautiful." Many of the Jewish families living in rural New England today are there specifically because they desire a more full-fledged connection to place, an experience of Judaism away from the synagogue and surrounded instead by the holiness of the natural world. Ritual is often enhanced, at least as several current-day rural New England Jews describe it, by the splendors of the land.

Bob Rottenberg speaks to this idea and expresses his affinity for a Jewish ritual practice liberated from the walls of a temple, "especially inside a building that was not receptive, or an institution that was not receptive to fresh air. Which kind of brings us back to the whole of Judaism as a place-based religion. What I started—it started becoming clearer and clearer to me as I was here and as I was living in a very rural setting—that Judaism started coming alive." For some Jews, the natural environment takes on a special spiritual significance and invites its own variety of ritual. Rabbi Howard Cohen uses an outdoor setting as a starting point for a deeper attention both to his own and his congregants' spiritual growth. Before studying for the rabbinate, Cohen was an outdoor educator. In recent years, he developed a program called Burning Bush Adventures, which combines Jewish ritual practice with environmental awareness—"Judaism in an outdoor context," as Cohen puts it.

Just that alone sets it up as a Jewish experience. The fact then that they're being led by someone who is also a rabbi is another level of affirmation that these things aren't alien. And so those are just two levels of barrier breaking. And then when we're out there, depending on the group that I'm out with, we might do things as structured as have different people lead davening, either traditionally or in some creative way, but just the regular worshiping service. We study; we'll study text in an informal way. I'll put out text and depending on . . . when we do the winter, we do the dogsled trip, we study text related to Jewish views on treatment of animals. We study text on sacred place—what makes a place sacred? Does it have to be a certain place? What's sacred time? So one has this experience, like, "This is like wow, this is such a wonderful, special place," and so we'll ask, "What makes it special?" And we'll ask from a Jewish point of view, and this text says this, this text says that—things like that; the conversations, the dialogues, the discussions that emerge, the comparisons and contrasting with home life.

That Judaic practice can be enhanced by access to the natural environment is hardly an innovation of rural New England Jews. Jewish residents of the region may, however, be more obviously disposed to share in such a view, having made the deliberate choice to forgo more densely populated Jewish centers in favor of the countryside.

Current-day rural New England Jews may at times go out of their way to seek worship opportunities outdoors. From the individual blessing offered in thanks for the sight of a single beautiful natural object to self-consciously outdoor Jewish adventures, the role that may once have been fulfilled by formalized, indoor practice can now be filled elsewhere. Joe Kurland of Colrain, Massachusetts, mentions a blessing that comes to mind for him as he steps out his front door, which overlooks the Cold River on its way to join the Deerfield. As Kurland puts it, "There are blessings that are traditionally said when you see a beautiful object—a beautiful thing in nature, and even though I don't know the particular traditional blessing, I just feel like to go outside and look at the mist rising off the hills is a blessing. And to go up the hills and see the first leaves coming out, it's a blessing. It's a thing that is just . . . you just focus on that and, you know, just take in the spiritual nature of being in this spot at this time." David Arfa of Shelburne Falls, Massachusetts, cites an early experience from his growing up in Michigan as a source for his present-day observance of one Shabbat principle. He tells the story of how his rabbi instructed him in a new way to walk outdoors. "When I would go to his home for Shabbat," Arfa says, "I noticed he went to the end of the sidewalk and then he turned, he didn't cut across the grass, on Shabbat I remember asking him—because it was shorter just to cut across the grass—and he would say, 'David Arfa, on Shabbat we don't destroy anything and even the grass, walking on the grass.'" This Shabbat practice is supplemented for Arfa by another sort of walking meditation—in this case, one that is particularly appropriate to his adoptive home in the New England hills. Such practice involves him in

> thinking of different Jewish blessings . . . as I'm walking, just discovering the seasons changing around me. Of seeing, you know, if it's late winter as the snow melts I see birds building nests. I see insects coming out, the first mosquitoes of the year are all kind of ways—I mean it's just a really small way for me of marking that. Of birds coming or as they leave for the winter, they go back up north for the winter, when they come back for the fall, at different markers. The maple time, the maple sap, and having it so throughout the year. . . .

The ritualization of ordinary practice, which renders otherwise unnoteworthy daily activities as significant from a Jewish perspective, may very well distinguish the current generation of rural New England Jews from its predecessors. In such a context, Judaism has become inseparable from one's habitation of the natural world, and all of New England becomes, in this respect, a sacred place.

For Shmuel Simenowitz, the outdoor life occasions more than inspiring vistas or even contact with the sacredness of the natural world. From an experiential point of view, outdoor activity—especially in an agricultural context—revives a generations-old Jewish connection to the world of forest and field. Simenowitz, an Orthodox Jew, has undertaken to reacquaint his largely urban-based Orthodox brethren with the outdoors. Many Hasidim are, in Simenowitz's words, "crowded, stacked up a mile high over Newark and Williamsburg and Brooklyn. But the [outdoors] is really in their DNA."

> They sit around every Shabbos and every night telling stories about the Baal Shem Tov taking a wagon ride through the forest and going by wagonloads to see their Rebbe. And they very much appreciate what we're doing. Whenever we have a chance and we have some

bochurim come up to the farm, and we'll take a wagonload of them and *fabreng*. They walk away absolutely transformed, because it's in their DNA as Hasidim and it just kind of lays in there inchoate. And we get to actually animate a part of their lives that's been there and never really been inflated before. So you get some guy who's going to go out and become a *shliach* somewhere and tell the story about a Baal Shem Tov traveling in a wagon and he'll spend an afternoon with us and we'll go through the woods in a wagon bouncing and telling stories and everything. And when he goes out and tells that story, he's not just telling it from his mind, he's telling it from the essence of his being because now he feels the bumps of the road and everything else about the story in a very different way.

Enacting this sort of adult education for urban Jews is Simenowitz's way not simply of legitimizing his own agricultural existence but of imparting long-lost rural values to a constituency that, in his view, has lost its vital connection to a physical spirituality that once lay at the heart of its dearest teachings.

In the early days of Jewish settlement, as well as in the current period, a given family's commitment to perpetuating a Jewish future—its willingness to arrange for its children's Hebrew school education—was a factor of equal importance to that of upholding ritual. In the days before World War II, Hebrew school was an option open only to young men and offered training toward the bar mitzvah. Often enough, going to Hebrew school actually meant pursuing a tutorial with a rabbi. As Jewish communities grew in size, Hebrew school evolved into more of an institution, open to boys and girls and operated as an adjunct to an already existing synagogue congregation. Hebrew schools in small-town New England today extend their operations to students both younger and older than the bar or bat mitzvah age. Their primary function as a medium for moving young people toward the ceremony marking their official adult entrance into the synagogue community ensures the longevity of this ritual marking an important entry point into the Jewish life-cycle.

Jack August attended a traditional *cheder* in his hometown of Northampton. The "school"—it was taught by one man—provided a grounding in all aspects of Jewish ritual.

We went to *cheder*. . . . We learned to read Hebrew. We learned how to daven. . . . We used to read the Bible. We read Genesis. Translated it into Yiddish. So, this is where I learned a lot of things. I learned a lot of things. We didn't have a teacher. So they finally got a teacher. A teacher came to Northampton who was called a Rebbe. Not a Rabbi, but a Rebbe. A teacher. He used to have classes after school every day. Different groups of kids would come in and we'd sit, he would teach them how to read and how to write and how to translate and how to pray. And this was part of the curriculum. The rabbi, for those who couldn't come to the *cheder*, I'd say $1.50 a week and he would come to your house. He would teach the kids at home. His total income couldn't have been more than $15.00 a week. A man with three or four kids of his own would have to scrimp and do without a lot of things.

In a small-town New England context, especially in the early days of settlement, the very existence of such a school was a marker of a deep commitment to Jewish practice.

Milt Adelman, who grew up in remotest northern Maine, was able to build and maintain his sense of connection to Judaism, as well as his Jewish identity, by means of his early participation in Jewish education. On high holidays, Adelman's family traveled to nearby Woodstock, New Brunswick, "outside of Houlton[, Maine] . . . about 50 miles from where we lived." "They had enough Jews there at that time that they had a rabbi," Adelman says. Hebrew school education, on the other hand, could only be arranged by other means. The rabbi's name was A. B. Mag, and Hiram Adelman took advantage of his versatility. Adelman recalls: "My folks wanted me to be bar mitzvahed, so the only way that A. B. could get from Woodstock to Mars Hill was by train, and he used to come over once a month or once a week." Adelman's older brother had had a partial Jewish education, but did not complete the course of study. "They shipped him to Bangor to study," Adelman says, ". . . [but] he never was bar mitzvahed and he came back." Milt Adelman's more positive experience proved to be a catalyst for the building of Aroostook County's Jewish community. "At my bar mitzvah, they decided that they ought to get together as a group and do some more," Adelman says. "So from that bar mitzvah, they formed the Aroostook Hebrew Communities. Our shul was called the Aroostook Hebrew Community Center. But it's really a shul. We used to be a center. That way people got together for social. Then we formed the B'nai Brith organization, Number 1289." Natalie Cohen was a beneficiary of this community, even though she lived on the Canadian side of the border. "We had a big Jewish community in Aroostook County," she says, "so they decided we'd have a Sunday school. So Sundays we would get in the car with our Sunday school books and our regular school books. We would go to Sunday school and then we would go back to Caribou, Maine, which was 12 miles from Presque Isle." At the early pioneering stage, Jewish education was conducted for the most part at home or at some remote site outside the immediate community. Steve Steinberg, whose grandparents settled in Whitefield, New Hampshire, recalls that his two great-uncles "did not live in Whitefield in the winter, but were parceled out to relatives in Portland or Boston where they could receive a religious education to prepare them for bar mitzvah." Gertrude Crockett Shapiro, a resident of Stonington, Maine, tells how her family made a similar choice. "I have two much younger brothers," she says. "When they were old enough to study for their bar mitzvah, my parents decided that that my mother would move the family to Boston, where they could study Hebrew and get ready . . . [while] my father stayed in Stonington to run the business."[6] Assembling a minyan for synagogue worship posed enough of a challenge in and of itself that early rural New England Jews knew better than to try to build Hebrew schools too early.

Sonny Chertok's experience matches that of Milt Adelman. He would go to a public hall that had been hired for purposes of Jewish education. "After school we had a *cheder* at 4:00, 5:00, or something like that where he prepared the boys and taught and the boys and girls Hebrew. Some took to it, some of us kind of goofed off wherever we could. But that was the attempt of the community to instill Judaism in their children. And when I got to be 12 years old, Mr. Cohen used to come over the house every day, and I'd have to study to get ready for my bar mitzvah. I had it in August of 1927." Pal Borofsky of Brattleboro, Vermont, shipped out to nearby Keene, New Hampshire, for his Jewish education. In Turners Falls, Massachusetts, where Phyllis Nahman grew up, the pressures of work and school, coupled with the relative isolation of small-town life, precluded her brothers, the Rubin boys, from following through with their Jewish education. Indeed, only in the postwar period, when an increasing number of synagogues were able to build Hebrew school programs into their activities, did large numbers of rural New England Jews begin to undergo bar or bat mitzvah ceremonies.

Rabbi Max Wall of Burlington, Vermont—the same rabbi who helped to eliminate separate seating for women and men from the Burlington synagogue—also had a hand in creating that congregation's first religious school. "I started complaining about the size of the synagogue because the *talmud torah* was in a separate building, and I ran the *talmud torah*. We had one teacher and I the first summer I came for official duty in August, so he and I went literally from Jewish home to Jewish home and registered about 90, 95 percent of all the Jewish kids who were available." Developments such as this one were not only healthy expressions of Jewishness in their own time. They all but guaranteed the longevity of Jews in rural New England and enabled a miniscule population to maintain both its presence and visibility.

Yet the growing strength of Hebrew schools—their accessibility to both boys and girls and their existence as adjuncts to synagogues throughout the region—could hardly in and of itself guarantee the long-term viability of Jewish communities. Members of the second generation of rural New England Jews were just as likely to leave their small-town homes upon reaching adulthood with or without a Jewish education. Rather, Hebrew school programs in the area grew over the years not so much by educating the children and grandchildren of the first settlers as by filling the needs of newer arrivals. As more Jewish families began arriving in the area in the 1970s, existing Hebrew schools, like the synagogues that had established them, experienced a revival.

"When people have children," observes Julie Chamay of Pownal, Vermont, "it sort of calls into question how [they] want to address child-rearing and religious training." Current-day Hebrew schools appeal to this need within an increasingly assimilated and often intermarried Jewish community. Almost as if to underscore the relative ease with which Jewish families can now blend in and disappear, Shana Tinkle talks about how her Hebrew school training distances her and her more strongly Jewish-identified friends from their classmates. In public school, she says, "I'm the only Jewish kid in my class. I remember a couple of other kids were half-Jewish or sort of Jewish but don't practice, and then one or two other Jewish kids who I also know through my synagogue and Hebrew School."

Michael Docter, who describes his own Judaism as entirely cultural, none-theless feels the need to expose his own son growing up in Hadley, Mas-sachusetts, to a Jewish education. "It didn't have much to do with me," he indicates, calling attention to his own secularism. "My son's devout," he says, owing in large part to the foundation of his Hebrew school training at the Jewish Community of Amherst.

In a contemporary context, one makes Jewish *choices*, especially in a rural area where Jewishness is all but invisible. Beth Weissman, a resident of Colrain, Massachusetts, describes how her son Cale decided to pursue a Jewish education. Her own upbringing, as well as that of her husband, was more or less secular. But as her sisters-in-law became more observant and her own children began to attend bar and bat mitzvahs, their interest was piqued. Often enough, the Hebrew school education of a child proves to be the impulse for an adult's reacquaintance with Judaism. Again, in the context of small-town New England life, one has to go out of one's way in order to practice Judaism. Lacking the familial pressure that would, dur-ing the earlier generations of Jewish settlement in the area, have supplied a sufficient impulse to even the most isolated rural families to make sure that a Jewish education was in the offing, rural Jews in the current genera-tion might find it just as easy to forgo Hebrew school entirely. On the other hand, in the culturally tolerant atmosphere of rural New England, men and women who have the luxury of choosing to pursue their own belated Jew-ish education may find it increasingly easy to do so. Shana Tinkle speaks of how her mother, who was raised in a relatively nonobservant household, chose to attend a program for adults. Steve Pyenson, whose grandparents first settled as farmers in Otis, Massachusetts, in 1904, grew up celebrating Jewish holidays at home but not attending a synagogue, let alone a Hebrew school; for a farm family, the distance to the nearest shul was too great. However, with his own children now grown and his family's farm business well enough established in the area, he has of late decided to attend adult Hebrew classes. He explains how his relative lack of exposure to Jewish custom, over time, led to his recent decision. As a child, he says,

we always celebrated Hanukkah, but we celebrated Christmas too. I don't know why, but we did. My grandfather could read Hebrew and of course they would talk in Yiddish, you know, or whatever it was—you could make out some of the words. It just wasn't a factor. I remember my cousins being bar mitzvah and bas mitzvahed . . . and at the time it might of bothered me. It bothered me to the extent that I wanted to take the Hebrew lessons finally after I'm 61 years old. I have recently been asked many times to do *aliyahs* at nephews' bar mitzvahs and I have grandchildren that will be bas mitzvahed and I just want to be able to do it and I can't do it so I want to be able to do it, so that's why . . . I'm taking the lessons now. I don't know, it just became a little more important than it was when I was growing up.

The legacy of Hebrew school education, like the evolution within the region of synagogue affiliation, illustrates the general trajectory of Jewish life in the area. Where Jews once knew only orthodoxy and limited Jewish education toward the bar mitzvah, current conditions emphasize openness and choice.

Jewish weddings and marriages, too, have undergone an analogous sea change. In the Orthodox days, even in the remotest sections of rural New England, Jewish weddings were strictly Jewish affairs. Like the bar mitzvah, courtship and marriage—at both formal and informal levels—were means of assuring the growth of the Jewish community. The first generations of small-town New England Jewish families recount both the courtship and wedding as integral aspects of their having been able to maintain a firm Jewish identity in the relative isolation of rural life. Some parents required or strongly encouraged their children to date only Jews; others—recognizing how extremely difficult such a requirement was in such isolated circumstances—looked the other way as their children courted outside the Jewish fold.

Lillian Glickman explains that her parents cared very little about whether her school friends were Jewish or not in their hometown of North Adams, Massachusetts. "Except," she says, "when it came to a dance, you know, and actually dating. It was very important to my parents that I date a Jewish boy. So that when it came to the . . . prom, I had to import a boy from Pittsfield. My first date was the junior prom, because I was the chairman of the prom, and so I had to have a date, and so I got a very nice boy my brother knew from Pittsfield." Eva August, who grew up in Holyoke, Massachusetts, recalls the Saturday night dances held at the YMHA for Jewish youngsters. A friend of hers had told her about "the nice boy from Northampton" who was interested in her.

I said, "That shrimp?" We were fifteen years old at the time. I says, "Not me. Noo! He doesn't even know how to dance good and I always dance with tall boys." So all of a sudden he walks over . . . to the boy I was with. He knew him. He says, "Dave, do you mind if I dance with your lady friend?" Dave looks at me . . . I didn't want to tell him yes. He says, "Yeah, go ahead. You can dance with her." Well, do you know I didn't go home with the other one. I went home with him. We were married at 19.

Such communal structures for courtship and marriage existed, presumably, to keep young Jews from being tempted out of the fold. For her part, Eva August was eager to follow along with convention in order to avoid traumatizing her family. She tells a story about why she adhered to the traditional path. "See, the way I married him was I was going with another fellow and he was bugging me to elope."

I says, one thing I wouldn't do to hurt my people, my father and mother, was to elope. My oldest sister was going with a fellow who came from Tumsk, Russia. Siberia. He couldn't speak Yiddish. He just spoke Russian. My father and mother felt he wasn't Jewish. He told them his grandfather was a rabbi, but because he couldn't understand Yiddish, they didn't think he was Jewish. So he asked my father to marry her. . . . My father—"Never!" he says. "I'll kill you first before you marry my daughter! You're not a Jew." He says, "If you don't let me marry your daughter, I'll elope with her." My mother started screaming and crying. So when I saw that little experience, when this fellow asked me to elope, I says, "Harry, never will I hurt my people to elope."

Well, I was in a quandary. He bothered me and that one bothered me, so my chum, this girl said to me, "There's a colored woman outside of Holyoke that tells fortunes." I never believe in that. She said, "Why don't you go and see her? It's a nice experience" . . . so I went up to this woman. I opened the door. I just opened the door and she says to me, "Your name begins with an E." My name is Eva. I looked at her. I said to myself, "How the devil does she know?" I says, "Yes." She says, "Come in, come in. Sit down" So she takes my hand and is reading it. She says, "You're in a quandary." She says, "Two men, two fellows are after you." She says, "You're going to marry a man whose father has a barn." He was a cattle dealer. His father was a cattle dealer. "You're going to be very well to do and you're going to have five children." Which I did.

Notwithstanding the pivotal involvement in this courtship tale of the fortune-teller, Eva August's story suggests the importance in her mind of minimizing her parents' fears of their daughter leaving the fold. She was fortunate, of course, to have had two (Jewish) pursuers in the first place. Whoever she was or whatever her sources of foreknowledge, the fortune-teller told Eva August exactly what she needed to hear.

Often enough, even Jewish youngsters who succeeded in marrying other Jews could only do so by looking beyond the immediate community. Lena Sandler, who grew up in New York City, met her husband when she and her family went up to the Jewish colony in Sandisfield, Massachusetts, to spend summer vacations. Jack Sandler, also a New York City native, had moved to the country in order to farm. Lena tells the story of their courtship. "He never had a very good car," she says, "and he had a broken window and somehow my mother's hand got caught on it, and she said, 'You know, you could never tell, but the bloods could combine.' And somehow, I don't know, it just happened, and I married my husband a short time after I came here." Ruben Tablitz, another one of the Sandisfield settlers, married a woman whose family had also recently moved from New York City. He was introduced to her by a business connection.

Well, I happened to help out a man in the public market on a Sunday. And a fellow comes over to me and introduces himself. He says to me in Jewish, "Are you still single?" We used to talk under the nose. I say, "Yes."

"I got for you a wife. Something nice—very nice woman." Well, I made up with him a date. And I'll never forget when I took the train to Great Barrington. Most of them used to do their business through Great Barrington, not Connecticut, over there. And little by little, corresponding, I got married. . . . It was moonlight outside. With lamps. I'll never forget.

In nearby Otis, Massachusetts, farmer Maxwell Pyenson met his wife while he was away at summer camp. He continued to court her by making frequent excursions to New York in his capacity as an agricultural extension agent. Before she came to live permanently on a farm in the Berkshires, Mrs. Pyenson had been a resident of Brooklyn.

Surely, the likelihood of a Jewish girl or boy finding a Jewish mate in her or his own small town was quite small. Traveling more widely—to Pittsfield from North Adams, for instance—was a more likely means of making a fitting acquaintance. Alternatively, one might find a mate in another community through family connections. Folklorist Carolyn Lipson-Walker describes a similar region-wide phenomenon among the Jews of the South, where long-distance courtships have typically occurred as a result of summer camps, college fraternities, and kinship ties that unite Jews living throughout the states of the former Confederacy.[7] Small-town New England Jewish families who have kin in other small New England towns or in adjacent cities, for that matter, lend substance to such a parallel. They also constitute direct evidence of the existence of a Jewish cultural life specific to rural New England.

Within the oral tradition of rural New England Jews there seems to be an equal measure of recollection that speaks to the inordinate strain that the dating dilemma might have brought. Amy Jo Montgomery talks about how her mother had tried to encourage her to find a Jewish mate even though her family lived in tiny Bennington, Vermont. "She sort of gave up on me," Montgomery says,

> even though she would have preferred for me to be with someone Jewish. [But] looking at who was in my surroundings in Bennington and I had no romantic interest in any of the three or four boys that were in my class. I think she sort of gave up on that and said it would be fine if you married outside of your religion as long as, you know, you were in love and he was a respectable person. But I think she gave up. . . . But, she kind of relented after awhile. She really realized that it wasn't going to happen here.

I asked Amy Jo Montgomery if the handful of other Jewish families that she knew in her southern Vermont community assumed a similar attitude. Speaking in collective terms, she explains the gradual process by which parents' attitudes on courtship and marriage softened. "We were always pushed towards marrying the Jewish men or women. But, you know, when you go away to college and sort of break out of that and decide if you want to be in love with someone else. Some of the families accepted it and some of them probably never did. You know, some of the Catholic girls went out with the Jewish boys. I don't know if that was really kosher, as they say. So it was a problem, but I think my mother was a little bit more liberal." In the end, Montgomery met and married a local Bennington boy, someone with whom she had gone to high school. Although he did not convert to Judaism, Bob Montgomery is quite active in the Bennington synagogue.

Pal Borofsky, who grew up in Brattleboro, Vermont, remembers having experienced a similar lassitude on the part of his parents. He himself had had a bar mitzvah, but neither his father nor his mother were strict in their observance. Sam Borofsky, who had first settled in Brattleboro immediately after World War I and had established an Army and Navy store there, wasn't, according to his son, "a religious person."

> He wasn't educated as far as the religion was concerned. In other words, he was not an authority. He didn't really understand an awful lot. I don't believe he read Jewish; he read Hebrew very well but certainly there were instances where there were problems but my mother never pressured me to marry a Jewish person. As a matter of fact, when I started going out with my wife now, who wasn't Jewish, I said to my mother, "I'm going to start going out with this girl . . . she's not Jewish." And my mother said, "Don't let that bother you." So at that particular point, my mother was not concerned about it and my father never passed any judgment in that way.

Mrs. Borofsky converted to Judaism, and the Borofsky sons were raised, accordingly, in a Jewish household. From the point of view of a parent, Irene Moskowitz recounts the attitude she assumed with her children. "Both of my sons married non-Jewish girls," Moskowitz begins. "My younger son married a non-Jewish girl from Atlanta. But all [of the wives] were converted, years after they were married; they said that if their children were Jewish, *they* wanted to be Jewish. . . . We had this thing. My children could marry whoever they wanted; it was all right with me, as long as they were decent people." Like Amy Jo Montgomery, Pal Borofsky, and Irene Moskowitz's sons, Milt Adelman and his son Todd also found non-Jewish mates. During the interview I was conducting with them, Milt's wife, Gloria, had been sitting quietly. As they spoke of their family's having so successfully weathered three generations of an integrally Jewish experience in remotest Maine, Milt spoke of his wife's role in that achievement. "Things could have been different," he says. "She took conversion seriously. It wasn't just because she was marrying me. It probably was, but I mean, we realized the kids ought to have something to hang their hat on." Mrs. Adelman spoke of having grown up in the "next town over" in Aroostook County. "I get emotional," she says, as she contemplates the perseverance of the family, her six children, many more grandchildren and their collective rootedness in their ancestral soil of Aroostook County. For his own part, her son Todd grew up knowing how unlikely the prospect was of finding a Jewish mate in northern Maine. "My mom is not Jewish; she converted. My wife's not Jewish; she converted. . . . We were brought up that this isn't your future, and your wife is not in this community. It wasn't spoken, but when we dated people in high school . . . we were always kind of being trained or taught to look out, that there's something out there." Jews who wished to remain in places like Mars Hill, Maine, would have to make just these sorts of adjustments.

Intermarriage, once a relatively rare phenomenon even among rural New England Jews, has in recent years become much more common. Sumner Winebaum describes a ceremony that he witnessed recently. His son had married a woman named Dominique,

> and Nathan my grandson was born, then Dominique converted after he was born, and she did the mikveh and everything. [Nathan] then was about seven, six, the rabbi said to him, at the time, "Nathan, you know you're not Jewish. You're going to go to Hebrew School, if you want, but you have a choice when you're thirteen. You can choose to be Jewish or you don't have to." So he did and had the bar mitzvah, and the thing that was so great about it, and this is a real Portsmouth story, was in April, maybe in May. There's no mikveh in Portsmouth, we had gone to Portland and the rabbi said, "Well, we're going to go down to the beach at Newcastle. There's another young boy who's bar mitzvahed and converted and I have a young couple intermarrying and they're going to convert." So the three of them took their clothes off on the beach and they went into the unbelievable cold.

As Orthodoxy and its fairly standard rituals have become more or less a thing of the past among small-town New England Jews, a more improvised ceremony has become more common. Steve and Julie Chamay were married near their home in Pownal, Vermont. Ahead of time, Julie made it clear to her husband how important it was to her, as she put it, to have "a Jewish household." She explains: "I wanted our home to be Jewish and any children that we raised would be Jewish. So when we got married, we picked a minister to marry us; we didn't know any rabbis at the time, and we had a *klezmer* band at the wedding, which was a lot of fun and a *chuppah*, so it was sort of like, you know some restaurants aren't kosher but they were a kosher style; we had a Jewish style wedding and then gradually became more and more involved in the synagogue's community in Bennington." Often enough, intermarriage seems to be an occasion for a deepening of Jewish connection, a renewal of faith, and an expansion of the communal base.

Helene Meyerowitz, a resident of Maine who grew up in an Orthodox household in New York City, married a Micmac Indian. She jokingly refers to what she terms similarities between her background and that of her husband.

[I was] brought up with lox; he was brought up in a reserve in New Brunswick in northern Canada. They're on the Marmashee River, which is where the best salmon comes from. So he was raised on salmon—real salmon, and I was raised on lox—smoked salmon. He also was raised on salt herring; I was raised on pickled herring. One of his relatives or his grandmother's last name was C-a-p-l-a-n; they pronounced it Cape lin; my grandparents' name was Kaplan. And we just more and more talk about the similarities. My grandparents coming from Russia—that was a very cold environment, as is New Brunswick, and both being nomadic. My husband's name now is George and he left the reserve at 17 and has traveled the world. Once I got married, I guess I left the nest in the Bronx and became nomadic as well.

The couple was married, nonetheless, "in a Jewish ceremony":

We found a rabbi from Portland who would perform mixed marriage ceremonies. His name was Rabbi David Sandmel, and we were married right here in Rockland. We were married at the Samoset, which is one of the largest resorts in Maine, and they have a little chapel;

it's right off the golf course. My mother had made a bedspread that could be used as the *chuppah*, so we built the *chuppah*, and the rabbi came up, and, as I said, we had a Reformed ceremony. George being a recovering alcoholic, we did not partake in wine but we had white grape juice for the ceremony, which was neat. George wore a yarmulke and it was great.

The frequency of intermarriages among small-town New England Jews, in other words, isn't necessarily equivalent to the dissolution of Judaism as a vibrant religious tradition within the region. Now, as Massachusetts, Vermont, and Connecticut have instituted either gay marriage or its near equivalent, new rituals and a climate of still greater tolerance are taking shape. The rainbow flag that now hangs from the Bennington synagogue, as Amy Jo Montgomery explains, had been part of hers and her husband's ceremony. Earlier, when her sister "and her partner had a commitment ceremony . . . in New York City, they used the rainbow flag for their ceremony, so she wanted to pass it on to us." Intermarriage has also had a transformational effect on Jewish burial customs in the region. As Evelyn Slome describes it, her home synagogue in Portsmouth, New Hampshire, is "50 . . . or closer to 70 percent intermarried. There is now an addition," she says, "and I gather this is tradition, there is an addition to the cemetery for mixed burials. I think that has characterized in many ways the change."

Phyllis Nahman, who married a South African–born Jew when her parents sent her to Israel in the 1960s for the express purpose of having her find a Jewish mate, speaks at length to the evolving contexts within which small-town Jews, from her grandparents' generation to that of her own grandchildren have worked to raise Jewish children in relative isolation. "It's interesting to see how that has come down over the generations," she says. "So who knows where it will go? But it's interesting to see with the changes in religious life—in Jewish life—in this country, and what the possibilities are. There's been a lot of loosening up. We have moved, certainly in my lifetime, from the Turners Falls shul that was Orthodox, and everything about it was Orthodox, to the Greenfield synagogue, which now has an interfaith cemetery and welcomes interfaith families and just sees the richness of that. So times have changed." In general, that rural New England Jews have been so long surrounded by non-Jews has hardly meant that their Judaism has been in jeopardy. Direct exposure—which today takes the form of interfaith dialogue and collaboration—only seems to increase both Jewish visibility and viability within the region.

"We're Not Afraid to Go to Each Other's Houses of Worship": Interfaith Encounters

Early specifically religious encounters between Jews and non-Jews were likely to have been more or less haphazard—accidents of proximity rather than deliberate attempts at sharing traditions. Sonny Chertok and Jack August mention the tendency of some of the old Yankees in their respective communities to seek out the biblical expertise of that town's earliest Jewish settler (see chapter 3). More often than not, an interreligious encounter would occur as a result of people's social and economic lives being closely intertwined. Phyllis Nahman, for instance, recalls a time when she accompanied a Catholic friend of hers to Midnight Mass. Her parents were not pleased at the prospect but, as she indicates, they did permit her to go.

> It was a very big deal for doing this at night. And the priest was talking about Jews killing Christ, and it was a small town; everybody knew everybody else. And here was this Jew sitting up front with her friend, not knowing whether I was supposed to kneel when they knelt or stand up or what and feeling very self-conscious and a little scared, and when I heard that I was *really* scared. But things have changed; we're not afraid to go to each other's houses of worship, people go back and forth regularly, and there's an interfaith council.

Deliberate ventures to bring Jews and Christians into religious dialogue are quite common now, and many towns have existing institutions to allow for such endeavors. Whether interfaith dialogue is intended to bring about actual collaboration or merely mutual recognition, that the councils exist in the first place is an indication that Jews and non-Jews have, in some capacity, stopped seeing each other as threats and acknowledged each other's integral role in the cultural life of the region.

In the earlier days of Jewish settlement, the absence of deliberate ventures hardly prevented dialogue or encounter. Louis Plotkin tells a humorous story about how in his town of Orange, Massachusetts, mutual appreciation came about between himself and a local Catholic priest, Father McCormick. Plotkin, who had by this time attained status as a sort of town father, had tried to draft McCormick, the newcomer in town, into the local Kiwanis Club. McCormick declined, explaining that Kiwanis night conflicted with a Christian doctrine class that he taught regularly. On the one occasion on which he was available to make a guest appearance at the club, Plotkin was away on business in Boston. "Two or three weeks after he [McCormick] had spoken," Plotkin explains,

> He meets me on the street and he says, "Huh! Fine guy you are. You turned out to be a real friend of mine. You knew I wasn't a good speaker. You never did want to hear me speak. What did you do? You deliberately found an excuse to run away to Boston so you wouldn't have to listen to me speak." I started to answer him, and he says, "Wait a minute. Under the circumstances, I don't blame you. Let me tell you what happened. Several weeks ago I was having my Christian doctrine class. One of the questions that I asked them was, 'Who is the father of the Jewish people?' This kid raises his hand and he wants to be absolutely sure that he gets attention and that nobody else is going to answer that question. He says, 'Father, I know.'
>
> " 'All right, sonny, who is the father of the Jewish people?' He says, 'Louis Plotkin.' " He says, "Anybody that is the father of the Jewish people does not have to listen to Father McCormick speak." It's one of my favorite stories which is true.

In the days before Father McCormick's tenure, a Father Healy had been the leader of the Catholic church. Healy, as Plotkin recalls, was not only present for the ceremony, but actually laid the cornerstone for the synagogue's new building.

In Northampton, Massachusetts, the grand opening of a new synagogue building in the 1950s witnessed another large-scale community event. The congregants, according to Jack August, expected between 1,500 and 2,000 visitors and prepared refreshments for that number. Ultimately, 4,000 townspeople showed up, including "every member of the clergies in [the] area." In North Adams, Massachusetts, Eugene Wein recalls the halcyon days of the athletic "inter-religious church league, at the old YMCA," when mutual exposure came about as a result of sportsmanlike competition. "We had a team," he says, referring to the town's synagogue.

And St. Francis Church, St. Anthony Church, [the] Baptist church, Congo church. It was a friendly competition. We all got along well. At the end of every year we would have an end-of-the-year banquet. We rotated among the different churches. And one year we got it at the synagogue. . . . The women prepared a nice meal, [a] meat meal. But the kids wanted milk, and we told them that because we were a kosher kitchen we couldn't serve them milk, we had to give them soda instead. So they couldn't quite understand that. But outside of that it was a good feeling.

Such shows of good will notwithstanding, the oral tradition suggests that formal and intentionally spiritual channels for interfaith collaboration did not exist in small-town New England until well after the period of earliest Jewish settlement.

That an interfaith council exists today in northern Vermont is largely the result of the early efforts of Rabbi Max Wall who, in the 1960s, initiated an effort to bring visibility to his own congregation. "I started bring mostly church groups to the synagogue for tours," he says. Ultimately, Wall's involvement in interfaith dialogue took on a life of its own, in which more than mere sharing occurred. "Part of my service to this [Jewish] community," Wall explains, "was breaking into the larger community. Not giving up my Judaism but affirming it in public." The earliest stages of this process were hardly painless. "One day in 1964," begins Rabbi Wall, "I got a call from the secretary of the president of Saint Michael's College, which is a Catholic college."

He said, "The president wants to apologize to you for the churlish letter that was in the *Free Press* this morning about Jews." One of the faculty members was an anti-Semite and a vicious anti-Semite. So I said, "Well, why is the president apologizing? He didn't write the letter." He said, "Max, I'm trying to do something nice. Please don't give me a hard time." I said, "I mean it. If you don't like him, why don't you get rid of him?" He said, "Well, he's got tenure." And I said, "And anti-Semitism is not the college." So I said, "I have a suggestion for you. Since you're a Catholic school, you're not bound by the church-state problems, and you have lots of clergy who teach there, I would suggest you get at least another Jew who can speak a Jewish point of view if you can't shut him up. That would be fair.

And since you have so many clergy who are teaching there as professors, I would suggest the equivalent would be a rabbi, and I know just the rabbi."

Rabbi Wall was indeed invited as a lecturer before a student body of 38 nuns and 5 seminarians. When one nun asked for his help in choosing a research topic, he suggested "The Church and Anti-Semitism" and recommended some books to her. The nun returned three days later, her confidence in her church entirely shaken. "If any of this is ten percent true," she told Wall, "I don't know where I stand with my church." Wall continues:

So for the next three weeks, you find the interesting anomalous experience of a rabbi counseling a nun to keep her faith strong. In the middle of the semester, we had a confraternity of Christian doctors. They would bring in all teachers of religion from the parochial schools for a conference showing the latest educational materials since I was new on campus. So they asked me to bring materials from the talmud torah and Jewish education and so on. And I was introduced by a priest that was a very close friend of mine at the time, with whom I had become friends when I first came to town, Monsignor Fitzsimons. He gets up and he says as follows: He raises his hands and he says, "These hands have either been too often raised in shedding Jewish blood or have hung idly by our sides in no protest when it was being done. And therefore, I welcome this special opportunity to welcome Rabbi Wall and to welcome a new approach to the Jewish people and the Jewish religion." And introduced me. I gave my speech and I saw a nun, Sister Elizabeth, walking towards me. Did you ever see the motorboats clean the water, peel the water aside? She was peeling people aside with a beatific look on her face. She comes over to me finally and says, "Thank you for your speech." I said, "You look wonderful Sister, what happened?" She said, "Now that Monsignor has said it, I can write it!" She went on to get a doctorate at Brown in Judaic studies.

Wall is unapologetic as he represents his own qualifications as "an ordained expert" to help to translate Judaism in a Christian context. He went on to teach Hebrew for Episcopal clergy, "putting on seders in churches during the week of Easter because they got to realize matzoh and wafer as the

same thing." His overall view was that such experiences were transformational not only for Christians but, more important, from his own standpoint, for Jews themselves. "What I did was effectively change the attitude
of the Jewish people," he says. "They didn't behave as the old *shtetl* people.
They began to walk straight, upright, which was, of course, a remarkable
psychological thing."

Interfaith encounter and dialogue have only increased as rural New
England Jewish populations have grown as a result of the post–baby boom
influx of ex-urban and ex-suburban Jews. Tradition-bearers who describe
such endeavors will often emphasize both the frustrations of having to
explain Judaism to an ignorant gentile populace and, by the same token,
the rewards of successful exchange. Bob Rottenberg speaks to both sides
of the equation, but even his accounting of a certain arrogant ignorance
of the past on the part of some neighboring Christian clergy is couched in
somewhat equivocal terms. Like Rabbi Wall, he finds a considerable lack of
grounding in scripture as he discusses theology with his Christian counterparts. Nonetheless, an encounter that might have turned ugly, as he tells it,
offered an opportunity for unanticipated growth. I had asked him a general
question, in the interest of hearing a little bit about how his identity as a
Jew affects his sense of himself as a rural New Englander. "I'll tell you a
little story," he began.

I was with a group from the interfaith council several years
ago . . . the theme of the service was a Jubilee—the forgiveness of
debts—so we were all supposed to be looking for readings from our
scriptures to talk about forgiveness of debts. You know, it's simple.
And so this one Catholic priest came up with a reading, talking about
Jesus, when Jesus was a young man he showed up in the synagogue
and read a passage from Isaiah, and he said, "Today in your hearing,
this scripture is fulfilled." You know, they're all sitting around saying, "That's nice." And I said, "Pardon me; I don't get it." You know,
what's this got to do with forgiveness of debts? Well, it's in the scripture, they said. I said, "No, no; this is Jesus, talking about something
that hasn't happened yet." Clearly, it didn't happen. He says your
scripture is fulfilled, but what happened? I said, "Find me something
else. There must be something in your tradition that talks about
forgiveness of debts." So they all went scurrying, and they actually

found some stuff, but it was one of those moments when they could
have said, "Who the hell are you?" you know? "Get out of here; we
know what we're doing." And they needed somebody to sort of wake
them up, you know. "Hey, you may be the dominant religion around
here, but that doesn't mean that you can't pay attention to what
you're doing. Get real," you know? It said . . . to me that these people
were definitely interested. They were open to some input from the
outside world—from a Jew.

If a spirit of mutual recognition and respect exists between Jews and their
Christian neighbors, it is the idea of shared traditions that makes such a
thing possible. Small-town New England offers a workable context for
interfaith Thanksgiving services like the one that Bob Rottenberg was
part of.

Indeed, this spirit of interreligious kinship can extend beyond the
parameters of a single holiday. Joyce Selig describes how in her hometown
of Laconia, New Hampshire, a joint Thanksgiving service represents only
one aspect of a shared tradition. In Laconia, a geographically based kinship
exists as well. "We have a lot of interfaith services," she says.

We have a Thanksgiving service, and there's always a Jewish component to the interfaith services, so we have had the interfaith service
for Thanksgiving at the temple, and if it's not at the temple, we're
always part of wherever it is. And then I serve also on the spiritual
care committee at the hospital with the chaplain of the hospital and
the other religious leaders in town. If we had a rabbi here, it would
be the rabbi serving on that, but I take the place of being the rabbi
for that event. There's something called Sister Lakes. Lake Winnipe-
saukee has been made a sister lake with Lake Kinneret, and there's
been a back-and-forth dialogue, and some people have come to this
lake and done environmental studies on the lake. It was started by
somebody named Jim Braver. And they're about to have a respite
program and bring some victims of terrorism in Israel to the Lakes
Region, and the interfaith group is very interested. They want to be
part of that, and they want there to be at least a service that they
can be part of it. We'll come and welcome them, be involved with a
dialogue with the people who come. I think the community is very
open to the Jewish people.

More often than not, as Judaism is viewed by so many Christians as a "parent" religion, the connections between Jews and Christians follow this sort of teaching trajectory.

Rabbi Wall is not the only tradition-bearer I spoke with who represented the Passover seder as a hallmark occasion for Christian appreciation for Jewish ritual. Joyce and Bob Selig indicate that the Laconia synagogue has long welcomed Christians—among whom number Baptist ministers—who, as Bob Selig puts it, "knew the Hebrew at least as well as we do and know the order of the service"—to the temple for its "mock" seder (the meal is served as lunch). Bill and Mary Markle speak similarly of a seder that is held annually in their home community of Randolph, Vermont. "One time, " Bill Markle says, "I was asked if I would do a seder at a local church—United Church of Christ."

> They asked me if I would conduct a service as if I was doing it in my own home, and so I talked to our rabbi friend out in Illinois and he sent us a bunch of old Reform haggadahs. . . . It was really quite amazing. The thing sold out. They couldn't take any more reservations. First night seder—I did the first night seder, and so they turned around . . . 20 people away or something. So quick in a hurry, we arranged to do a second night seder. . . . We took over a local restaurant in town and did a seder in town for about 40 or 50 people and we invited the people who couldn't get into the one in town to be our guests. . . . They asked me if I would do others. I said, "Look, you all learn to do the one. I'm giving you the haggadahs; you figure out what to do with them." But the thing that amazed me about that seder was the emotional impact it seemed to have on the people who attended. There were people who were actually in tears.

As a window into the Last Supper, among many other Christian reference points, the seder offers a particularly poignant opportunity for mutuality, especially in the context of a centuries-old practice of increased anti-Semitism at Easter, which some of my tradition-bearers remember quite well and bitterly.

If a shared interest in ritual and scripture serves to bring Jews and Christians together in small-town New England, a mutual spirituality that may well exceed the bounds of tradition is a factor as well. Bob Rottenberg reflects on how both a sense of tradition and a growing affinity across faiths for spiritual growth have converged as a result, he says, of the area's tolerance. Jews who, on a certain level, are isolated as a result of their rural surroundings, find themselves able to survive, *as Jews*, because this sort of small-town environment and spiritual quest create a kinship of sorts between them and many of their non-Jewish neighbors. As an Orthodox Jew living in southern Vermont, Simenowitz indicates that his neighbors nonetheless have "great respect" for him.

> You know they're not Jewish but what we had in common, they're religious. They're *frum* Americans and *frum* Christians, and we're *frum* Jews. So they respect someone who puts their principles before their pocket. I play some guitar, and we had a neighbor's house burn down and they organized a benefit concert to raise money to help them rebuild, a community effort. And they asked me to headline the show. And you know, they called me up to say that the church choir was performing, would I be offended? I told them no, but it was nice that they called. They thought enough to ask, so I'd have to say there are more nice considerate things like that than anything. Has it been an idyllic, halcyon paradise? No, but people are decent, I have to say, by and large.

This spirit of openness both encourages cooperation among faiths and, importantly, instills a sense of increased Jewish purpose and identity. For Rottenberg, settling in rural New England and living a richly Jewish life there served almost as a substitute for his attending rabbinical school.

> What we find is that Jewish ritual and Jewish tradition is really very appealing to people of faith. Because they see something that they don't find in their own faiths. It's fascinating to see that. And yet, because we are few in number, and because of the geographical, logistical challenges of living in these small towns, it's not that easy to congregate in any kind of ongoing, meaningful way. So that's the challenge we face, and you find, around here, Jews who are very committed to living a Jewish life that is frequently not necessarily tied to synagogue life—to institutional life. And that's somewhat of a paradox, and somewhat of a challenge, to the organized part of Judaism. And it's an ongoing challenge.

The quest for a spiritual existence—some might view it as an infusion of "New Age" thinking into both Jewish and Christian theology—offers Jews a means of sustenance in an environment that lacks many of the conventional sources of strong Jewish identity.

David Arfa, a resident of Shelburne Falls, Massachusetts, is a member of a fledgling cohousing community of four mixed Jewish and Christian families. As the community was searching for common ground upon which to build not only its dwellings but its communal life, the spirit of Shabbat occurred to all of the members as an ideal vehicle for a shared ritual that would be neither Jewish nor Christian but well adapted to life in community and a small New England town. "Everyone [in the group] is comfortable with having Shabbat," he says. The future of Judaism in small-town New England, like much of its past, seems in large part to be in the hands of those who would embrace such opportunities for transformation, even if it means appearing to shed the seemingly reliable and stiff-necked approaches to retaining identity.

"If You Know What Shabbat Means, Give Us a Call": The Unifying Role of Yiddishkeit

If Jewishness were merely the expression of religious tradition untethered from folk practice, it is quite likely that all Jews besides the most Orthodox would long ago have been absorbed into the American, not to mention, rural New England mainstream. Indeed, in the golden age of Reform Judaism in the mid-nineteenth century, when educated and modernizing Jews from Germany and other western European countries began coming to America in large numbers, their expression of Judaism *did* in many cases follow an assimilationist tendency. Some Reform Jews opposed circumcision, and all deemphasized the use of Hebrew in liturgy. Religious incorporation in America could very easily tempt Jews to practice an invisible Judaism in which incidentals—the Saturday Sabbath, for instance—might exist as the only traces of Jewish difference. Jews did not, however, disappear, even in the relative isolation of rural areas. Instead, in part through their practice of an unmediated Judaism but also owing to a strong sense of Jewish ethnic, or folk, identity, they have persevered as a visible, if numerically small presence in such places. The vibrancy of Jewish folk practice—some of which might fall under the heading of *Yiddishkeit*—has in many ways represented the least susceptible strand in Jewish identity. Jews have differed historically in their religious practices and beliefs. Even as the spectrum of self-identified Jews has included the most Orthodox and those who profess to be atheist, a sense of Jewish identity retains strength on a cultural level. Owing in part to the power of *Yiddishkeit* to define Jewish identity and in part to a tendency among non-Jews—especially in the early days of settlement—to notice and set Jews apart from the mainstream, small-town New England has proved to be a place where Jewishness far exceeds the bounds of religious practice.

When Jews first came to rural New England at the turn of the century, many of them spoke Yiddish, and the maintenance of that mother tongue, though its actual use was nearly always restricted to first-generation immigrants who had not learned English fully, served—and to a lesser degree continues to enforce—a keen sense of Jewish ethnic or folk identity. Jack August recalls that his mother took ten years to learn English, even as a resident of Northampton, Massachusetts. She stopped speaking Yiddish only when the family "moved into a new section of town" where "she had had to talk English because she had nothing but English-speaking neighbors." Rabbi Max Wall describes his predecessor, an elderly gentleman whom he came to know on his first arrival in Burlington, Vermont, shortly after World War II. Reverend Natelson was "an old-fashioned Eastern European Jew. He spoke 'Engels,' not English." Indeed, when Wall was brought to Burlington to audition there as a rabbi, he almost left in disgust at what he—a European-born Jew himself—perceived as a backward cultural milieu. "Here in Burlington," Wall says, "they were speaking Yiddish." He had anticipated conducting his service in English and Hebrew. "Don't I speak in English?" he asked. "Well," the congregants told him, "tomorrow night you'll speak in English. Sunday night." On Shabbat, apparently, Yiddish was still the lingua franca. "So that's the way it was," Wall says. "I decided right then and there this is one place I'm not coming." It took a considerable amount of additional coaxing on the Vermonters' part to convince him to take a job in a place that, to him, felt like a *shtetl*.

Since the oldest of the tradition-bearers I spoke with are of the second generation, their experience with Yiddish and with the overall sense of a self-enforced Jewish separateness was different from the world that Wall describes. Like many other modern-era Jews throughout the world, they

experienced Yiddish as the language spoken by elders who didn't want to
be understood by their children. The second-generation rural Jews rarely
spoke it themselves. May Schell explains: "I understand Yiddish perfectly.
I can't speak any phrases except that I remember." Selma Mehrman con-
curs, but lets on that the parents were not quite as savvy as they may have
thought.

> And they also talked Yiddish when they didn't want me to under-
> stand, you know always. I don't know if you came from a household
> where they spoke that. I told you my parents spoke Yiddish when-
> ever they didn't want me to know something, and finally, of course,
> after a while you pick things up. It's amazing how you can pick up
> a language just sitting there and listening long enough but I never
> said anything, so I just sat there, and probably a year or so or more
> until one day my father said something and it just cracked me up
> completely. And they looked at me and said, "You understand?" And
> I said, "Yeah, I do."
>   "How long have you . . . ? "
>   "Oh, quite a while."

Younger people, in other words, may not have conducted their daily lives
in Yiddish, but they inherited enough of it to be part of the folk group that
still relied upon having its own mark of cultural difference.

Lillian Glickman, like Selma Mehrman, says that her parents spoke Yiddish, "when they wanted to keep something." For her own part, she "loved
it. When my brother got into looking for cookies," she says, her mother
"used the expression '*geh avek fun danen*, go away from there.' " She continues to use Yiddish in small doses, especially as she refers to various Jewish
foods. "I love to say '*lochshen kugel*,' instead of 'noodle pudding,' " she says.
"It hurts me to say 'noodle pudding' when it's '*lochshen kugel*.' " Although
she grew up only hearing but not speaking Yiddish, May Schell became
attached over the years to various Yiddish expressions, and took their use
for granted. Retention of their meanings, in her experience, is a generational marker. "I find myself using them," she says. "My son sneezed, and
I said, '*Zie Gesunt*,' and he said, 'What's that mean?' and I was shocked. I
was shocked that he didn't know the meaning of 'Good Health.' So I guess
in our own home, we didn't speak any Yiddish." As Yiddish speaking was
hardly retained in *any* non-Orthodox American Jewish community beyond

the second generation, that it passed out of ordinary daily usage among rural New England Jews, who would have had less occasion to use it than anyone else, is hardly surprising. Indeed, its longevity—even in fragmented form—is a testament to the strength of Jewish folk expression in the most isolated communities.

Folk groups defined by ethnicity often find their foremost mode of traditional expression to be foodways. Small-town New England Jews from their first arrival to the present have continually asserted their Jewishness and imparted it to younger generations through the preparation and eating of traditional—and adaptations of traditional—Jewish foods. In part because Jewish religious life imposes a set of dietary laws and in part because so many Jewish holidays are commemorated by eating certain foods, Jewish cultural identity can often be most readily asserted—and, for that matter, rejected—through dietary practice. Moreover, in a geographical context, food is of equal importance as a means of asserting regional affiliation. New England's diet, unlike that of the South, has never been hugely distinct from that of the rest of the nation's, but a few regional foodways survive into the twenty-first century, and to the extent that some Jewish residents of the region adapted local ingredients such as maple syrup to their own distinct cultural foodways, they have in effect asserted a specifically rural New England Jewish cultural identity.

When Jews first came to the area, those of them who were religiously observant often expressed their adherence to Judaism and Jewish tradition through the maintenance, often at great pains, of kosher dietary practices. As she grew up in Easthampton, Massachusetts, May Schell recalls that her "mother always kept a strictly kosher house, not because she believed in it . . . but because they had a certain pride and they didn't want that in any way to be chipped off." Perhaps as if to underscore the temptations that rural life might have brought to Jews in the early days, Louis Plotkin explains the importance of kosher butchering and the need within a Jewish community for a proper *shochet*. "You cannot go out into the forest and shoot an animal and eat it," he says. Even though as an adult he dispensed with such strictures out of the home, in the early days Jews in his community were fastidious in their observation of kosher regulations. The same was true for Natalie Cohen's family in Maine and New Brunswick. "Our house was strictly kosher," she says, "and everybody respected us. We kept very strict Jewish rules, and everybody in town knew it. And if I was invited to somebody's home, they never served me bacon or any of that stuff. And all our meats came from Montreal." Cohen recalls that as a Jew living on the Canadian side of the border, she was often surprised to encounter the apparent laxity of American Jews. "The Americans didn't celebrate as much," she says. "I can remember one year we were at a cousin's house, and she was serving milk and meat, and my kid brother who was about four years old then said very loudly, 'How can you do that and you're in a Jewish home?' From that day on, she never served meat and milk with us around, or especially with him around. But our family was known. I mean, we ate out, but our home was strictly kosher." To maintain a kosher kitchen was hardly an easy prospect for a family living in a rural area. The first generation's adherence to the practice was an expression of its commitment to maintaining a strong sense of Jewish identity.

In most cases, kosher food could be procured only either as a family member traveled to a city to bring it back to the country or as a traveling *shochet*—more often than not, an itinerant rabbi in town for a Shabbat or High Holy Day service—could oversee the slaughter of a locally raised chicken or cow. Sonny Chertok describes how his mother would arrange from month to month to purchase the family's supply of meat. Before Laconia has its own rabbi and slaughterer, Chertok's mother "used to order meat from a butcher in Manchester, Adler. He had a grocery store in Manchester, and he sold meat also. And mother would send down a penny postcard and order a pound of this or two pounds of that. He would get it the next day, immediately wrap up whatever had to be sent, send it right out parcel post. Mother would have it the following day, and then once a month she would settle up with him. He'd send a bill, and she'd send him a money order or a check for it." Alternatively, one might make the trip him- or herself if the city and butcher in question were not too far away. Phyllis Nahman's mother traveled from Turners Falls to Greenfield, Massachusetts, every week to bring kosher meat home until the family decided to give up on keeping kosher meat around. "By then the trains that went through Greenfield and brought kosher meant weren't running any more," she says. "So they had to go to Springfield or Worcester to get meat. So that kind of went by the wayside." Bob Selig of Laconia, New Hampshire, remembers his mother making the trip to Manchester herself, "which is an hour away now [but] more than that then." Jews in Maine routinely traveled to Bangor for the same purpose, according to Julius and Charlotte

Goos. Another coastal Mainer, Gertrude Crockett Shapiro of Stonington, recalls something similar. "Meats had to be brought from Rockland by boat or by land from Bangor," Shapiro says. "[My mother] would order extra meat in the summer, which she cooked and prepared and steamed in jars."[8] As May Schell tells the story of her own birth, her mother's having gone shopping for kosher food figures as the starting point.

> My mother had gone to Northampton to buy food, kosher food, for us
> for the whole week, you see, and, apparently, the heavy packages and
> bundles brought on the early birth. And the doctor said that there
> was no point in trying to get me to Northampton where there was
> the only incubator. I think that he really thought it was a waste of
> time and he didn't want to take his horse and buggy because that's
> what he would've had to do. And my mother, of course, obviously
> didn't throw me out but found the largest shoebox in my father's
> store; probably size 12, and filled it with cloth and soft material and it
> was in March, so the stove was going and she put me in the oven.

Jewish families who adhered to kosher dietary laws might not always have gone to such lengths, but even their intermittent willingness to do so bespoke a deep commitment to Jewish tradition in a place where leaving such practices behind would certainly have been much easier.

Those who might want to avoid making the trip to a distant butcher would often take advantage of the availability, at least occasionally, of a *shochet*. Natalie Cohen's family often brought in the rabbi from nearby Woodstock, New Brunswick. "He would drive about 40 miles," as she tells it, "come in, give us Hebrew lessons, and then before he left my mother had brought live chickens and he would kill them because he was a *shochet*. We would bring them home, and my mother would boil them and get them all feathered, and we'd have our chickens." In Great Barrington, Massachusetts, the local Jewish population took advantage of their rabbi's qualifications as a *shochet*. Rabbi Axelrod would, like the rabbi recalled by Natalie Cohen, go from house to house giving Hebrew lessons. He then, as Jake Pevzner remembers, "went around to all of the [Jewish] farmers, and he used to kill the chickens, so they would have kosher chickens." Sonny Chertok speaks of his community's rabbi, "a man named Mr. Cohen," who would do the same. "He'd kill the chickens on Friday, and he'd have kosher meat set up once a week in his back shed. He'd lay it out on newspapers on the table, and the women would come, and he'd cut it up and sell it to them." A *shochet* might be called upon for more than ritual slaughtering of meats to be eaten in the home. Those few early settlers who retained any bits and pieces of Old Country folk medicine might have been disposed to put into practice the following remedy, or others like it. In any case, a *shochet* was needed in order to complete it properly. "In Russia," explains Jack August, "they had their little medical secrets." Shortly after the family had arrived in Northampton, August's brother had taken ill. He tells the story: "So they decided what my brother needed, this little infant, what he needed was a blood transfusion. Not a medical blood transfusion, through the arm, but they killed a pigeon. A *shochet* came to the house and killed a pigeon. They saved the blood in a glass and they fed it to the baby through the mouth with a teaspoon." Granted that, in the early twentieth century, such applications of folk medicine were probably infrequent, their perseverance among first-generation western Massachusetts Jews suggests that traditional folklife was hardly something to be casually abandoned in a new land.

Preparation and consumption of kosher meats were hardly the only means by which the first generations of rural New England Jews expressed their allegiance to the foodways that derived from their *shtetl* origins. Lillian Glickman's mother prepared, among other things, *kneidelach, lochshen kugel,* and blintzes. When she prepares these traditionally Eastern European foods now, however, Glickman makes use of ingredients that were not available when her mother cooked. "When I make a brisket—she [my mother] would fry the onions and peel the carrots, to give it more flavor and everything—nowadays I open up a can of cranberry sauce . . . and use onion soup mix and put it over the brisket, put it in the oven, and it's wonderful." Pal Borofsky's mother prepared potato latkes and matzoh brei. In Otis, Massachusetts, the Pyenson family grew up eating traditional Jewish foods—including *hamentaschen* for Purim—even though they rarely attended shul. Cooking and eating Jewish foods, as well as maintaining a kosher kitchen, offered a way for the most isolated rural Jews to feel Jewish. Such practices also helped to instill a sense of Jewish cultural identity in younger generations, for whom the traditional Jewish cultural life of Eastern Europe was merely a story told—or often enough *not* told—by parents and grandparents.

As Jewish life and Judaism have, in the more recent past, been reinvented by people now three, four, and five generations removed from the Old Country, the terms of its expression, at least on the level of folklife, have shifted greatly. Jews who live in rural New England today enjoy many means of participating in Jewish activities and giving voice to their ethnic allegiance. Referring to the intensive weekend-long Conference on Judaism in Rural New England gatherings that began in the mid-1980s and only recently have been phased out, Julie Chamay speaks of such engagements as "a joyous way to be around other people doing Jewish things." She uses a term coined by Rabbi Zalman Schachter-Shalomi to describe such activities—"Jewing." A similar spirit appears to have infused the efforts of Suzie Laskin and her fellow White Mountain (New Hampshire) Jews who, in developing an advertisement to promote their now thriving *havurah*, spoke not just to Jewish religious expression but to a broader cultural allegiance that they assumed would have a still wider appeal. She and a friend of hers worked for a local radio station and had the means to put the word out. They released their advertisement

> right around Christmastime, and it said something like "If you're tired of being the only one on your block without a Christmas tree and if your idea of comfort food is lox and bagels and if you know what Shabbat means, then give us a call." And it was something like that and "we'll get together for a Shabbat potluck supper . . . and give us a call and we'd love to meet you." So we had the commercial on the air for maybe a week or two, and it was a Friday night; we did a Shabbat potluck supper . . . and about 50 people came. And we all came and everybody said, "We never knew there were so many Jews around." And we all went around the room and introduced ourselves and we all discovered that we were all here because we love the mountains and we love the environment and we weren't real religious and we didn't go to shul but we felt a need to reach out to other Jews, and we felt a need to have some kind of Jewish connection.

Having chosen, in other words, to settle in an area where this sort of "Jewish connection" is a rarity, the Jews of the White Mountain *havurah* have had to choose, subsequently, to pursue their connections by means that their predecessors would not have anticipated. Jewish life in the early days of settlement was an extension of the synagogue and the product of localized interactions among established Jewish families. It now operates by an entirely different set of guidelines and builds itself as an assemblage of individual or, as Rabbi Howard Cohen refers to them, "self-actualizing" choices.

Betty and Eli Gordon, who moved to the White Mountain region of New Hampshire after retirement, have sought and found most of their "Jewing" connections through nonreligious means. Both raised in New York City and skilled as folk musicians, steeped in Eastern European and Zionist traditions, the two began playing at coffeehouses throughout the region, where they found enthusiastic audiences, Jewish and non-Jewish alike, for their ballads about World War II Jewish partisans and the founding of Israel. Food preparation too offers current-day rural New England Jews a means of "performing" their Jewishness in a broader context, often enough comprised of non-Jews as well as of Jews. When Helene Meyerowitz first came to Aroostook County, Maine, in the 1970s, she and some friends collaborated on giving a seder.

It was Passover, and our friend, who worked at the mental health center with my husband at the time, his wife was an Episcopal or a Presbyterian minister and she wanted to have a seder to kind of educate her community. And Presque Isle was not known for having any ethnic food readily available, so I volunteered to make matzoh. Yeah. All I did was mix whatever I had to mix, flour and water, and came out with some sort of discombobulated form of a cracker and that was our matzah. We could have had it if somebody had thought ahead to order it from Bangor. Bangor was a three-hour trip south of Presque Isle and they would order ethnic food, but nobody thought of doing that, so we did have a seder with Helene's homegrown matzoh.

Later on, as a schoolteacher, Meyerowitz had occasion to share the Chanukah tradition of preparing potato latkes with her pupils.

Being a minority in Presque Isle, Maine, came December, and they did Christmas stuff, I would come in and do Hanukkah stuff, and I introduced latkes to the children and we would make it together. And it was very unusual. One or two children wouldn't like it, and I'd say, "Gee it's just like hash brown potatoes and we're living in potato country." But most of them enjoyed it and they were fascinated by learning about the ceremony of the candles and playing with the

dreidel. I proceeded to take that with me when I worked in the mid-
coast here to the point that when I retired in 2000, they would ask
me back on a yearly basis to come and cook latkes for them. That
has since ended but they certainly know about Hanukkah, and I've
introduced matzah to many children who had no idea what that was
all about. . . . So I've done that much as far as promoting that culture
which ordinarily these children really know nothing about. They live
in these little cocooned towns and their life is just their life and very
little practical experience as to what there is in the outside world.

Perhaps because rural New England Jews have become so broadly assimilated in the life of their communities, much more of the sort of Jewish
folklife that their predecessors may have kept to themselves is now *visible*,
if only on an incidental level, to the region's population as a whole.

A Jewish folklife is still, however, a vital means by which Jews pursue
engagement with each other and maintain an open dialogue on what
it means to be a Jew in changing times. Outside of a rural context, it is
difficult to imagine the following debate taking place. At Adamah in Connecticut, where farming interns spent time investigating whether or not
it was appropriate to milk goats on Shabbat, an even more surprising discourse was the one held, also during the summer of 2004, on pigs. Shamu
Fenyvesi, who oversees the intern program, explains:

We have just a tremendous amount of food waste, especially in the
summer, because the seniors are served at their table. . . . We're talking about 50, 60, 70 gallons a day of food waste. And that's not really
backyard composting scale, right? And we don't have that much land,
so it can't be really far from where people are living, so we've got
to keep this mountain of waste down and have to keep pests down.
We've moved it further away from the kitchen when we had a rat
problem, which was successful, and now there's no rats, but we do
have skunks around. . . . From an ecological point of view the most
efficient use is to have a pig, or a few pigs. Because pigs would eat all
the food waste; we wouldn't have pest problems, or odor problems,
and we'd have great manure. Right now we're buying quite a bit of
organic compost because we don't have enough animals—we have a
few chickens and goats—but not enough animals to make enough

manure to grow an acre and a half of vegetables. These pigs would be part of that. And yet we're Jewish.

So the concern is not just legally, could we have pigs; the concern is symbolically, culturally, what that does. To have people say, "Oh, they have *pigs* there!" . . . We have a rabbi who's been looking into that, and we could actually do it—we could have pigs here. We wouldn't eat them; we could give them away; someone else would eat them. Or we could keep them until they're old and let them die. But we could, legally, do it.

That such a *Jewish* debate is so closely in keeping with a current debate on sustainability in agricultural practice and food use offers insight into just how commensurate Jewish life and the current-day rural New England mentality are with each other. Such debates bode well for the future of Jews living in such places because they offer evidence that allegiance to one constituency doesn't dilute one's allegiance to the next.

The Rewards of Hard Work

How Small-Town New England Jews Might Be Helping
to Reverse a National Decline

o o o

The story of Jews living in small-town New England bears implications both for the life of the region and for the history of Jews in America. On the one hand, since American Jews remain a primarily metropolitan population, the notion of small-town Jewish life will always *seem strange*. To be sure, as of the late 1980s, 95 percent of American Jewry could be located in a metropolitan area; indeed, 4 out of 5 American Jews lived in one of ten specific metropolitan areas.[1] Such figures offer startling confirmation of the general perception, but they are also mitigated by accompanying data pertaining to the broad trend within American demography that has been shaping itself since the late nineteenth century. Since approximately 80 percent of all Americans also live in metropolitan areas, the Jewish concentration in cities might be just as indicative of Jewish *Americanism* as it is of Jewish particularism. Moreover, for all their concentration in major metropolitan areas, urban and suburban Jews are hardly immune to the various disillusions, compromises, and unsettling trends that face American Jewry in the first part of the twenty-first century. Having known exceptional and strange-seeming experiences for all or most of their lives, on the other hand, Jewish people who live in rural districts may be in a unique position to shed light on the Jewish future in America.

Much of the contemporary scholarship on the current state of American Jewish life poses what Seymour Lipset and Earl Raab frame as a single question: "What is wrong with American Jewry?"[2] The question arises as multiple data sources indicate an imminent decline in the American Jewish population. Jewish population in the United States grew exponentially in the years of the large migrations first from Germany and then from Eastern Europe; it peaked in the period immediately following World War II. But it has been undergoing a steady freefall ever since, owing to low birth rates, a high rate of intermarriage and—perhaps most alarmingly—the gradual waning of Jewish religious and communal institutions. Ironically, the root cause of every one of these trends can quite clearly be marked out as American life itself, which has continually blessed Jews with political and social equality, religious tolerance, and material bounty. Being an American Jew has become easier and easier with every generation. As Eric Alterman writes, life has "never [been] safer, more prosperous and more secure in more than 5000 years of history."[3] The very comforts afforded by American exceptionalism have caused Jews to assimilate more fully and to abandon their Jewish exceptionalism. Notwithstanding declining rates of attendance at synagogue services or membership in Jewish organizations and any number of other traditional markers of Jewish identity, the *meaning* of Jewish life in America has shifted immeasurably.

In the "gigantic affirmative action program" to which Karen Brodkin refers in her 1998 book *How Jews Became White Folks*, the majority of American Jews used their educational achievements to pull themselves out of the non-white working class and into the comforts of middle-class, largely suburban life.[4] Jewishness vanished as a marker of difference and—startlingly—revealed itself as an indicator of one's status as a member of the American *majority*. All of the accoutrements of membership within this majority—economic ease, educational credentials, geographic mobility—couldn't help but peel away centuries of Jewish separateness. In the chastening words of the late Rabbi Arthur Hertzberg, Jewishness in America has now devolved into a sort of doldrum state in which a poorly conceived and petty "ethnicity"—bagels, Seinfeld, and *Hava Nagilah*—has replaced an immersion in Jewish intellectualism and traditional prayer. Where ethnic style becomes inoperably amorphous, Hertzberg argues, another even more troubling identity marker takes its place—*tsoris*, or the story of Jewish suffering.[5] That Jewish distinction should follow from the mere fact of historical oppression, and from the tendency on the part of both American Jews and non-Jewish Americans to associate Jewishness with past suffering, would be of obvious concern to anyone raising Jewish children. For all of the incalculable benefits derived from the relatively high rate of Holocaust awareness among Americans, that Jews should be identified primarily as the historical victims of Nazi genocide can hardly be expected to promote a positive self-image. Jewish identity in America, as Hertzberg and others argue, must necessarily be built out of more solid elements than superficial markers of ethnicity and collective *tsoris*.

If the integrity of American Jewish life is threatened, however, the temptations of assimilation can only be part of the problem. Indeed, in Hertzberg's view, American Jews must bear significant responsibility for failing to promote their own Jewish education and awareness. The comforts of ethnicity, by the same token, are merely comforts, and threaten to fool American Jews into thinking that eating certain foods or pronouncing certain Yiddishisms will keep them Jewish. The conditions of Jewish life in the metropolitan United States, as so many small-town New England tradition-bearers whose own origins and relatives still reside there say, tend to make being Jewish too easy. As Lipset and Raab put it, Jewish life in mainstream America presents us with "the conundrum of individual Jewish success amidst the dissolution of the American Jewish community."[6] Whether or not metropolitan Jews are tempted into becoming more American than Jewish, the terms of their Jewishness are compromised to begin with.

Certainly, temptations to assimilate can only be greater in areas of lesser Jewish density. Isolation has loosened the bonds of Jewishness for many small-town New England Jews. In America in general, but especially in its rural districts, "increasing contact between Jew and Gentile,"[7] in Earl Raab's formulation, cannot help but accelerate the pace of dissolution. If sheer numbers were the only marker of Jewish integrity, of course, then historical trends in rural America would hardly be the place either to worry about or, for that matter, to exult in. Contemporary prophets of American Jewish dissolution—or, for that matter, revival—are reacting to more than numbers, however. When the *quality* of Jewish life is taken into account, the experience of small-town New England Jews takes on a new significance. For all the perceived disadvantages of living away from a center of Jewish population, Jews in small-town New England who have self-consciously sought to retain and enhance their Jewish identity have had to create the institutions necessary for doing so themselves. In sending their children fifty miles distant for bar mitzvah training or devoting a day of the week to procuring kosher meats, as so many of the earlier generation did, the founding generation of small-town New England Jews had to go out of their way to be Jewish. Something similar holds true today, even as extreme geographical isolation is less of a factor. Jews who have moved to the country in recent years and then worked to revive and even build Jewish institutions were hardly turning their backs on their Jewishness; if anything, as so many of the tradition-bearers with whom I spoke have suggested, life in small-town New England has inspired Jewish choices. Even the apparent compromises, on closer reflection, suggest a depth of commitment and seriousness that, in a metropolitan setting, might be less stark. As small-town New England store owners felt compelled for business reasons to keep their shops open on Saturday, as some tradition-bearers tell it, the Shabbat meal at home with the family meant all the more to them. When, as Todd and Cathy Adelman describe it, time spent in the synagogue on High Holy Days offered respite from the physical toils of the potato harvest as opposed to the humdrum drudgery of grade school, being a Jew can be said to have acquired a dimensionality that it would otherwise not have had.

The current debate on the future of American Jewish life seems primarily to center around two opposing views as to its trajectory. The "assimilationist" view (which is hardly an endorsement of assimilation), espoused by Hertzberg and others, suggests that generations of exposure to non-Jews and to mainstream American culture will eventually exact a high toll and eliminate any sense of Jewish difference. The more optimistic "transformationalist" view suggests that many of these same exposures—quite prominently including the enormous trend toward intermarriage but also including such things as broad Jewish participation in (non-Jewish) educational institutions—can only aid in the eventual solidification of American Jewish life. The creation of so many interfaith families, in this view, only builds a broader base for the Jewish community. Moreover, in an age in which so much Jewish life occurs outside the immediate confines of the synagogue, an increasingly "wide range of ties to Jewishness," as Calvin Goldscheider puts it, allows and forces the Jewish community to be all the more inclusive.[8] Earl Raab echoes the sentiment, even as he offers the qualification that the bonds of Jewishness have been loosened in recent years: in contemporary America, "the organized Jewish community has in some ways more resources than it ever had," he asserts.[9] Indeed, something of this effect may have been apparent to the group of Jews who founded the Conference on Judaism in Rural New England in the 1980s. The recent dissolution of that group seems to have come about as a result not of a waning of Jewish life in the region but of its opposite: so many organized

Jewish resources and institutions exist in rural New England now that an overarching conference—which was initially created to fill a vacuum—is no longer needed.

Neither the "assimilationist" nor the "transformationalist" view can fully explain or encompass the experience of small-town New England Jews, either at the turn of the twentieth century or at the turn of the twenty-first. Naturally, the relative smallness of the Jewish population in the region has always stood as an impediment to more obvious forms of "growth," and long-standing Jewish residents would obviously be all the more susceptible to fully assimilating. But if Jewish agency is accounted for and if depth of commitment is important, then Jewish families living in predominantly non-Jewish communities are, by virtue of the greater sacrifices called forth from them, the more likely to resist the most damaging assimilating tendencies. As its opponents point out, on the other hand, the transformationalist view is weakened by a certain lack of substance that underlies so many of today's Jewish choices. The breadth of resources available to contemporary American Jews—from Internet dating services to "Birthright Israel"—belies a lack of true Jewish literacy or the ability, as Arthur Hertzberg puts it, "to know which end of the siddur is up." [10] Small-town New England Jews, though hardly immune to such elements within contemporary Jewish life, may experience less frequent exposure to them. Any ambivalence on their part toward their Jewishness must necessarily result in a total lack of affiliation; no one is going to meet them halfway. Regardless of the rate of intermarriage or any other traditional marker of a lack of solidity within the Jewish community, committed Jews in small-town congregations know that they must rely on themselves alone to maintain their Jewishness. From the strictly observant to the nonbelieving, Jews who participate in Jewish activities in smaller communities must all do so together.

Occasionally, these sorts of convergences can bring about striking moments of Jewish visibility in unexpected places. In 1980, then graduate student Aaron Lansky, who lived at that time in the so-called Five College Area of western Massachusetts, became aware of the world's quickly diminishing supply of books in Yiddish. With the help of some friends, he managed to find a serviceable storage area for rescued books and issued an international call for their recovery. Within six months, this group had recovered 70,000 books. Today, the National Yiddish Book Center is housed at Hampshire College (in South Amherst, Massachusetts) in a building whose architecture is modeled on that of the wooden synagogues of pre-Holocaust Eastern Europe. Its holdings include 1.5 million volumes and are enhanced by a digitalization capability funded by Steven Spielberg. The National Yiddish Book Center is more than a mere repository, however, for dusty old books written in a dying language. It stands as perhaps the most spectacular but hardly the only reminder of a latter-day Jewish revival that has touched all of rural New England in the last few decades. Its location in the rolling hills of western Massachusetts is an indication not of an ephemeral presence but of the strong roots that Jews have planted in the area going back to the late nineteenth century. This Jewish presence, as I hope to have shown, has been vibrant and has come about as a result of an active collaboration among disparate constituencies.

Beginning in 2005, an assortment of Jewish congregations, agencies, and community groups collaborated to create an annual festival for the harvest festival of Sukkot. Sweet Harvests is held on the grounds of the Yiddish Book Center on the Monday of the Columbus Day weekend, which also happens to be the peak period for "leaf-peeping" in New England. The five hundred attendees at the 2006 festival found themselves wandering the lush gardens and looking off into the distance at the redolent foliage of the Holyoke Range. Dozens of artists, musicians, falafel and latke vendors, and craftspeople were on hand, as organizers brought about activities as diverse as the raising of a timberframe *sukkah*, the recital of a Yiddish-language chorus, and a series of hourly yoga sessions held in the midst of an apple orchard. Sweet Harvests brought out every element within the current-day Jewish population of the region—Hasidim from Longmeadow, Massachusetts, organic farmers from the Berkshire Hills, Hebrew school children and families from the surrounding communities of Amherst, Northampton, and beyond. All of this seemed perfectly normal and fitting. The present-day demographic in places like western Massachusetts, as it is in other non-metropolitan sections of New England, is hardly homogeneous, if it ever was. Prominent and festive displays of a Jewish harvest holiday tradition appear, in this environment, to be every bit as indigenous as jack-o-lanterns, leaf piles, and Thanksgiving turkeys. Attendees at such events, by the same token, achieve a singular state of Jewish unity and diversity, one that is rarely achieved in more urban or suburban settings.

And so we are brought, perhaps not unexpectedly, to an old element of small-town New England life, succinctly relayed in Emerson's famous essay "Self Reliance": "Your goodness must have an edge to it—else it is none."[11] Generations of small-town New England Jews have persevered not because it has been easy for them to do so but because life in the region has both compelled and inspired them to be both committed Jews and small-town New Englanders. Indeed, the very convergence of Jewish exceptionalism and New England exceptionalism seems to have constituted an underlying solidifying force behind that perseverance. Notwithstanding the ancient tribalism that has cemented collective Jewish survival through successive centuries of oppression and, more recently, postwar prosperity in America, the surrounding contexts within which this survival has taken place are each possessed of their discrete properties. Modernity, which has both conferred upon and imposed the terms for this perseverance over the last several hundred years, has always functioned as a double-edged sword. Expansive economic and social opportunities, leading as they have to a stripping away of ghetto walls, have, as we have also seen, loosened communal ties. The false securities of an Enlightenment or a Weimar Republic or a New World Order, give way, periodically, to latent tribal and authoritarian impulses on the part of anti-Semites, and life in the Diaspora exacts its toll. On the other hand, any flat rejection of modernity cannot help but bode ill for minority populations, for whom economic and social mobility, as opposed to mere genealogical provenance, offers the surest means to survival and prosperity.

The conditions of life in small-town New England, perhaps quite inadvertently, have long been shaped by the inherence in the region's very founding and settlement patterns of a simultaneous cultivation of tradition and an openness to innovation. Small-town New England's steadfast adherence to the tradition of valuing a commitment to place, to neighborliness, and to strong communal structures has served all of its residents, oldtimers and newcomers alike, well. By the same token, the region's tendency, born perhaps of material scarcity as well as of Puritan or Yankee ingenuity, to adapt to changing conditions and shifting populations, has stood its Jewish settlers and various other ethnic minorities in good stead. New England— hardly utopian in its hardscrabble topography and flinty-edged mores—has made upon those who have chosen to love it demands that lead to just the sort of earthly rewards from which the proverbially good Jewish life can be shaped.

APPENDIX 1

A NOTE ON METHOD

Ethnography requires preparation and flexibility in roughly equal measures. In order to write meaningfully about the cultural life of Jews in small-town New England, I had to undertake a fairly systematic effort, at the outset, at least. I needed to cast a wide net. I sought tradition-bearers who could represent roughly equal proportions not only of men and women, but of various sub-regions, walks of life, and so forth. I structured the interview sessions themselves, which generally spanned anywhere from three quarters of an hour to an hour and a half, around a fairly uniform set of questions. For all of this apparent symmetry, however, the best field research often comes about as a result not simply of uniformity in approach but of the researcher's receptivity to the unanticipated turns that an interview can take. Not surprisingly, some of the interviews I conducted were more successful than others were—they yielded more detail, greater candor, broader enthusiasm. The subjects of ethnographic research, like everyone else, have their discrete areas of interest and expertise. In order to conduct the fieldwork that comprises the foundation for this book, I had to create a uniform context whose parameters were based on my expectations and upon my gradually increasing base of knowledge on small-town Jewish life in New England. At the same time, I knew full well that the success of the venture depended, in large part, upon exactly the sorts of responses and results that I could never have anticipated. Research can take shape only as we *act*, at least, as though we know what we are doing and can make sensible predictions based on prior knowledge. That same research is meaningful and instructive, however, only insofar as it generates at least a measure of surprise. If our theories are merely confirmed by our field investigations, what have we truly learned?

As a scholar whose work is of interest from both a folkloric and an oral historical point of view, I have found myself once again, in the fieldwork and composition of this book, preferring to elide such all-too-tidy disciplinary distinctions. For this reason, I refer consistently in the text to the interview transcripts as indicative of an *oral tradition*. Much of what people told me in the course of the interviews would, indeed, be of interest to anyone pursuing the study of vernacular, or folk, expression. As tradition-bearers verbalized their immersions in *Yiddishkeit*, for instance, they were enacting "artistic communication in small groups," to borrow Dan Ben-Amos's universalizing definition of folklore.[1] Responding to my questions and promptings about their families' settlement history in small-town New England, these same tradition-bearers could just as easily hold forth with authority on historical matters. Oral tradition is comprised of the sorts of materials we associate with folklore, such as legends, jokes, and songs, but to the extent that such materials are communal in origin and have been passed informally and intergenerationally, historical accounts—of the immigrant experience, for instance—can be traditional in nature too. My work in the field was informed by an interest in matters both cultural and historical, and based on the assumption that the *taxonomy* of the material I encountered would prove less important (and less interesting) than its overall contiguity as the collective product of an identifiably integral constituency. I make no claims either for universal cultural authenticity or for universal historical accuracy in the accounts that the book examines. On the other hand, the most salient indication of these accounts' broad relevance to the lives of small-town New England Jews is their consistent corroboration of each other (and, where pertinent, of existing documentation) as informally rendered *representations* of the group experience.

Ethnography can be informed by any number of scholarly orientations, and this book is no exception. Writing in 1965, the late folklorist Alan Dundes suggested that despite the tendency of many non-folklorists "to divide folklore into literary or anthropological categories"[2]—or, for that matter, many folklorists' training in *either* the humanities or the social sciences—fieldwork cannot help but yield materials that are relevant both to the study of human *expression* and to the study of human *behavior*. My own training and—more important—daily practice certainly fall in the former category. For all my formal education as a "literary folklorist," with an American Studies Ph.D. that I earned within an English department, it is my employment as a folklorist who teaches two or three literature courses for every folklore course within a department that grants bachelors' and masters' degrees also in *English* that most greatly influences my practice as a researcher. The practice of conducting interviews and generating written transcripts from these interviews places folklorists in league with every other kind of field researcher. The *interpretation* of those transcripts, at least as I practice it, is in many ways a literary critical enterprise. As I often point out to the students who enroll in the folklore courses I teach, many of whom are English majors, we can learn a great deal by treating the words on the page of a given interview transcript with the same thoughtful attention we might otherwise accord to a page from *Othello* or *Huckleberry Finn*.

In certain respects, the field of folklore studies would appear long ago to have outgrown such practices. Folklore-as-literature was a popular pursuit among ethnographers before the 1960s and 1970s, when the practitioners of the "performance school" began to point out that the dynamism inherent in the *act* of folklore transmission precludes undue attention to folklore as it is reduced to, or frozen into, print. The habit of interviewing, transcribing, and interpreting has hardly been entirely curtailed, however. Instead, we work to account and compensate for the artificiality of such renderings by paying simultaneous attention to the contexts in which folklore is performed. As we account, in various ways, for what the ethnomusicologist Jeff Todd Titon refers to as the "indeterminacy principle" that underlies any print rendition of a field experience, such texts become more viable as the bases for research. The inherent intertextuality of folklore items—their relationship, in other words, to other folk items and to their performative contexts—guarantees their instability. On the other hand, as Titon points out, transcripts of interviews, for all their susceptibility to such critiques, provide us with more than a mere window into the folk process; they also supply "pleasure." "Transcription," Titon writes, "has the advantage of taking a performance out of the past and permitting the folklorist to experience it as an aesthetic object."[3] As long as we recognize that this "object" is not "the real thing" but a limited representation of it, a transcripted interview can offer a useful and, indeed, pleasing mode of access to the verbal culture of everyday life.

My own approach to reading the interview transcripts has been shaped in large part by my interest, as a "literary folklorist," in modes of expression. Had my background as a literary scholar been the sole determining factor, however, I would have organized the materials represented here in a much different fashion. Literary study has, by necessity, to be equivalent to genre investigation. Literary critics read poems, in other words, by comparing them to other poems and by studying a given poem's adherence to

or departure from existing practices of poetry. A purely literary folklorist—
and I doubt the existence of such a person in the current age of folklore
study—would study one legend alongside other legends in order to say
meaningful things about what legends do and how they work. Clearly, this
would have been a very different and, I daresay, less compelling project
from my own point of view, as well as from that of the reader, had I taken
such an approach. Much of the material here can, in some capacity, be
categorized according to existing definitions of folk genres; the personal
experience narratives, for example, comprise a large proportion of the texts
included here. So too do the various personal legends and anecdotes represented within the transcripts. This book is not a genre study, however, and
in this respect it departs quite drastically from the literary model.

Instead, I have organized the materials here in accordance with my own
interest, and the interest I anticipate on the part of readers, in historical
patterns. The book tries to tell a story, in other words. It invests the 60
tradition-bearers whom I interviewed with a certain kind of collective historical authority. It presents them as witnesses, as people whose expressions
of experience and insight—in composite form, especially—can be made to
comprise an actual narrative. This narrative's adherence to the "real story"
of Jews living in small-town New England appears, on the basis of its inter-
nal corroboration, its resonance with written history, and its convergence
with existing research on Jews in other non-metropolitan areas of the
United States, to be legitimate. Elements within the narrative could, for
all we know, be *out* of keeping with the facts of history and still be accurate
in important ways, however. The book is meant, after all, not so much as a
study of the *events* of the past as it is of the collective psychic experience of
small-town New England Jews. Ultimately, then, the book's pursuit of *oral
tradition*, as an elision of folklore and oral history, of literary and of socially
based interests and methodologies, is of a piece with the materials themselves. In writing about the folklorist Lynwood Montell, who has written
extensively about the vernacular oral traditions of the upland South, Barre
Toelken points out that the folk items Montell collected "are more accurate in their portrayal of *local values* [my emphasis] . . . than they are about
the facts."[4] The same may very well be true here.

LIST OF INTERVIEWS

Author-conducted interviews

Cathy Adelman, Malibu, California
Milt Adelman, Mars Hill, Maine
Todd Adelman, Rollinsford, New Hampshire
Interviewed in Rollinsford, October 11, 2004

David Arfa, Shelburne Falls, Massachusetts
Interviewed in Shelburne Falls, June 24, 2003

Robert August, Whately, Massachusetts
Interviewed in Whately, May 20, 2005

Toby Axelrod, Berlin, Germany; formerly, Great Barrington, Massachusetts
Interviewed by e-mail, February 12, 2004

Leta "Lee" Bagdon, Bethlehem, New Hampshire
Interviewed in Bethlehem, August 9, 2004

Stanley "Pal" Borofsky, Brattleboro, Vermont
Interviewed in Brattleboro, May 29, 2003

Julie Chamay and Steve Chamay, Bennington, Vermont
Interviewed in Bennington, July 20, 2003

Edwin "Sonny" Chertok, Laconia, New Hampshire
Interviewed in Laconia, September 27, 2004

Rabbi Howard Cohen, Bennington, Vermont
Interviewed in Bennington, April 25, 2003

Natalie Cohen, Augusta, Maine
Interviewed in Augusta, October 27, 2004

Michael Docter, Hadley, Massachusetts
Interviewed in Hadley, October 20, 2004

Leslie Dreier, Bethlehem, New Hampshire, and New York City
Interviewed in Bethlehem, September 15, 2004

Shamu Fenyvesi, Falls Village, Connecticut, and Portland, Oregon
Interviewed in Falls Village, August 5, 2004

Jacob Elisha Fine, Amherst, Massachusetts
Interviewed in Amherst, September 8, 2004

Lillian Glickman, North Adams, Massachusetts
Interviewed in North Adams, June 23, 1998

Charlotte Goos and Julius "Zeese" Goos, Augusta, Maine
Interviewed in Augusta, October 27, 2004

Eli Gordon and Betty Gordon, Freedom, New Hampshire
Interviewed in Freedom, June 9, 2003

Joe Kurland, Colrain, Massachusetts
Interviewed in Colrain, May 8, 2003

Susan Laskin, Chatham, New Hampshire
Interviewed in North Conway, New Hampshire, June 8, 2003

Elizabeth Lerner, White River Junction, Vermont
Interviewed in Amherst, Massachusetts, July 22, 2003

Mary Markle and William Markle, Randolph, Vermont
Interviewed in Randolph, May 24, 2004

Selma Mehrman, Beverly, Massachusetts (formerly of Ashland, New Hampshire)
Interviewed in Beverly, May 25, 2004

Helene Meyerowitz, Rockland, Maine
Interviewed in Rockland, June 29, 2004

Amy Jo Montgomery and Robert L. Montgomery, Arlington, Vermont
Interviewed in Bennington, Vermont, April 25, 2003

Irene Moskowitz, Great Barrington, Massachusetts
Interviewed in Great Barrington, August 16, 2004

Phyllis Nahman, Greenfield, Massachusetts
Interviewed in Greenfield, August 11, 2004

Saul Perlmutter, Amherst, Massachusetts (formerly of Burlington, Vermont)
Interviewed in Amherst, June 9, 2004

Jack Pevzner, Great Barrington, Massachusetts
Interviewed in Great Barrington, August 16, 2004

Maxwell Pyenson, Otis, Massachusetts
Interviewed in Otis, January 24, 2005

Steven Pyenson, Otis, Massachusetts
Interviewed in Otis, January 13, 2005

Robert Rottenberg, Colrain, Massachusetts
Interviewed in Greenfield, Massachusetts, February 5, 2003

Rhoda Sakowitz, Bethlehem, New Hampshire
Interviewed in Bethlehem, September 15, 2004

May Schell (deceased), Slingerlands, New York (formerly of Easthampton, Massachusetts)
Interviewed in Slingerlands, August 6, 2003

Beala Stark Schiffman, Sheffield, Massachusetts
Interviewed in Great Barrington, Massachusetts, August 16, 2004

Robert Selig and Joyce Selig, Laconia, New Hampshire
Interviewed in Laconia, July 6, 2004

Rabbi Shmuel Simenowitz, Longmeadow, Massachusetts, and Readsboro, Vermont
Interviewed in Shelburne, Massachusetts, May 27, 2005

Evelyn Slome, Portsmouth, New Hampshire
Interviewed in Portsmouth, May 30, 2003

Stephen Steinberg, Acton, Massachusetts
Interviewed in Concord, Massachusetts, February 9, 2005
(Also provided unpublished memoir)

Shana Tinkle, Portland, Maine
Interviewed in Lyndonville, Vermont, June 23, 2003

Genevieve Uris, Waitsfield, Vermont
Interviewed in Waitsfield, July 8, 2003

Rabbi Max Wall, Burlington, Vermont
Interviewed in Burlington, October 18, 2004

Eugene Wein, North Adams, Massachusetts
Interviewed in North Adams, June 23, 1998

Beth Weissman and Cale Weissman, Colrain, Massachusetts
Interviewed in Shelburne, Massachusetts, June 3, 2003

Sumner Winebaum, York, Maine (formerly of Portsmouth, New Hampshire)
Interviewed in York, August 21, 2003

Trudy Wolf, Waitsfield, Vermont
Interviewed in Waitsfield, July 8, 2003

Archived interviews

Eva August, Northampton, Massachusetts
Interviewed by Joel Halpern, September 20, 1976

Jack August, Northampton, Massachusetts
Interviewed by Joel Halpern, May 19, 1976, and September 20, 1976

Maurice Carlson, Northampton, Massachusetts
Interviewed by Joel Halpern, June 26, 1976

Louis Plotkin, Orange, Massachusetts
Interviewed by Joel Halpern, September 15, 1976

Lena Sandler, Sandisfield, Massachusetts
Interviewed by Carrie and Michael Nobel Kline in Sandisfield, May 11, 1992

Ruben Tablitz, Winsted, Connecticut, and Sandisfield, Massachusetts
Interviewed by Carrie and Michael Nobel Kline in Sandisfield, May 11, 1992

NOTES

Introduction: *A* Shtetl *on a Hill*

1. Lee Shai Weissbach, *Jewish Life in Small-Town America* (New Haven, 2005), pp. 4–5.
2. Quoted in Michael Barbaro, "In Wal-Mart's Home, Synagogue Signals Growth, "*New York Times*, June 20, 2006.
3. Stephen Nissenbaum, "New England as Region and Nation," in *All Over the Map*, ed. Edward Ayers and Peter Onuf (Baltimore, 1996), p. 52.
4. Randolph Roth, "Rural Communities," in *The Encyclopedia of New England*, ed. Burt Feintuch and David Watters (New Haven, 2005), p. 55.
5. Mark Bauman, "The Southerner as American: Jewish Style" (Cincinnati, 1996), p. 16.
6. Ewa Morawska, *Insecure Prosperity: Small-Town Jews in Industrial America, 1890–1940* (Princeton, 1996), pp. 32, 72, 135.
7. Steven Feldman, ed., *Guide to Jewish Boston and New England* (Boston, 1986) pp. 152–53.
8. Quoted in the introduction to *The Encyclopedia of New England*, p. xv.
9. Donald Hall, foreword to ibid., p. xiii.
10. Andrew Delbanco, "Introduction" to *Writing New England: An Anthology from the Puritans to the Present* (Cambridge, 2001), p. xxvii.
11. Stephen Whitfield, "The Smart Set," in *The Jews of Boston*, ed. Jonathan Sarna, Ellen Smith, and Scott-Martin Kosofsky (Boston, 1995), p. 311.
12. Mark Bauman and Bobbie Malone, "Introduction: Directions in Southern Jewish History," *American Jewish History*, 85.3 (1997), 192.
13. Bauman, "The Southerner as American," p. 29.
14. Ibid., p. 19.
15. Eric Goldstein, "How Southern Is Southern Jewish History?" unpublished essay, 2005 (quoted with author's permission), p. 10.
16. Barre Toelken, "Folklore and Reality in the American West," in *Sense of Place: American Regional Cultures*, ed. Barbara Allen and Thomas Schlereth (Lexington, KY, 1990), p. 15.
17. Weissbach, *Jewish Life in Small-Town America*, p. 350.
18. Ibid., pp. 338–48.
19. www.clas.ufl.uses/cometz.
20. www.clas.ufl.uses/cometz.

21. Gary Okihiro, "Oral History and the Writing of Ethnic History," in *Oral History: An Interdisciplinary Anthology*, ed. David K. Dunaway and Willa K. Baum (Nashville, 1984), p. 208.

1. Settling the Landscape of the Present and Future

1. Dona Brown, *Inventing New England* (Washington, DC, 1995), p. 9.
2. Joseph Conforti, *Imagining New England* (Chapel Hill, 2001), pp. 263–309.
3. Abraham Lavender and Clarence Steinberg, *Jewish Farmers of the Catskills: A Century of Survival* (Gainesville, FL, 1995), p. 174.
4. Conforti, *Imagining New England*, p. 6.
5. Philip Roth, *The Plot against America* (New York, 2005), p. 17.
6. Weissbach, *Jewish Life in Small-Town America*, p. 350.
7. Jonathan Sarna, *American Judaism* (New Haven, 2004), pp. 151–52.
8. Weissbach, *Jewish Life in Small-Town America*, p. 348.
9. www.ajcarchives.org
10. Weissbach, *Jewish Life in Small-Town America*, p. 348.
11. Ibid., p. 11.
12. James Gelin, *Starting Over: The Formation of the Jewish Community of Springfield, Massachusetts, 1840–1905* (New York, 1984), p. 50.
13. Celia Risen, "Leave a Good Name: The Story of Hiram Adelman Is the Story of America—the Land of Opportunity," *Northern Maine Journal* 31 (1996), p. 17.
14. Weissbach, *Jewish Life in Small-Town America*, p. 341.
15. Howard Epstein, *Small-Town Jews: Legends and Legacies* (Santa Rosa, CA, 1997), p. 138.
16. Judith Goldstein, *Crossing Lines: Histories of Jews and Gentiles in Three Communities* (New York, 1992), p. 47.
17. R. D. Eno, in *Guide to Jewish Boston and New England*, ed. Feldman, p. 168.
18. Ibid., p. 171.

2. "I Remember Being in the Barn"

1. Lisa Krissoff Boehm, "Environment and Ecology," in *American Regional Cultures: New England*, ed. Michael Sletcher (Greenwich, CT, 2004), p. 43.
2. Hal Barron, *Those Who Stayed Behind: Rural Society in Nineteenth-Century New England* (Cambridge, England, 1984), p. 54.
3. Mark Lapping, Foreword to Howard Russell, *A Long, Deep Furrow: Three Centuries of Farming in New England* (Hanover, NH, 1983), p. xii.
4. Uri Herscher, *Jewish Agricultural Utopias in America, 1880–1910* (Detroit, 1981), p. 28.

5. Ibid., p. 25.

6. Ibid., pp. 25–26.

7. Morton Gordon, "The History of the Jewish Farmers in Eastern Connecticut" (diss., Yeshiva University, 1971), p. 5.

8. Ibid., 11, 14, 15.

9. Alexander Feinsilver and Lillian Feinsilver, "Colchester's Yankee Jews," *Commentary* 20 (July 1955), p. 70.

10. Thomas Hubka, *Big House, Little House, Back House, Barn* (Hanover, NH, 1983).

11. Russell, *A Long, Deep Furrow*, pp. 308–9.

12. Gordon, "History of the Jewish Farmers," pp. 29–30.

13. Wallace Nutting, *Massachusetts Beautiful* (New York, 1923), p. 208.

14. Ibid., pp. 208–9.

15. Mark Raider, "Jewish Immigrant Farmers in the Connecticut Valley: The Rockville Settlement," *American Jewish Archives* 47 (1995), 213–42.

16. Feinsilver and Feinsilver, "Colchester's Yankee Jews," p. 67.

17. Ibid., p. 69.

18. Herscher, *Jewish Agricultural Utopias*, p. 51.

19. Weissbach, *Jewish Life in Small-Town America*, p. 107.

20. Herman Levine, *The American Jewish Farmer in Changing Times* (New York, 1966), p. 51.

21. Gordon, "History of the Jewish Farmers," p. 23.

22. Horwitt and Skole, *Jews in Berkshire County*, p. 5.

23. Ibid., p. 5.

24. Ibid., p. 7.

25. Quoted in Raider, "Jewish Immigrant Farmers in the Connecticut Valley," p. 219.

26. Gordon, "History of the Jewish Farmers," p. 68.

27. Ibid., p. 65.

28. Ibid., p. 108.

29. Lavender and Steinberg, *Jewish Farmers of the Catskills*, p. 199.

30. Herscher, *Jewish Agricultural Utopias*, p. 18.

31. Risen, "Leave a Good Name: The Story of Hiram Adelman," p. 18.

32. Ibid.

33. Julie Wiener, "From Varied Pasts, Group Plans Collective Kosher Organic Farm," www.jta.org.

3. *A Good Place for Jews to Live*

1. Weissbach, Jewish Life in Small-Town America, p. 229.

2. Morawska, *Insecure Prosperity*, p. 11.

3. Ibid., p. 54.

4. Goldstein, "Crossing Lines," p. 43.

5. Stella Suberman, *The Jew Store* (Chapel Hill, 2001), p. 3.

6. Morawska, *Insecure Prosperity*, pp. 72–122.

7. Suberman, *The Jew Store*, p. 116.

8. Risen, "Leave a Good Name: The Story of Hiram Adelman," p. 17.

9. Quoted in Lavender and Steinberg, *Jewish Farmers of the Catskills*, p. 54.

10. Morawska, *Insecure Prosperity*, p. 13.

11. Quoted in Goldstein, "How Southern Is Southern Jewish History," p. 60.

12. Morawska, *Insecure Prosperity*, p. 16.

13. Ibid., p. 41.

4. *"Just Enough to Make a Minyan"*

1. Sarna, *American Judaism*, p. 287.

2. Brown, *Inventing New England*, p. 6.

3. Sarna, *American Judaism*, p. 278.

4. Ibid., pp. 162, 182.

5. Ibid., pp. 284–85.

6. Epstein, *Small-Town Jews*, p. 112.

7. Carolyn Lipson-Walker, "Weddings among Jews in the Post World War II American South," in *Creative Ethnicity*, ed. Stephen Stern and Allan Cicala (Logan, UT, 1991), pp. 171–83.

8. Epstein, *Small-Town Jews*, p. 141.

Conclusion: The Rewards of Hard Work

1. Stephen Whitfield, "American Jews: Their Story Continues," in *The American Jewish Experience*, ed. Jonathan Sarna (New York, 1986), p. 285.

2. Seymour Lipset and Earl Raab, "What Is Wrong with American Jews?" in their *Jews and the New American Scene* (Cambridge, 1998), p. 3.

3. Eric Alterman, in *The Chronicle of Higher Education* (November 3, 2006), p. B4.

4. Karen Brodkin, *How Jews Became White Folks and What That Says about Race in America* (New Brunswick, NJ, 1998), p. 3.

5. Arthur Hertzberg, "The Jews in America: An Uncertain Future." in *American Jews in the Twenty-first Century*, ed. Earl Raab (New York, 1991), p. 34.

6. Lipset and Raab, "What Is Wrong with American Jews?" p. 7.

7. Raab, *American Jews in the Twenty-first Century*, p. 1.

8. Calvin Goldscheider, "The Continuing American Jewish Context: Continuity, Israel, and Challenges for Leadership," in ibid., p. 27.

9. Raab, *American Jews in the Twenty-first Century*, p. 2.

10. Hertzberg, "The Jews in America," p. 32.

11. Ralph Waldo Emerson, "Self Reliance" (1841), in *Emerson's Essays: Second Series* (New York, 1890), p. 38.

Appendix 1: Note on Methodology

1. Dan Ben-Amos, "Toward a Definition of Folklore in Context," *Journal of American Folklore* 84 (1971): 5–15.

2. Alan Dundes, "The Study of Folklore in Literature and Culture," in *Folk Groups and Folk Genres*, ed. Eliot Oring (Logan, UT, 1989), p. 350.

3. Jeff Todd Titon, "Text," in *Eight Words for the Study of Expressive Culture*, ed. Burt Feintuch (Champaign, 2003), p. 73.

4. Barre Toelken, The *Dynamics of Folklore* (Boston, 1979), p. 23.

INDEX

Michael Hoberman is associate professor of folklore and English at Fitchburg State College. He is a graduate of Reed College and received his MA and PhD in American studies from the University of Massachusetts Amherst. Hoberman is the author of *Yankee Moderns: Folk Regional Identity in the Sawmill Valley of Western Massachusetts, 1890–1920*. He lives in Shelburne Falls, Massachusetts, with his wife, Janice Sorensen (whose photographs accompany the text of *How Strange*), his daughter, Della, and son, Lang.